Praise for THE BOY WHO

"Doane has written an engrossing
ultimately doomed young man, and
sprawling portrait of a remarkable community of bluewater sailors, a
tribe of humans who prefer ocean to land."

–Mark Bowden, bestselling author of *Black Hawk Down* and
other titles

"Doane dissects the freedom one finds at sea and in any life close
to nature, a powerful siren call even to those who will never venture
there."

–Steve Callahan, bestselling author of *Adrift: Seventy-Six Days
Lost at Sea*

"Lyrical, engaging, and true. Doane reconstructs the searing
tragedy, apparent resilience, and ultimate vulnerability of a brilliant
young man better suited to navigating the sea than life itself. It's
gripping—a thriller to the last page, and much more than just a sea
story."

–W. Jeffrey Bolster, prize-winning historian and author of *Black
Jacks* and *The Mortal Sea*

"A very thought-provoking read. Thomas was so at home on
the sea that shipwrecked his youth, literally and figuratively, that his
life on shore became a train wreck, in spite of all his good qualities.
His old-school sailing parentage and pedigree was cool, but not cool
enough to make Thomas whole, or his story any less heart-breaking."

–Tania Aebi, author of the bestselling memoir *Maiden Voyage*

"In this fast-paced, richly detailed work of investigative journalism
Doane invites us into the world of bluewater cruising by uncovering
the life of one of its most complex characters. This is a must-read for
every sailor and would-be global wanderer."

–Prof. Christopher L. Pastore, author of *Temple to the Wind* and
*Between Land and Sea*

"A fascinating chronicle of the life and voyages of a damaged yet brilliant iconoclast, and a gripping exploration of the dark tensions between minimalism and seamanship, between individualism and egocentricity, and between a storied, demanding father and an ambitious, orphaned son."

—Tim Zimmerman, contributing editor at *Outside Magazine*, co-writer of the documentary film *Blackfish*, author of *The Race*

"The tragic life of Thomas Tangvald is like none other. Doane has teased out the tale with skill and tact. He recounts it for us in the raw in this well-researched book."

—Tom Cunliffe, BBC broadcaster, yachting journalist and author of *In the Wake of Heroes* and other titles

"I spent time with both protagonists of this story when my husband Larry and I sailed into Manila onboard our own engine-free cutter, *Seraffyn*, many years ago. The father charmed and intrigued me. The son, at the time only two years old, stole my heart. This book destroyed any romantic notions I had of the father; it made me almost weep for the son. With its amazing research, amazing cooperation from interviewees, and fine writing, Charlie Doane's *The Boy Who Fell to Shore* kept me reading late into the night."

—Lin Pardey, award-winning voyager and author of *Storm Tactics Handbook*, *The Self-Sufficient Sailor*, and other titles

"Charles Doane's latest book is a mesmerizing account of a young man who was born at sea, was at one with the sea, and finally was lost at sea. From the first page you are drawn into the mysterious, terrifying, triumphant and tragic life of Thomas Thor Tangvald. This tale is impossible to put down; you just keep reading until it breaks your heart."

—John Kretschmer, author of *Sailing to the Edge of Time*, *Cape Horn to Starboard* and other titles

# THE BOY WHO FELL TO SHORE

# The Boy
## Who Fell
# to Shore

The Extraordinary Life and
Mysterious Disappearance
of Thomas Thor Tangvald

# Charles J. Doane

The Boy Who Fell to Shore:
The Extraordinary Life and Mysterious Disappearance of Thomas Thor Tangvald

Copyright © 2022 Charles J. Doane

Book and cover design by Kevin Breen and Jon Gosch
Cover image used with permission from Greg Bowl

ISBN: 978-1-957607-06-1
Cataloging-in-Publication Data is available upon request

Manufactured in the United States of America

Published by Latah Books
www.latahbooks.com

For Gaston and Lucio

"I see things, terrible things. It's strange. I see you die, but it's not you who gets killed. And then you find what you're looking for . . . at last. But only to lose it all over again."

—Hugo Pratt, *Corto Maltese: The Golden House of Samarkand*

"And now it was that he felt the certainty of change—in the weight of the atmosphere, perhaps, or in the very breath of the world. He was in that other island, the one he had glimpsed but never seen again."

—Michel Tournier, *Vendredi ou les Limbes du Pacifique*

# PREFACE

## Two Questions

DURING THE TIME I spent researching and writing this book, one question laypeople sometimes asked me was how in the world had I ever learned that such a person as Thomas Thor Tangvald even existed? It seemed they could not fathom how a putatively normal person like myself, living an apparently normal life, in a house on land (most of the time anyway), might somehow catch word of such an unusual and enigmatic creature. A boy who was literally born at sea and lived on a sailboat, roaming the world's oceans, through all his childhood. Who initially had such limited contact with human society he believed for years that most people must live on boats, just as he and his family did. A boy with a genius IQ who mostly educated himself, studying the books on his father's boat and the natural world of sea and sky that surrounded him. Who was fully fluent in three languages, loved mathematics and physics, and later had little trouble gaining admittance to prestigious universities. Whose early life was scarred by a number of searing calamities, yet who seemed so outwardly resilient these events had—for a time at least—little apparent effect on him. A boy who as a young man, once

1

introduced to modern society and life on shore, saw clearly how it was going astray. Who consequently was fiercely determined to live simply, sustainably, and independently on his own terms. Who in the end disappeared without a trace, leaving no evidence of his fate and more than a few questions behind.

Bluewater sailors who learned of my project, on the other hand, asked me a different question. Had I ever met Thomas?

The answer to that question, sadly, is no, I never did meet Thomas Tangvald. I first sailed into Culebra, a Puerto Rican island that played an important role in his life, in late 1999, a few years after Thomas had last stopped there as a teenager and just a few months before he returned as a young man. I next sailed to the Spanish Virgin Islands in the spring of 2013 and visited both Culebra and its sister island Vieques, about a year and a half after Thomas sailed away from Vieques for the last time. The last time I visited the area, in 2019, while I was researching this book, I was honored to have Thomas's wife and two sons aboard my boat as guests.

As far as Thomas and I are concerned, it seems our individual orbits through the Spanish Virgins were roughly coterminous but bound never to coincide. Still I like to think that if only the continuum of our lives were shifted but slightly, I might have spotted him, at Culebra say, anchored out behind the reef at Dakity. I certainly would have noticed him—a very striking Rasta-Viking lad with long blond dreadlocks flowing down his shoulders, presiding over a raft of dilapidated boats—and would have been pleased to make his acquaintance.

As to the first question, I initially learned of Thomas's existence during the opening phases of my own career as a bluewater sailor. I spent the years 1992 and '93 crewing around on other people's boats, crossing the North Atlantic from the U.S. to Europe and back, and emerged from this adventure determined to go to sea on a boat of my own. This in spite of the fact that my first transatlantic voyage, aboard a large wooden schooner, had ended in a shipwreck on the coast of Spain. Over the next few years, as I cobbled together a very modest bluewater sailboat and set out voyaging on it, I inhaled large doses of sailing literature. One of the more memorable books I encountered was *At Any Cost*, an autobiography by Peter Tangvald, Thomas's father, published just a few years earlier. The book's final pages, written as an epilogue by Thomas, who was then still a boy, are remarkable.

I immediately recalled those pages during my second cruise through the Spanish Virgins in 2013, when I happened upon an article in a local sailing magazine, also written by Thomas, now a young man with a family, about a certain voyage he was planning. I cannot tell you how happy I was to connect those two dots over that chasm of 20 years. Though I had never met him, I at once felt bound to Thomas. Soon afterward, as events unfolded and I learned more about how that voyage turned out, I became a bit obsessed with him and ultimately embarked on a quest to tell his story, the results of which you now hold in your hands.

The difference between those two questions I was asked while engaged on my quest illustrates where the community of bluewater sailors stands in relation to the rest of human society. For the fact is most people living on land don't even know such a community exists. Just as Thomas for a time could not imagine there was a much larger society beyond the harbors and anchorages where he touched land, those on shore can't see that those littoral refuges and the sea beyond them are home to a much smaller society. The land-people may wander down to a harbor on the coast near where they live and see a collection of sailboat masts, or "sticks" as we sailors sometimes call them, and never realize some of the boats under those sticks are not simply playthings, but people's homes. A more discerning eye will quickly distinguish these craft—which ones really are playthings, left tied up and rarely used; which ones may be floating vacation homes that never go very far; which ones are raced or used only for a few hours at a time; and which ones are permanently and truly mobile homes, equipped to cross oceans, part of a far-flung network of such vessels that encircles the world.

Once inside the bluewater cruising community, you soon realize how small and tight-knit it is, with only one or two degrees of separation between most persons within it. You realize also how spread out and dissipated it is, and how, in spite of this, people often run into each other again and again. We are, I've always liked to think, a small tribe spread out over a very large territory. The first couple of times you are amazed. Someone you met once on a boat in an anchorage a whole ocean and half a world away suddenly appears before you in a very different anchorage, in a very different place, and you cannot believe your eyes. But soon enough, after a few such encounters, you stop being surprised and are simply pleased to see them. This is the essential alchemy of the bluewater tribe: our paths crisscross in seemingly miraculous ways wherever there is water enough to float a boat, and in each crossed wake a unique bond is formed.

So it was during the years I spent researching this book. I was never surprised but always pleased to learn that some sailor I was already familiar with happened to have once spent some time with Peter or Thomas, or the both of them. Often I found I had friends and acquaintances in common with new sources I had diligently unearthed, and at times I found unlooked-for sources entirely at random while sailing about the western North Atlantic on my own boat. Such are the interstitial connections that make up the fabric of any human tribe.

Though most of my career as a journalist has been conducted within the sailing community, I have been schooled in the tenets of traditional journalism and even practiced law for a while, so I do understand the value of maintaining an objective critical distance from one's subject. This is necessarily more challenging when one member of a small tribe is reporting on the doings of another member.

Arguably, it may be impossible. I have, inevitably perhaps, become enmeshed in this tale and with certain people in it. As a member of the tribe of bluewater sailors, I gained access and trust that might well have been denied to others, and while I do feel an obligation not to betray that trust without good cause, I have also felt a strong obligation not to betray the story itself.

A few of my sources did ask to read the parts of this book that are directly relevant to them prior to publication. While I agreed to this in those particular cases, I never agreed to change anything I had written on demand. This has, I believe, made this work stronger. It saved me from some factual errors and elicited some telling details I might not have discovered otherwise. Though I did make a few small textual changes to spare feelings here and there, I have changed nothing that directly impacts the truth of this story as I see it.

I should note also that I have written this story for both constituencies. I do believe the tale of Thomas's life will be of great interest to a general readership, so I have limited or explained any technical terminology or nautical esoterica that might obscure the core of it. I have at the same time strived not to insult the intelligence of my fellow sailors. No doubt I have stumbled off this line in certain instances and will have confused or annoyed disparate elements of my audience, but I do have faith that the power of Thomas's story will in the end earn me some measure of forbearance.

One final note regarding quotations: a good part of the material you will find in here is derived from Thomas's own correspondence, first written letters, then later e-mails. He had idiosyncratic punctuation and capitalization habits—for example, for a long time he refused to capitalize the first-person pronoun I—and when writing e-mails was often simply sloppy, as many of us are. To avoid confusion and distraction I have regularized punctuation and capitalization and have corrected obvious typographical errors in quoted correspondence, but I have not changed any text or meaning.

The correspondence between Thomas and his wife Christina that appears later in the book was all conducted in Spanish and has been translated. Other small bits of correspondence involving Thomas's father Peter were also originally in French and have also been translated.

# 1. IN HIS FATHER'S WAKE

AT ABOUT 2 P.M. on Thursday, July 18, 1991, a bluewater sailor known as Peter Tangvald hoisted anchor and set out from the island of Culebra, off the east coast of Puerto Rico, on a short voyage south. His intended destination was the island of Bonaire, in the Netherlands Antilles off the north coast of Venezuela, a distance of about 400 nautical miles.

This was in certain respects a perfectly routine venture. Like any cruising sailor based in the Caribbean, Tangvald was worried about the advent of the North Atlantic hurricane season, which officially begins in June. Though Culebra is one of the few small islands in the Caribbean with a perfectly landlocked harbor that can be described as a "hurricane hole," a place where a boat might conceivably survive a storm, the safest strategy always, for those who live on boats, is to get outside the heart of the hurricane zone by mid-summer. Most transient sailors who find themselves in the Caribbean at the end of spring are happy to head north to the more temperate waters and cooler climates of the eastern United States or Europe. But for those who want to stay within the Caribbean, staying safe means moving deeper into the tropics. The Dutch "ABC" islands (Aruba, Bonaire, and Curaçao) and also Trinidad and Tobago, all of them quite close to South America, are far enough south that they have never been plagued by storms. So every year in the late spring and early summer, there is a small exodus of sailors who migrate out of the heart of the Caribbean to these peripheral islands.

In other respects both Tangvald and the passage he was undertaking were anything but ordinary. Unlike most modern yachtsmen who sail production-built fiberglass boats equipped with all sorts of electronics and modern conveniences, Tangvald sailed a strikingly primitive wooden boat he had designed and built himself many years earlier. Though it now looked a bit shabby, with peeling white paint, its lines were traditional and quite beautiful. It was built all of teak and had a graceful clipper bow. There was a handsome wineglass transom, an archaic gaff rig, and an elegant wooden taffrail in place of the ugly steel stanchion posts and wire lifelines that rim the decks of modern sailboats.

Tangvald was very much a purist. He believed a serious cruising sailboat should carry no equipment its owner could not easily repair and rebuild without assistance. His boat, which he had named *L'Artemis de Pytheas*, after the vessel sailed by the ancient Greek mathematician and explorer, therefore had no modern gear. As one of his sailing friends remembered it: "There wasn't a wire on that boat." No auxiliary engine, no radio transmitter, no electronic sensors or navigation equipment, no refrigeration, no electric pumps or lights, not even a toilet. For light Tangvald preferred oil lamps; to relieve himself he squatted over a bucket.

Tangvald was also unusual in that he'd been living full time on his boat, and on two previous boats, for much of his adult life and through several marriages. Throughout the latter half of the 20th century bluewater sailing had become increasingly popular, thanks largely to pioneers like Peter Tangvald. Many had come to see it not merely as a sport and as a means of travel, but more fundamentally as a way of life. There were more and more people now exploring the planet in boats they sailed themselves. Most however only did this for a few years before eventually returning to their regular lives on shore. Tangvald was one of a handful who lived permanently afloat with no fixed address. He'd done this for decades now. He had written one influential book about his early cruising life. More recently, in his original home country of

Norway, he had published a full autobiography that soon would appear in English in the United States. Over the years his exploits had been featured in many sailing magazines, as well as in a few mainstream publications, most particularly in Norway. To many in the sailing community Tangvald was a legendary figure and highly respected, though in recent years his reputation had declined. To some his method of sailing and his very simplistic lifestyle had come to seem extreme and anachronistic. There were also vague dark rumors concerning the fate of certain women who had sailed with him.

For this was what was most unusual about Peter Tangvald. He was now a single parent with two children to care for—a young girl, Carmen, age 7, and an older teenage son, Thomas. Cruising sailboats with children aboard have never been a rarity, but normally these are manned by couples—usually by young couples. Tangvald however was not only alone, but was now 66 years old. A veteran of seven different marriages, he had always been a handsome man. He had piercing blue eyes, a trim physique, an almost elfin air about him, and a very serious yet somehow magnetic personality. As one old Caribbean sailor once put it: "Peter Tangvald was a good seaman, but also a very strange character who attracted women like bears to a honey pot."

Unfortunately, the break-up of Peter's last marriage three years earlier had disarmed him. Soon after his young wife decided to leave him, he suffered a serious heart attack. Not long afterward he suffered another lesser heart attack. He'd also been badly incapacitated by kidney stones and persistent angina attacks, and for some time now he'd been acutely aware of his mortality.

Thomas and Carmen—born to different mothers, one French, one Asian—had lived all their lives aboard *L'Artemis de Pytheas*, roaming the planet with their father and his different wives under sail. Thomas, at age 15, was now just old enough to start asserting himself. He was a taut, wiry lad with a tousled mop of blond hair, an earnest smile, and a sharp mind. During the past year he'd taken jobs working on other people's boats, and the previous fall had used some of the money he earned to buy himself an old wooden sailboat. Given his upbringing, it was the only mode of independent existence he could conceive of. The boat he purchased was just 22 feet long, less than half the length of his father's, and had a large open cockpit and a very leaky deck. Thomas had proudly named her *Spartan* and immediately moved aboard.

Over the previous months Thomas and his dad had sometimes moved their two boats through local Puerto Rican waters in tandem. Rather than sail independently, however, Peter had towed the barely functional *Spartan* behind *L'Artemis*. Of course, for a boat without an engine to tow another any distance was inherently challenging. To make sure there was a strong connection aboard *Spartan*, Peter had passed 20 feet of 3/8-inch chain around the base of her mast. Then, to ensure that neither boat would be harshly jerked about as the larger one pulled the smaller one through the water, he led 300 feet of 5/8-inch nylon rope from the chain to a strong point on the deck of *L'Artemis*. Both the length of the rope, and the great elasticity of nylon, served to act as a shock absorber between the two boats as they moved along.

This system had worked well enough when *L'Artemis* was sailing short distances in Puerto Rican waters. But sailing 400 miles across the open Caribbean, where the persistent strength of the easterly tradewinds routinely builds waves into steep breaking seas, was another matter entirely. Peter, ever jealous of his own independence, had briefly pondered whether he could now leave Thomas on his own in Puerto Rico. Thomas, like his father, was a fiercely competent sailor and had spent time living aboard *Spartan* well away from *L'Artemis*, in a different harbor on a different island. But Peter knew the boy was not yet mature enough to take care of himself. Only recently he had complained to friends that Thomas sometimes "acted like a complete idiot" and did not choose his companions wisely.

So together father and son laid out a plan for the long tow to Bonaire. Aggravated by how little Thomas had done to make *Spartan*'s deck watertight, Peter helped him finish the necessary repairs. But even with the deck secure, Peter knew that *Spartan*, with an open cockpit running half her length, might be swamped and sunk by the lumpy seas of the open Caribbean long before they reached Bonaire. Thomas, he decided, would therefore have to stay aboard *Spartan* for the duration of the passage, which he expected would take three to four days. Thomas then could periodically bail out the water coming aboard his boat, while Peter handled the mothership and minded Carmen on his own. If the two boats were somehow separated, Peter was confident that Thomas, who had taught himself celestial navigation when he was younger and had built his own sextant from scratch, could reach shore safely on his own.

TO ANY OBJECTIVE PERSON with a modicum of nautical common sense, this scheme must at least have seemed ambitious. Factor in Peter Tangvald's failing health and it might more accurately be condemned as foolhardy. A few of Peter's Caribbean sailing friends and acquaintances had told him they thought this passage was a bad idea, but out of deference to Peter's great experience and his reputation, none had pressed the point. There was however one very experienced mariner, Edward Allcard, Peter's oldest sailing friend, who now lived in the tiny mountain nation of Andorra between France and Spain, who had no such compunctions. When Peter wrote to Edward describing what he proposed to do, Edward at once wrote back, told him not to be such a damn fool, and practically ordered him to stay put in Puerto Rico.

We cannot know for certain if Peter Tangvald ever received Edward's warning before he and his children set out with their two boats from Culebra. We can only speculate as to what he was thinking. There's no doubt he must have felt anxious about the prospect of hurricanes, as already there'd been one storm that season. Little more than two weeks earlier Tropical Storm Ana had suddenly formed in the Bahamas and had swept back and forth across Florida before shooting out into the open Atlantic Ocean. As a young man Peter had never been too shy about taking chances with hurricanes and typhoons. He'd tangled with such storms before, both in harbor and at sea. But now he was much older, palpably weaker, and could not delude himself that Culebra, with its landlocked harbor, might be a bulletproof safe haven. Just two years earlier Hurricane Hugo, a strong Category 4 storm with winds gusting to 240 miles an hour, had swept right over the island, destroying all but 20 of the 300 boats that had sheltered there.

Given the geography of the Caribbean basin, a more conservative hurricane-avoidance plan would have been to island-hop short distances with *Spartan* in tow, north through the Bahamas and then up the U.S. Eastern seaboard, or south down the chain of the Lesser Antilles to Grenada. And it seems Peter had considered this. In his earlier correspondence with Edward he had laid out initial plans to tow Thomas and *Spartan* downwind to either the Dominican Republic or the Bahamas. But Peter Tangvald was a stubborn man, always rather self-absorbed, and he was used to going where he wanted. He and his children had easily sailed on *L'Artemis* down to Bonaire and Curaçao the two previous summers, though without another boat in tow, and had enjoyed themselves. Though Peter found Curaçao a bit boring, he appreciated Bonaire and felt the people there had much better manners than those in Puerto Rico. Thomas, meanwhile, ranked Bonaire as one of his favorite islands. It had been easy there for him to find friends his age, easy to find work, and the windsurfing and snorkeling were excellent. Most likely he'd been trying to talk his father into returning.

One thing Peter Tangvald never considered in planning this passage was whether it really was necessary to leave Thomas aboard *Spartan*. His fanatic aversion to modern technology prevented him from conceiving, much less implementing, what to many contemporary mariners might seem an obvious solution to the problem of keeping *Spartan* afloat at sea. Rather than have Thomas bail out the boat while underway, a strong electric bilge pump with an automatic float switch, properly secured and plumbed, wired to a 12-volt battery and a solar panel, could have been installed aboard to do the job instead. With a rig like this on *Spartan*, Peter then would have had a much easier voyage, with his highly experienced son by his side to help manage *L'Artemis*.

DURING THE FIRST THREE DAYS and nights of their passage, Peter and Thomas—each isolated on his own boat, but joined by the long tether between them—sailed on a course that was slightly west of south. The wind was not too strong, at least not for the Caribbean, but it did blow from the southeast, perhaps even from a bit south of southeast, so that *L'Artemis* and *Spartan* were on what is known as a close reach. At this sailing angle the wind and seas were coming at the two boats from slightly ahead of the beam, rather than from behind, and their motion therefore was aggressive.

When sailing on the ocean for extended periods, motion is everything. It is a cosmic constant, never-ending, a perpetual dance between a sailor, his or her vessel, its rig, and the immense, amorphous elements of liquid and air that surround them. It focuses the mind acutely, forcing the sailor to live in the present moment. This meditative acuity, combined with the extreme and isolating nature of the sea itself, gives rise to what psychologists have termed "oceanic feeling"—an innate sense of connection between an individual and the rest of creation.

When wind and seas are favorable, coming from abaft the beam, and a boat's motion is kinder, sinuous and rolling, a sailor's close connection with the elements can feel pleasurable and seductive. It was this sensation that helped lure Peter Tangvald away from his existence on shore when he was a much younger man and helped keep him at sea through most of his life. For Thomas, it was never anything he chose; it was the ether he was born into.

Tighten up a boat's sailing angle so that it points closer into the wind, and its motion becomes sharper. The boat stops rolling, starts pitching and yawing instead, sometimes slamming into waves rather than yielding to them. The closer the angle and the steeper the seas, the more slamming there will be. The need to live in the moment then becomes even more acute, because it is impossible to accomplish any task without focusing on it exclusively. The connection to the elements meanwhile is unbroken and becomes stronger, because now it is tinged with violence.

Both Peter and Thomas were familiar with this sort of uncomfortable motion. If you sail on the ocean for any length of time, it is inevitable. You grit your teeth and endure it. In this case it could only have been aggravated by the towline that joined their two boats together.

The wind and the slapping of the waves against the boats inevitably sent a good deal of spray flying through the air, so that Thomas, bouncing along behind *L'Artemis*, had to bail out *Spartan* at least once every three hours to keep her from being overwhelmed. He had little chance to sleep for very long, probably felt seasick (at least at first), and most likely wasn't eating well. Even when anchored in calm water, Thomas's life aboard *Spartan* had never been comfortable. According to one friend who visited Thomas on the boat not long before he and his father left for Bonaire, he had no stove to cook on and no mattress aboard. To sleep he stretched out on open wooden boards with only a beach towel to cover himself. Even with such amenities as blankets and mattresses aboard, an open-water passage in such a small, crude boat in a lively sea, with only a cramped cabin for shelter, was bound to be an ordeal.

Aboard *L'Artemis* the unpleasant motion would also have inhibited Peter's ability to take accurate sextant sights. Although most sailors by now were shifting from old-fashioned celestial to modern satellite GPS navigation, Peter Tangvald had no interest in this new technology. He'd relied on his skill as a celestial navigator to find his way clear around the world when he was a younger man; he could now certainly find his way across the Caribbean. But one drawback to working with a sextant, which requires that you carefully catch the celestial object you are shooting in a tiny mirror and then swing it precisely down on to the horizon, is that rough conditions on a boat make it much harder to take accurate sights. It is also quite aggravating, so there was a good chance that Peter, who had his hands full sailing singlehanded with both a boat and a young daughter to tend to, wasn't bothering to break out his sextant. As an experienced navigator, it was a fairly simple matter for him to estimate his position through a process known as dead reckoning. By keeping careful track of his course and speed and the elapsed time, allowing also for his boat's westward drift due to the relentless easterly wind and current, he could quickly deduce where he was by solving a few basic equations.

Fortunately, on the fourth day of the passage, Sunday, the wind shifted more to the east so that it was blowing from slightly behind *L'Artemis* and *Spartan*. This eased the motion of the two boats and reduced the amount of spray in the air—not a vast improvement in conditions, but it was an improvement. If he was dead reckoning, Peter might have seized on this as an opportunity to check himself and take some sextant sights, or he might have thought this unnecessary. At some point that day in any event, not long before sunset, Thomas shouted to his father across the 300 feet of bumpy water that separated the two boats. He asked hopefully if they would reach Bonaire that night. His father nodded his head affirmatively.

THOMAS WOKE UP AND CHECKED on his boat three times that night. The third time he found the water inside *Spartan's* tiny cabin had risen up several inches above the floorboards, so he got up to bail. It was a little before 3 a.m. and still very dark with no moon showing.

Stepping out into his boat's cockpit, Thomas looked around and saw they were now well within sight of land. No, he could not actually see any land, but he could see lights that were obviously on land. Behind him to the right, high on the horizon, he saw one lighthouse shining quite brightly. Straight ahead he made out another, much lower and shining only dimly, that he knew must be some distance away. To the right he could see the soft glow, or loom, of more lights that were not directly visible. Thomas checked the chart he had onboard and quickly deduced they must be sailing down the east coast of Bonaire. The light behind him, he surmised, was Spelonk, on the island's easternmost headland; the one ahead was Willemstoren, at the island's southern tip. The loom of lights to the west, he figured, must be from Kralendijk, the main town, on the other side of the island.

"I stood up," Thomas later wrote, "thinking about anchoring amidst the yachts at dawn, meeting new people, cleaning my boat out. I felt good."

But he didn't feel good for very long. The problem was, from a navigational point of view, they were on the wrong side of the island—the windward side, which was open to all the long, powerful waves driven west across the Atlantic Ocean and the Caribbean Sea by the relentless easterly wind.

Thomas would not have been too surprised by this. He knew celestial position plots were often several miles in error, most particularly on the trickier east-west axis of longitude. If his father had been dead reckoning, the most likely axis of error, again, was east-west, due to the uncertainties of estimating drift in the easterly tradewinds. Thomas might well have wondered why his father hadn't changed course earlier, once he had the island in sight ahead, so as to sail down its western coast. But now that they were here on the exposed eastern coast, he must have assumed his father planned to maintain a safe distance from shore while circling around the island's southern end into the safety and shelter of its lee side.

Gradually, however, Thomas sensed they were much too close to the shore. He could see that the southern Willemstoren light in the distance was swaying to either side of *L'Artemis* ahead of him as the boat yawed back and forth under her imprecise wind-driven self-steering gear. He could also feel his boat's motion starting to change as the waves beneath it steadily grew steeper in anticipation of finally reaching some land to crash into.

Growing nervous now, Thomas guessed that his father must be down below in the cabin of *L'Artemis*, studying his chart and plotting a course change to the east, away from the shore. Any moment, he prayed, he would see his father pop out on deck to make the necessary adjustments to the boat's self-steering gear.

If only Peter Tangvald had been willing to tolerate a bare minimum of technology in his life afloat, Thomas in this moment of crisis might easily have taken action. With a pair of handheld VHF radios, commonly carried by all modern sailors, and a few AA batteries to power them, Thomas and Peter could have been in regular communication, and Thomas might now have hailed his father, waking him if he were asleep, so they could discuss the situation.

But Thomas was powerless and could only watch what happened next. He spotted three rocks on the horizon directly ahead, and he panicked. His mind leapt to an irrational conclusion: this must be somewhere else, perhaps Aves, a dangerous coral atoll some 30 miles east of Bonaire. Then, through the darkness, he finally saw the shore in full and a long white line of waves crashing on to it.

As he later noted: "That is probably the most unpleasant sound in the world for any sailor."

Thomas watched the surf pull *L'Artemis* up and into the shore and could only scream in disbelief. This couldn't be real; it must be some sort of nightmare. Then he saw the towline that connected his boat to *L'Artemis* go slack. In the next instant he heard over the roar of the waves a sharp cracking sound as the mast on *L'Artemis* broke in two and crashed down onto her deck. Instinctively he rushed to save himself. He jumped back into *Spartan*'s cabin, extracted the small surfboard he had stowed there, and leapt with it into the water seconds before his boat followed his father's into the vicious maw of the surf line. He was wearing no pants, just a wool shirt and a waterproof windbreaker.

This was a particularly nasty piece of coastline, a flat low shelf of very sharp, jagged coral known locally as the Iron Shore. Thomas's immediate instinct was to paddle in closer and somehow scramble ashore so that he could join his father and sister, but the action of the surf on the coral was violent and extremely intimidating. He described the ordeal of the rest of that night in some detail in an account he wrote for his father's American publisher little more than a month later:

> I stayed as close to *L'Artemis* as possible, waiting for a break in the waves to dash in and jump ashore. Under the light of the stern lamp, I could see the boat being destroyed with ghastly efficiency. She would leap up in the air with the rising water and, as the water went back out, the boat would drop 10 feet onto the sharp coral with the sickening noise of cracking wood and my sister's hysterical screams coming from inside. For a minute or two, I saw my Dad sitting in the companionway shining a flashlight out to sea and then across the reef. I put my surfboard up in the air, but I don't think he saw me.
>
> Then *L'Artemis*'s stern lamp went out from the successive shocks, leaving her completely in the dark. I paddled out and away from the breaking waves. After a little while, I didn't feel panic at all. Instead it was a lot like a dream. I figured I just had to keep paddling to stay warm, and wait until sunrise when I could climb the coral and find them both waiting for me.
>
> After some three hours, the sun finally came up and I could see the coast. It was Bonaire, after all. Edging closer to the reef, I spent another two hours trying to get in, timing it so I would reach the coral as the wave went down. But there was a current pulling me away from the coast. The important

thing wasn't timing, the idea was to get in. As I headed north again, I saw something on the reef. It was the remains of *L'Artemis*—part of the stern here, a bit of dagger board there, fenders floating around, millions of little bits of teak.

At around 9 o'clock, I finally got on shore without too many scratches but, after staying six hours on the surfboard, I had massive friction burns. Immediately I set about searching for my father and sister—but they weren't there.

By the end of that day Thomas found himself lying in a bed in room number 16 at the Hospital San Francisco in Kralendijk. Kaye and Jack McOustra, Canadian expatriates from Curaçao who were visiting Bonaire at the time, recalled later that Thomas was "a shell-shocked and really grazed-up kid." He did not cry, nor even seem sad, Kaye wrote, which was, she assumed, the result of his being traumatized.

The very next day Thomas was asked by the local authorities to return to the scene of the wreck to identify a body. He agreed and was led to a grisly tableau where he saw the mortal remains of his father lying on the unforgiving coral with his face cut up and all smashed in. To Thomas it looked like he must have been caught between the hull of his boat and the sharp coral. The body of his little sister Carmen, meanwhile, had apparently gone missing. But the following day it too was found, afloat near the shore.

Now, quite suddenly, Thomas Thor Tangvald was an orphan, all alone, with no immediate family left anywhere in the world.

22

# 2. AFTERMATH

MANY YEARS LATER, when she was much older and her memories of those days had begun to fade, Clare Allcard still vividly remembered the phone call. It came via a circuitous route.

The people on Bonaire who were immediately helping Thomas—the local police and the staff at the Hospital San Francisco—had divined he was a U.S. citizen and quickly consulted one of the more prominent Americans on the island, a Baptist missionary named Jack Ludlum. Ludlum in turn had contacted the nearest American consulate on Bonaire's larger sister island of Curaçao and spoke with the vice consul there. This was a young woman named Elizabeth Moore, on her first overseas assignment with the U.S. State Department. She spoke with Thomas over the phone and recalled later that he was "in total shock." She was keen to learn who might come to collect him, now that he was orphaned. Thomas could provide her only with three first names: an ex-wife of his father's, Simonne, who lived in southern France; and Edward and Clare, sailing people who now lived in the remote micro-nation of Andorra.

Vice consul Moore reached out to the U.S. consulate in Marseille, which had no way of identifying who Simonne might be. She also contacted the consulate in Barcelona, the closest major city to Andorra. The U.S. Consul General there, a woman named Ruth Davis, happened to mention the situation over dinner to her counterpart at the British consulate, and this gentleman knew immediately who Edward and Clare must be.

The call from the British consulate to the Allcards was made in the early evening. It was Clare who answered the phone, and when she heard the news—that Peter Tangvald had not followed her husband's advice and had sailed south to Bonaire, towing Thomas's boat behind him, and had been wrecked on the Iron Shore, and that both Peter and young Carmen were now dead—she screamed. "Loud and clear," was how she remembered it. It was the first time in her own decidedly tumultuous life that she'd ever done this, so angry was she with Peter and so upset at what had happened.

First thing the next morning Clare and Edward hastily organized a trip to Bonaire. Edward, at age 76, was still hale and hearty, but he was suffering with an inguinal hernia at the time. The scheduled surgery to repair this had to be postponed, and then a chain of travel legs as circuitous as the chain of phone calls that had reached them the night before was booked. First a pre-dawn bus ride from Andorra three hours down out of the mountains to Barcelona. Then a transcontinental flight from Barcelona to Amsterdam, followed by a long transatlantic flight to Curaçao, followed by a short puddle-jumper to Bonaire. Unfortunately, the agent in Andorra who strung together this itinerary was a novice and made a terrible mess of things. Hence there was a good deal of anxiety, confusion, and improvisation along the way, with poor Edward, ever the stoic, carefully clutching his gut through all of it.

Though they were certainly surprised and shocked by the violent, sudden manner of Peter Tangvald's death, Edward and Clare, like Peter himself, had anticipated his end might come sooner rather than later. Peter, not long after suffering his first major heart attack in the summer of 1988, having been told he might have only a year to live, had written to Edward, despairing over what would become of Thomas and Carmen. At Clare's suggestion Edward immediately responded, volunteering that he and Clare would be happy to take care of the children should anything happen to Peter.

Peter was effusively grateful—"I had trouble keeping back

my tears," he wrote—and there followed an involved train of correspondence in which Peter laid out the arrangements he was making. Though he very much hoped to prove the doctors wrong and live several more years, he wanted to be prepared and so executed a new will: Edward would serve as executor of Peter's meager yet convoluted estate; Clare and Edward together would be foster parents and guardians to his surviving children.

PETER AND EDWARD HAD BEEN GOOD FRIENDS ever since they first met in November 1957, in the harbor at Las Palmas, on the island of Gran Canaria, in the Spanish Canary Islands, not too far off the northwestern coast of Africa. Edward, a reserved fellow with a slight physique, a trim beard, and a quick wit, was at the time already renowned as a bluewater sailor. In an era when such feats were still unusual, he had twice sailed alone across the Atlantic, in 1949 and '51, from England to the U.S. and back, in a 34-foot yawl named *Temptress*, becoming the first man ever to sail a full circuit of the North Atlantic singlehanded. That fall in Las Palmas he was preparing to complete yet another circuit, in a 36-foot ketch he called *Sea Wanderer*, which he'd previously sailed from New York to Plymouth, England, by way of the Bahamas.

Peter at that point was a mere novice in the bluewater sailing game. Originally named Per, he'd been born in Oslo, Norway, in September 1924 and first learned to sail at age 14 at the insistence of his father. Thor Tangvald, Thomas's grandfather, had led a very active life. He'd been a renowned skier and was several times national champion in cross-country and ski-jumping events. He also had served as an air force aviator, one of the first pilots in Norway, holding license number 12. He went on to found a successful company and became one of the top manufacturers of ski equipment in all of Europe. Not surprisingly then, Thor was horrified when he discovered his eldest son Per supposedly had a "delicate" disposition and was being fed sedatives each night before bed. He at once decreed that Per should receive no more medication and had a boat mooring laid in the fjord in front of the family's house at Nesodden. On that mooring he installed a sailboat; he also hired a man to teach his son how to sail it.

It proved a fateful decision. Per's private instructor worked him hard and had him out on the water 12 hours a day during the summer season. He not only taught Per the relatively simple process of sailing a boat, but also drilled him relentlessly in the more arcane details of close-quarters maneuvering and anchoring under sail. Per loved every minute of it, and as his father had hoped the rigorous tuition made the boy healthier and stronger. It also instilled in him a great love of the sea and a deep appreciation of the art of handling boats under sail alone.

Spoiled and self-indulgent, Per had stumbled haphazardly into adulthood. Eager to build up his skill as a mariner, he left school to join the Norwegian coast guard but found the service dull and tedious and soon quit. He had a similar experience in the Norwegian air force. Finally, again at his father's insistence, he'd taken up the tool-and-die trade and found he had an aptitude for it. Ultimately, in March 1949, he immigrated to the United States and eventually drifted to California, where he studied engineering.

Per, now more commonly called Peter, was by 1956 already married to a third wife, a Norwegian woman named Lillemor Thorkildsen, and was living in the Los Angeles area. He was working there as a prosperous engineer in a successful firm when his love of sailing was rekindled. Studying yachting magazines, he noticed that prices for used sailing yachts were much lower in England than in California. As he later wrote: "Why not go to England, buy a yacht at their favorable prices, and then sail it to Los Angeles, where I should be able to sell it with sufficient profit to cover all my expenses? I'd be able to get the most fantastic vacation any yachtsman could desire—for free."

On a whim he quit his job, flew to England in the spring of 1957, and purchased a 45-foot teak yawl named *Windflower*.

Lillemor had bravely joined Peter in his first adventure sailing *Windflower* a short distance down the English coast, from West Mersea to Dover. The couple unfortunately were caught in a gale, and the boat leaked badly. Lillemor was terrified and jumped ship as soon as they reached Dover. Peter, though he'd been badly seasick in the gale, carried on regardless. He spent months working on the boat, fixing her leaks and preparing her for sea. That October he struck out south alone from Falmouth on his first ocean passage. After just one stop in Vigo, Spain, he had arrived safely in Las Palmas.

Now Peter and Edward were two singlehanders in the same port, each preparing his boat for the same voyage—the long downwind run through the northeast tradewinds from the Canaries to the West Indies.[1] They quickly formed a strong bond. Peter had known of Edward, who had published two books about his exploits, and was flattered to be treated by him as an equal. Already, he thought proudly, he'd been accepted into the elite club of ocean-sailing yachtsmen.

As for Edward, he immediately felt a kinship with Peter. They were both esthetic men, sober teetotalers who reveled in the rigors of the sea.

"Peter and I found we had many things in common," he later wrote. "We had both given up good jobs in order to start to live; our ideas on smoking and drinking and physical fitness were similar,

---

1. The passage from the Canary Islands to the Caribbean basin, originally forged by Christopher Columbus in 1492, is the route most frequently traveled by modern bluewater cruisers. Where in the 1950s there was a handful of yachts making this seasonal migration, now there are well over 1,000 boats sailing the route each year.

and I admired Peter's complete candor with regard to himself, a refreshing honesty in these days when most people are doing their best to sell themselves with a lot of inaccurate boloney."

As they prepared their boats in tandem, Peter and Edward hit on the idea of making a race of it. They would sail out of Las Palmas together, and the first man to step ashore at English Harbour in Antigua, almost 3,000 miles to the west, would win one dollar. Edward's boat was nine feet shorter than Peter's, which technically gave Peter an advantage, as longer boats are generally faster than shorter ones. But *Sea Wanderer* steered herself downwind more easily than *Windflower* (this was in the days before reliable self-steering gear) and also had a more reliable engine, in case there were calms along the way, so the two men considered the odds to be more or less even.

A large crowd gathered along the waterfront to see the two boats off on November 20. Thirty-one days later, on December 21, 1957, Peter sailed into English Harbour, two days ahead of Edward, and so became the winner of what is today remembered by well-informed yachting historians as the first singlehanded sailboat race across the Atlantic Ocean.[2] There was a fair bit of publicity at the time, including a feature story in *The Times* of London. Peter framed the dollar bill he won from Edward as a prize and proudly displayed it in *Windflower's* cabin.

Once in the Caribbean the two men went their separate ways. Edward spent the next four years aboard *Sea Wanderer* sailing up and down the chain of tropical islands, earning money in the charter trade. With his bank account thus fortified, he later embarked on

---

2. The more formally organized Observer Singlehanded Transatlantic Race (or OSTAR) of 1960, sailed by five different men, including Sir Francis Chichester, who won the race aboard *Gipsy Moth III*, is most commonly cited as the first singlehanded transatlantic sailing competition. Though the course for this event, from Plymouth, England, to New York City, was mostly upwind and therefore more arduous than the Canaries-West Indies route, there is no denying that Edward and Peter's match race predated it.

an ambitious 100-day solo voyage to South America, where he cruised the desolate waters of Patagonia, one of the first modern yachtsmen since Joshua Slocum to do so. From there Edward ultimately sailed west across the Pacific Ocean on a peripatetic, often interrupted solo circumnavigation back to Antigua that took him 13 years to complete.

Peter meanwhile continued more expeditiously on his own voyage home to California. His wife Lillemor rejoined him aboard *Windflower* soon after he arrived in the West Indies, and she stayed aboard as they cruised together through the islands and while the boat later locked through the Panama Canal. She got off again, however, in Costa Rica, after she and Peter started bashing their way against the prevailing winds up the west coast of Central America. Peter finally arrived in Los Angeles late in December 1958, having thoroughly enjoyed a vigorous solo cruise up the Mexican coast. As he'd hoped, he was able to sell *Windflower* for a price that not only covered all his expenses, but also left him some profit.

Peter returned to the engineering office where he'd been working prior to his great adventure, but he immediately felt this was a mistake. He quit again after just one day on the job, this time for good, and promptly returned to England on his own to buy another sailboat. The immigration officer who stamped his passport immediately recognized him from his previous visit two years earlier. Peter could only smile. That *ka-thunk* of a passport stamp marked a new beginning, the inauguration of his new life as a full-time liveaboard cruising sailor.


THOUGH CLARE AND EDWARD RUSHED to reach Bonaire as quickly as they could, Thomas was still nearly a week on the island before they arrived. Using his surfboard as a shield and boarding ramp, he'd managed to clamber up the sharp coral littoral without suffering too much harm when he came ashore that Monday morning after the wreck. He had wandered inland over the barren wind-blasted landscape, half-naked with no trousers on, and came eventually to the only dwelling on that portion of the coast, an isolated chicken farm. He hoped he might find his father and sister waiting for him there, but was disappointed.

The residents of the farm provided Thomas with immediate relief—more clothing and most likely some food and water—and contacted the police to inform them of the tragedy that had taken place during the night. The one person who subsequently assumed the most responsibility for Thomas's well-being was the Baptist pastor, Jack Ludlum, who had set the gears grinding at the U.S. consulate on Curaçao.

Ludlum worked with a unique organization, Trans World Radio, a non-denominational band of American and other expatriate missionaries who had been spreading the Christian gospel around the world via an ever-growing network of radio stations since 1954. The station on Bonaire, which transmitted to the Caribbean basin, Central America, and northern South America, had been established in 1964, and its staff of 100 or so were led by Ludlum. One of the first people he called to help manage the crisis of Thomas's arrival on the island was a local businessman, Amado Felix. Felix, when he was a teenager, had helped to build the island's Trans World Radio station and later married one of the American staff. He was well known on the island as a man always willing to help others in need.

Pastor Ludlum and Amado Felix did all they could to aid Thomas, both emotionally and logistically. Ludlum spent much time counseling Thomas and simply sitting with him in the hospital. He also accompanied him to the crash site on Tuesday, when Thomas identified the mutilated remains of his father. Clare

Allcard, once she arrived on the island, bitterly regretted she hadn't been there to prevent this, as she thought it too cruel a chore to impose on the boy. Later, however, when Thomas told her of two dreams he had after the wreck, she changed her mind.

In the first dream Thomas's father came to him looking very different, but Thomas had no trouble recognizing him.

"Yes, it's amazing, isn't it?" said his father. "I'm all better now!"

In the second dream Thomas found himself studying a huge map of the world and was desperately trying to decide where to go to search for his father. Then he remembered he didn't have to look for him, because he was already dead.

"He might never have had that closure," Clare later wrote, "if he had not identified his father's body."

The following day both Ludlum and Felix accompanied Thomas when he went to identify the body of his little sister Carmen at the morgue next door to the hospital. For Thomas it was a particularly charged moment, as his relationship with his half-sister had always been difficult. She, like Thomas, had been a very bright child, but unlike him was also needy. Her father had occasionally neglected her. Other cruisers who knew the Tangvalds on Culebra remembered she sometimes had to wait on shore for hours until her father came from *L'Artemis* to pick her up after school. But Carmen was smart enough to get people to pay attention to her. She had little trouble charming women she met from other transient cruising boats and usually had "a cadre" (as one of these women once put it) of wanna-be surrogate mothers looking after her.

To gain attention from her father, meanwhile, Carmen at times simply cried. Thomas had resented this, and one of the reasons he'd wanted to move off his father's boat to one of his own was to get away from her.

Amado Felix recalled later that Thomas, as he confronted his sister's dead body, looked "completely broken."

Thomas certainly wouldn't have had any trouble imagining the last moments of Carmen's life. The night of the wreck, even over the roar of the surf, he'd heard the girl screaming from inside *L'Artemis* and he knew, from his own experience, exactly where in the boat she had been. Just as he'd been when he was younger, sailing alone with his father on *L'Artemis*, Carmen had been confined to the forepeak for safekeeping. This forwardmost cabin was effectively fitted out as a jail cell for children, a feature on his boat Peter Tangvald had always been proud of. It was equipped with a locked latch on the door and a fixed grate across the deck hatch overhead. Carmen therefore, as she heard and felt the boat being destroyed all around her, had had no hope of escaping and somehow saving herself.

Many years later, during a television interview, Thomas described the revelation that came to him that day. His voice was thin and filled with regret: "I thought I really hated her, but then I realized of course I didn't hate her at all."

Ludlum and Felix weren't the only members of the Trans World Radio community striving to do what they could to help. There were many donations of food and clothing, plus a suitcase to travel off the island with. One group went down to the Iron Shore and spent several days scouring the wreck site and the surrounding area for debris that might be meaningful to Thomas.

Terri Tangeman, a TWR staff member who helped lead this effort, remembered some of the items they recovered: a nameboard from the transom of *L'Artemis*, a wooden washboard, plus several tools. She especially remembered finding a wood carving Thomas's mother had made: "It was broken. One day we found one piece of it, and the next day we found another piece." Perhaps most significantly, the search party also found a sealed waterproof ammunition box full of photographs and slides that Peter Tangvald had collected over the years. Several of these would be used to illustrate Peter's posthumous English-language autobiography, entitled *At Any Cost*.

Funeral services for both Peter and Carmen were held on Thursday afternoon, the day after Carmen's body was recovered. There were no facilities on the island for properly preserving or embalming bodies, beyond temporarily freezing them in the morgue, and prompt burials were therefore standard procedure. In Peter and Carmen's case it was particularly necessary, as both bodies were already decomposing when discovered.

It was Amado Felix who arranged for and covered the cost of the burials, trusting that Thomas's new guardians, whoever they were, might eventually reimburse him. He recalled there was a small walking procession of TWR staff, led by Thomas, grim and silent, to escort Peter's body from the morgue next to the hospital just a short distance to the Alliance Evangelical Church Cemetery. Then the island's one hearse was sent back to retrieve Carmen's body. Pastor Ludlum conducted a brief service, and the two bodies, father and daughter, were commended to a pair of shallow concrete tombs.

THE ALLCARDS FINALLY APPEARED on Saturday. They stopped first in Curaçao and met with Elizabeth Moore at the consulate there, before flying on to Bonaire. Moore had done a bit of research and learned that Thomas's father had renewed his own U.S. passport in Curaçao just two years earlier, and she expected the documentation from that application would enable her to quickly replace the passport Thomas had lost in the wreck.

Clare was acquainted with Peter Tangvald only through her husband. Over the years she'd corresponded with him as he wandered the world aboard his boat, and she had thoughtfully sent small birthday and Christmas gifts to Thomas and later also to Carmen. She in return had received thank-you letters from the boy, but she'd never met him or his father. The first time she ever laid eyes on Thomas was that day in the air terminal on Bonaire. Walking down the stairs from the arrival gate, she surveyed the group below that had gathered to meet the flight. She spotted what looked to her like a very skinny young girl with fine features and curly blonde hair in a turquoise singlet standing next to a middle-aged man. That girl turned out to be Thomas; the man next to him was Pastor Ludlum. From that day forward Clare would assert that Thomas had been malnourished while in his father's care. (Thomas, ever protective of his father's memory, would always deny this.) Clare felt a strong urge to hug this odd, seemingly emaciated boy, but quelled it when she saw how very reserved he was.

"I didn't want to intrude on his private space," she later wrote. "I also sensed he didn't trust women."

Kaye McOustra, the Canadian expatriate who happened to be visiting at the time, was impressed with Clare. She, her husband Jack, and their three children had arrived from Curaçao the day after the wreck and were staying in the Trans World Radio guesthouse.

"Everybody really was out of their depth," Kaye recalled. "Here was a boy who had lost all his family, scraped up head to toe, shell-shocked, and no one was sure how best to help him. Then Clare came, and she was so business-like and sweet and compassionate with him."

That same day, realizing he now would soon leave the island, Thomas insisted on revisiting the wreck site. He was accompanied by Clare and Edward, who with his hernia had to take care clambering about the rocky coral shore. Pastor Ludlum and Amado Felix also came along. Clare remembered they found thousands of tiny slivers of teak lying about and also an empty brown glass ampule that had contained a dose of sodium amytal. Peter had been using this to treat angina attacks, and she now deduced such an attack might have been a cause of the wreck.

Amado Felix meanwhile remembered watching Thomas: "He just sat there and watched the ocean and watched the ocean. It was very hard for me. I'm sure it was much harder for him."

Before they left the island Clare took Thomas back to the hospital to thank the staff there. As there was no place else for him to stay, Thomas had been in their care for days while awaiting Clare and Edward's arrival. Even in the midst of this awful tragedy, the boy's adolescent hormones had been fully operational, and Thomas had developed a crush on one young nurse named Mayti. She wasn't there when he stopped in to say goodbye, but Clare left a box of chocolates for her with Pastor Ludlum, which he later faithfully delivered.

From Bonaire the two foster parents and their new foster child flew first to Curaçao, where they spent a few days waiting for Thomas's American passport to be processed. Here the new family visited with the McOustras, who had returned with their own children from Bonaire to their home on the island.

The McOustras' eldest child, Iain, aged 11, was very taken with Thomas. Here, his mother Kaye later recalled, was an older boy, who had just been shipwrecked no less, "with a scope of life that just blew my kid away."

Long afterwards Kaye liked to recount the story of what happened when Thomas jumped into their swimming pool. As far as anyone knew, it was the first time Thomas had swum in fresh water, and he was entirely unprepared for its lack of buoyancy compared to salt water.

"He just sank!" declared Kaye. "He was very surprised, and we all thought it amusing. It was the only amusing moment I remember from that time."

Elizabeth Moore, the vice consul, also met with Thomas at this time. Helping Thomas secure his paperwork was one of her first significant chores as a budding diplomat, and she carried clear memories of the encounter all through her later career. "There's no doubt in my mind he was very traumatized by what had happened," she recalled. "Certainly the way he acted he was sensitive and wary; like a cat he was carefully checking things out."

Finally, with new passport in hand, Thomas was ready to fly transatlantic with his new guardians, leaving behind him the bodies of his father and sister and the only life he'd ever known, always afloat on boats, for a new one he could not imagine, high up in the mountains in a landlocked country. Thomas was treated well on the KLM flight out of Curaçao and spent an hour in the DC-10's cockpit with the flight crew. He also fell asleep face down in a tray of food he was served and later, on arriving at the airport terminal in Amsterdam, again fell fast asleep on one of the benches there. Clare thought this only natural; of course the poor boy must have been exhausted. But it seemed entirely unnatural when she could do nothing to wake him up when their flight to Barcelona was called. She shook him and shook him, to no effect, and began to panic. They would miss their flight! Thomas was much too large and heavy for her to carry onto the plane, and Edward with his hernia could not help.

In the end Thomas did wake up at the last minute, and everyone was relieved. At the time it seemed like an anomalous event. Instead it proved to be a small hint of things to come.

# 3. A CHILD OF THE SEA

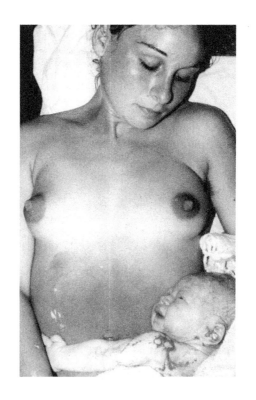

FOR THOMAS LOSING HIS FATHER and sister on the jagged Iron Shore of Bonaire was only the most recent in a train of tragedies that had snaked through all his early years. His father's life afloat had always been eventful and intriguing, for Peter Tangvald had long ago determined he would exist as much as possible on his own terms, at sea, where there were few boundaries to confine him. And yes, the consequences for those loved ones who sailed with him had often been positive. It is in the end impossible to quantify the great sense of freedom one experiences as a bluewater cruiser, or the value of one's exposure to undiluted nature and to foreign cultures. But in several instances those consequences had also been decidedly negative.

Not least among the loved ones who sailed with Peter Tangvald and suffered for it was Thomas's mother, a young Frenchwoman named Lydia Balta. She, like Thomas, had been born on a boat and for at least some part of her childhood also lived on one. Her father, Gustave Balta, was an adventurous French Catholic missionary. When she was born, in October 1953, he was working on the island of Lifuo in the western Pacific archipelago of French New Caledonia. Her mother was German. The story, as Thomas later told it, was that his grandparents met during World War II and encountered "quite some difficulties" pursuing their relationship.

There were no medical facilities on Lifou, so when Lydia was due to arrive, her parents arranged to travel to another island, Nouméa, aboard a local ferry boat named *Henriette*. They hired a midwife to accompany them, just in case, which proved prescient. Fortunately, the birth afloat went smoothly, and Lydia's full given name included those of the boat she was born on, her mother (Esther), and finally the midwife who delivered her (Emma).

Lydia first met Peter Tangvald in 1960, when she was but seven years old and he was 36. Peter at the time had only recently re-arrived in the Caribbean after sailing his second bluewater boat, a doughty 32-foot cutter named *Dorothea*, from England, where he purchased her, to the West Indies, again via the Canary Islands. He was anchored aboard *Dorothea* at Martinique, and the Balta family happened to anchor next to him on a much larger boat named *L'Aviateur* that they were cruising on. Inevitably, the two crews socialized. Peter later remembered *L'Aviateur* because, like his boat, she carried no engine. He was impressed that the crew, which did include a few "strong men" in addition to the family, could handle a boat this size, nearly 70 feet long with a heavy gaff rig, under sail alone. He also remembered Lydia. As he later related the story to Thomas and recounted in his autobiography, the precocious Lydia, one of six Balta children (five girls and one boy), had boldly declared to him that one day she would marry him and they would sail together around the world.

Peter Tangvald wasn't about to wait for her. In bringing *Dorothea* across the Atlantic, he again had sailed briefly—from England to Vigo, Spain—with his third wife Lillemor, who again could not abide the rigors of ocean voyaging. In Spain she put her foot down: Peter had to choose between her and the boat. For Peter it was an easy decision. "Any sailor will know that it is a lot more difficult to get a new boat than a new wife," he later wrote. Lillemor retreated to Norway and soon filed for divorce.

Feeling himself unbound, Peter, like Edward Allcard before him, chartered his boat while in the Caribbean to earn money, but had a different sort of experience. Edward had had no trouble signing up with Vernon Nicholson, the great pioneer charter broker based on Antigua, but Nicholson refused to book charters for Peter, as his boat had no engine. So Peter struck out on his own and picked up his first guests, a pair of American men he met on a beach in Martinique, by agreeing to take them on what amounted to a sex tour of nearby St. Lucia. From there he managed to book more guests with less prurient interests. He based himself on St. Lucia and in between charters began an affair with a young black woman named Bjula, the daughter of a voodoo sorceress. In a bid to keep Peter to herself, she pierced his left ear with a sail needle, installed a gold ring there, and cast a curse on him, apparently to no avail.

Peter was proud of his voodoo earring and wore it for years afterwards, but he was never faithful to Bjula. In September 1960 he met another woman, Simonne Orgias, a French schoolteacher who worked on Martinique, and soon moved in with her there. Eventually he convinced Simonne to take a leave of absence from her job and sail with him to the South Pacific.

SIMONNE IN MANY WAYS proved to be a perfect mate for Peter Tangvald. She was a gymnastics instructor, bold and athletic, and was immune to the discomfort of living on a small sailboat. She was absolutely devoted to Peter and was willing to tolerate some indiscretion on his part. From the Caribbean they sailed *Dorothea* clear around the world during the years 1961 to 1964, a grand adventure that Tangvald described at length in his first book, *Sea Gypsy*. One of its many highlights included an encounter with an MGM film crew in Papeete, Tahiti, who were then in the midst of shooting *Mutiny on the Bounty*, starring Marlon Brando and Trevor Howard. Peter worked as an extra in the film for seven dollars a day, playing a crew member aboard the replica ship *Bounty*, and ended up with a tiny speaking role. If you watch the film, pay special attention to the mutiny scene, where you can see

Peter for a fleeting instant insisting to first mate Fletcher Christian, played by Brando, that he will stay loyal to Captain Bligh.[1]

The route Peter and Simonne followed around the world was not particularly arduous. Known today as the Coconut Milk Run, it wends west from the Panama Canal through the South Pacific tradewinds, then west across the Indian Ocean. Sailing these waters in the proper seasons, a careful sailor can enjoy reliable tailwinds with no threat of serious storms. The one hard bit is getting around Africa—running north up the Red Sea, or west around the Cape of Good Hope, both against strong prevailing winds—before one eventually re-emerges in the Atlantic Ocean. Peter certainly wasn't the first cruising sailor to follow this path (he chose the Red Sea route around Africa), and today there are many more still following it. But *Sea Gypsy*, published in 1966, was one of the first full accounts of such a voyage and thus helped establish Peter's reputation in the sailing community.

It was during this great voyage, on the long passages across the wide Pacific, that Peter's commitment to pure sailing, with a minimum of technology, was confirmed and indelibly etched into his psyche. He had stripped the engine from *Dorothea* while preparing her for sea in England and never once regretted it. Any dedicated sailor will tell you some of their finest, most magical moments come in that instant when they switch their engines off,

---

1. The vessel *Bounty* on which Peter Tangvald served as an extra, launched in Lunenburg, Nova Scotia, in 1960, was the first replica of a large historical sailing vessel ever built for a film production. The original plan was that the ship would be destroyed by fire during the making of the film, mirroring the fate of the original *HMS Bounty*, which was destroyed by her mutineers after they reached Pitcairn Island. Marlon Brando, however, objected to this and browbeat MGM into keeping the vessel intact.

The replica *Bounty* served in various capacities for many years—as a sail-training vessel, as a prop in other films and TV shows, and as a charter vessel. Ultimately the ship was lost at sea 90 miles southeast of Cape Hatteras, North Carolina, on October 29, 2012, during Hurricane Sandy. There were two fatal casualties—the captain, Robin Walbridge, who had unwisely sailed the ship into the heart of the storm, and a volunteer crew member, Claudene Christian, who was a descendant of Fletcher Christian.

in the rush of silence where the abrasive roar of internal combustion is replaced by the organic whisper of wind and wave, and for Peter this became a religion. He wanted to remain permanently in that moment and was transformed, ultimately, into something like an ocean druid, at one with the elements and content always to rely upon them.

"It is a wonderful experience," he wrote in *Sea Gypsy*, "to cross a large ocean successfully under sail alone. It is hard to describe the sensation of happiness, of freedom and of general satisfaction given by such a voyage."

Peter's next great project after he finished his circumnavigation was to build a larger engineless boat—out of wood, of course—to a design of his own. He decided to do this in Cayenne, the main city of French Guiana on the northeast coast of South America, for two reasons. First, he could easily and cheaply acquire teak and other valuable tropical hardwoods there. Second, Simonne, who he had by now married, had no trouble getting a job teaching gymnastics in the local French school and could support him while he worked. The couple settled down in a comfortable house they rented in the suburbs of Cayenne, in an area known as Montjoly, just behind the beach east of the city. Next to the house Peter constructed an enormous shed in which he started building his "dream boat," the vessel that would become *L'Artemis de Pytheas*.

As any boatowner will tell you, job one when getting a new boat is to get rid of the old one first. So in early 1967, before he started working on *L'Artemis* in earnest, Peter set out alone from Cayenne aboard *Dorothea* bound for Fort Lauderdale, Florida, where he proposed to sell her. He had sailed about a third of the way there and was southwest of Barbados when the boat struck something solid in the water, shortly after sunset on the evening of March 12. Unfortunately, *Dorothea* was holed and quickly filled with water. Peter managed to escape in a seven-foot plywood dinghy. To save himself he erected a crude jury rig with a scrap of awning and an oar and sailed this tiny craft 55 miles downwind to the island of Canouan in the Grenadine archipelago south of St. Vincent.

Peter described this adventure in an article he promptly published in the September 1967 issue of the British magazine *Yachting World*. The loss of *Dorothea* was the biggest emergency he'd yet had to deal with at sea, and he seemed to take pride in this and in the fact that it might not be a singular tragedy, but one in a series, with presumably more to follow.

"I was so tired I felt sick," he wrote. "But I knew once more the words of the fortune-teller who had told me at the age of 15 that I was like the cat, born with nine lives, were still right. In fact, I should have two or three more to go!"

Peter returned to Cayenne and at once resumed work on *L'Artemis*. It was an enormous project for one man to take on alone. It took him nearly a year just to gather the wood, materials, and tools he needed to begin the job; it would take him several more to complete it. It was onerous, frustrating work, and many years later he confessed to his son Thomas that he came close at one point to ridding himself of his creation by setting fire to it. He was still in the midst of construction, hard at work in the shed behind his house at some point in 1971, when he was interrupted one day by two teenage girls in pigtails.

These were Lydia Balta and her sister Agnes. They and their family had just moved to the neighborhood, and the girls were curious about what was going on in the big shed next to their new home.

This was a remarkable coincidence—that Peter's old neighbors afloat from 11 years earlier were now his new neighbors ashore—but at first he did not credit it much. As he later wrote: "Little did I suspect that one of those young girls was going to become my wife and the mother of my son Thomas."

IT IS HARD TO SAY for certain exactly how Peter Tangvald negotiated his amorous segue from Simonne to Lydia. Peter's story was that this otherwise devoutly religious 17-year-old girl effectively set out to seduce him after they met again in French Guiana. He had a fast Moto Guzzi motorcycle he liked to ride around Cayenne, and Lydia, he claimed, one day laid a trap for him. She intentionally missed her bus ride to school, hid by the side of the road, and sprang out with her thumb up in the air when he came by on his bike. Peter gave the girl a lift to school, but when they got there she begged him to keep her aboard, pleading that "she just *loved* big motorcycles."

Peter acceded to Lydia's plea, and they continued on a long ride through the countryside.

"As we were banking in the long fast turns," he wrote, "I could feel her flat tummy and hard, small breasts against my body as clearly as if we were naked. I felt as if we were making love from all the sensations rushing through my body on that motorcycle, the sexiest machine man ever invented."

Lydia came to Peter's shed every day after that and from there, he implied to his readers, one thing inexorably led to another. He and Lydia were living "in a permanent state of ecstasy" until one day her mother suddenly died and her father Gustave announced he was moving the family back to France. To avoid being separated, Peter found Lydia a hiding place and waited for her father to leave the country without her. Which he eventually did, and subsequently Peter wrote: "Our nights were the most wonderful any lovers could dream about."

Simonne's version of how her relationship with Peter ended was more prosaic. As she later explained to friends, Lydia had been a favored student of hers. When Lydia's mother died and her father decided to move back to France, Simonne readily agreed that Lydia could move in with her and Peter so as to complete her last year of high school in Cayenne. Understandably, Simonne was very upset when she came home one day, just two weeks after Lydia had moved in, and found her in bed with her husband.[2]

However this truly played out, the end result was that when Peter finally finished building his boat and launched it off the beach in Montjoly in December 1973, it was Lydia rather than Simonne who sailed away with him on it. Some of the friends Peter had made during the seven years he lived in Cayenne were outraged by this; others remained loyal and gave him a bit of a send-off before he sailed away with his teen paramour.

Soon afterward, as the newly baptized *L'Artemis de Pytheas* lay a short distance up the coast from Cayenne at the town of Kourou, Peter also received a visit from none other than Edward Allcard, who was then sailing north aboard his boat *Sea Wanderer*. Edward had come from the Cape of Good Hope and was bound up the Atlantic for Antigua, where at last he would complete his solo circumnavigation of the world. It was a grand reunion for both men, with Peter just setting out on a new adventure, aboard a new boat, and Edward on the verge of completing one.

As to the question of Lydia, Edward was never inclined to judge Peter with regard to his romantic adventures and dealt with him always as one sailor to another. He was very impressed with *L'Artemis de Pytheas*, and to both men this was what mattered most. Besides, Edward himself was by now hardly in a position to throw stones over age-inappropriate relationships. Earlier that same year he had married Clare, who was 31 years his junior, and they had already had a child, now four years old.

---

2. Peter and Simonne also told different stories of how they came to marry. In *At Any Cost*, Peter wrote that he had warned Simonne from the beginning of their relationship he would never marry again, and it was only after she lobbied him that he relented and married her in Gibraltar in the fall of 1965. According to Simonne, it was all Peter's idea, as their marriage ensured he was covered by the generous French social security system.

THE BOY WHO FELL TO SHORE

As for Peter himself, he later justified his betrayal of Simonne with a jaunty French aphorism he remembered from his childhood, a pro-smoking slogan inscribed on the bottom of an ashtray in his parents' apartment in Paris: *Qui vit sans follie, n'est pas aussi sage qu'il croit.* Or in English: Whoever lives without folly is not as wise as he thinks. Peter enshrined this as the epigraph to his autobiography, wherein he also cited it explicitly as his rationale for taking up with Lydia.

PETER AND LYDIA SAILED NORTH from French Guiana and spent the rest of that winter and much of the following spring in the West Indies. Like Simonne before her, Lydia earned money to support the couple while Peter worked to perfect his new boat. Once the work was complete they set sail across the Atlantic bound for Europe. According to Peter's account in *At Any Cost*, this was a non-stop passage that took the happy couple right through the Strait of Gibraltar and across the western Mediterranean Sea, before they finally landed in the summer of 1974 on the French Riviera.

Again, however, Simonne had a different story to tell. What she later told Clare Allcard was that Peter and Lydia landed first on the west coast of Portugal, where Lydia for some reason left the boat. Sometime later Simonne took Lydia's place, and it was she who helped sail *L'Artemis* to Port Grimaud, on the south coast of France west of St. Tropez. Peter in his book wrote that he and Lydia spent 18 months together in Port Grimaud, save for one hiatus that winter of 1974, during which they lived in a tiny apartment in Paris, where Lydia again worked to support him. It seems in fact he may have been living with Simonne during some or most of this time and was seeing Lydia on the side.

The following summer Peter fell into his own employment opportunity. A yachting friend at Port Grimaud, identified only as "Claude" in *At Any Cost*, was designing a pair of boats for two wealthy clients and planned to have them built in Asia to reduce costs. Peter was preparing *L'Artemis* for an extended cruise to the Indian Ocean and southern Asia, and he proposed that he be hired as project manager to supervise construction of the two vessels. Claude and his clients readily agreed.

By August of that summer of 1975, Lydia was pregnant with Thomas, and Peter was anxious to start sailing east with her before the season waned. There were delays, however, as Claude and his clients finalized their arrangements. By the time contracts were signed in December, Peter had much less time to work with and more than twice as much distance to cover to meet his end of the bargain, as the build site for the yachts had been shifted from Sri Lanka in the Indian Ocean to Taiwan in the South China Sea.

In the end *L'Artemis de Pytheas* departed Port Grimaud, bound for southeast Asia by way of the Suez Canal and the Indian Ocean, on January 5, 1976. It was the dead of winter and Lydia's pregnancy was well advanced. The couple was soon caught in a strong winter gale east of Malta that lasted three days. Lydia was seasick, incapacitated and vomiting blood, and Peter was left to stand watch alone around the clock. It was a poor start to what promised to be a challenging voyage, and the couple was tempted, after they finally reached Port Said, Egypt, on January 23, to simply stay put until their child was born.

Lydia, according to Peter, had from the start pushed him to be more aggressive in his negotiations with Claude and his clients. Now in Egypt it was Lydia who argued that Peter's contract must be deemed void, as one of Claude's clients had failed to pay a promised advance on schedule. But when the funds did suddenly appear, she relented and claimed she was well enough to keep sailing east.

To save money transiting the Suez Canal, Lydia also insisted on handling the paperwork herself and spent four days haggling with Egyptian bureaucrats to get the earliest transit time at the lowest cost. The fact that she was such an unusual supplicant—a small blonde female obviously heavy with child, and unusually determined—must have helped her cause. In the end Peter spent only $55 US getting through the canal, instead of the $1,200 he expected to pay.

Once clear of Suez, Peter and Lydia spent 10 days sailing south down the Red Sea to the old French colonial city of Djibouti on the Gulf of Aden. Lydia again was seasick but cooked three proper meals a day while on passage, in spite of the ever more intense heat. After only a brief stay in Djibouti, the couple then set out across the Indian Ocean for Sri Lanka.

This was a long and grueling passage. Confronted with persistent headwinds intermingled with squalls and calms, Peter had to work hard for every mile gained to the east. Lydia meanwhile was often sick again, sometimes vomiting blood. Finally, after 40 days at sea, including two spent hove to during a gale near the Maldive Islands, *L'Artemis de Pytheas* arrived at the port of Galle in Sri Lanka.

Lydia by now was due to give birth in less than a month, and the couple fully intended to stay in Galle until the baby arrived. But Lydia was nervous about seeing a doctor. She reluctantly went along with Peter to an appointment he made, but then she fled when the doctor appeared in a foul lab coat covered with old blood stains. Peter pleaded with the doctor to visit them on *L'Artemis*, but the doctor insisted he would only take Lydia as a patient if she immediately checked into the hospital.

Lydia refused to do this and declared she wanted a midwife to deliver the baby on the boat in the harbor. When Peter couldn't find a midwife willing to do this, Lydia demanded they leave Sri Lanka at once. There'd be time to sail to Malaysia before the baby came, she insisted. Even if there wasn't, she was perfectly willing to give birth aboard the boat while underway, with or without a midwife. After all, she argued, she had been born on a boat at sea, and everything had turned out fine.

Peter reluctantly prepared to put to sea again. Citing Lydia's impending due date, the port authorities however refused to grant him clearance to leave the harbor. Lydia, wrote Peter, "became almost hysterical" when told this. She urged they should leave secretly at night, without any clearance, but in the end this proved unnecessary. The authorities relented and granted *L'Artemis* permission to leave Galle, but they also issued a stern warning: if Lydia's baby was born and died at sea, both she and Peter would be charged with voluntary manslaughter.


THOMAS THOR TANGVALD WAS BORN at sea aboard *L'Artemis de Pytheas*, south of the Bay of Bengal in the Indian Ocean, some distance west of the Malacca Strait, on May 23, 1976, at about 10 p.m. In leaving Galle when they did, Peter and Lydia were certainly taking a calculated risk. They hoped the winds of the summer monsoon, which normally blow consistently from the southwest in the northern India Ocean from June to September each year, would fill in early and speed them on their way east. If this happened they'd have no trouble covering the thousand or more miles to Malaysia in 10 days or less, which would leave some margin of error, as the baby by then was due in a little less than three weeks.

*L'Artemis* did enjoy fair monsoon-like winds for the first few days of her passage, but then the wind turned against her. Peter, with no engine to switch on, had to laboriously tack back and forth, zig-zagging against the wind, to keep going east, and the boat's progress became slow and tedious. After a few days it became clear they would never reach Malaysia in time.

Lydia, according to Peter's account, was in labor over two nights and one full day. Peter hove to, setting the sails to work against each other so that *L'Artemis* lay quietly and was stationary, and devoted himself to attending to the young woman he now thought of as his wife. It was quite hot, and Lydia lay naked on a saloon settee bench, soaked in sweat. All through both nights, the black sky, as a dramatic backdrop, was alive with vivid tropical heat lightning.

When the baby at last started to appear during the second night, Lydia, by now exhausted, asked Peter to help pull it out. In *At Any Cost* he described the process with reverence:

> I tugged gently at the head with a slow, rotating motion, as our books had explained, so as to better disengage the shoulders from the mother's basin. The baby had a total lack of expression on its face and I feared it was dead. Then the shoulders came free and the baby shot out at such speed that I nearly dropped it. I had trouble holding it, as it was covered with a slippery substance, which made it difficult to grasp firmly. I held it up by the feet with one hand, ready to give it the usual slap on the behind to make it gasp for air, when the infant got ahead of me with one huge wail. Its face wrinkled up to an awful and wonderful grimace, its arms started to wave like a windmill and the whole little creature came to life in my hands.
>
> That moment was the most extraordinary experience and the most fantastic adventure I have ever known: life itself!

Peter's attitude here belied the fact that Thomas was not his first child, but his fourth. For indeed he'd already had a son and two daughters with his first wife, Reidun Kathle, who immigrated with him to the United States back in 1949. She later left him in

California and sued for divorce after returning to Norway.[3] Peter never wrote of these earlier children, or ever mentioned them to friends and acquaintances, so we have no idea how he felt when they were born. But it would seem that those births did not make as much of an impression upon him as this one did.

Peter Tangvald had largely ignored his first three children, negligently if not deliberately. They were from the life on shore that he had sailed away from. Now he had a child who'd been conceived on a boat, who had been born on a boat—at sea no less, in the middle of a passage—and it appeared at last he was willing to let himself feel like a father.

Thomas fortunately had no trouble latching on to his mother's breasts and was apparently healthy. Lydia however had been badly torn while giving birth. Peter first proposed to stitch her up, but when she saw him cleaning a rusty needle from his sail-repair kit to prepare for this, she adamantly refused. Instead Peter patched her up with some sailcloth and glue, but still Lydia needed time to recover and couldn't get out of bed.

It was left to Peter to prepare meals and tend to both Lydia and Thomas while sailing singlehanded down the Malacca Strait, one of the most crowded shipping lanes on the planet. The biggest crisis came late one dark night, during a vicious rain squall, when Peter suddenly found himself sailing at top speed into the flank of a giant supertanker. He barely avoided a collision by violently jibing L'Artemis and laying her down on her side. Lying in her berth below with her infant boy, Lydia was convinced the boat had capsized and would sink.

After days of such drama—dodging freighters and squalls and nearly getting caught in a labyrinth of fish traps—Peter at last

---

3. Peter's second wife, shoehorned between Reidun and Lillemor, is identified in *At Any Cost* only as Helene. Peter evidently met Helene in southern California, but she left him, according to his account, after a business he started with his father in the Los Angeles area went bankrupt.

sailed *L'Artemis* into Singapore, by far the busiest port he'd ever visited, in early June 1976, two weeks after his son was born.

Peter and Lydia proudly displayed Thomas to the neatly dressed officials who came aboard to clear them in, expecting these men would be amused and impressed that the boy had been born at sea. Instead they were horrified. The infant had no papers for them to inspect and stamp, not even a birth certificate, and they had no idea what to do. For days afterward Peter hustled from office to office on shore, trying to get Thomas's birth documented, and to get him recognized as a French and/or American citizen, to no avail. Ultimately it would take six years before Thomas's paperwork was sorted out.

Papers or no, the family soon set out from Singapore, stopped in Hong Kong, and finally arrived in Taiwan in late July 1976. During these last two legs of their epic seven-month voyage from southern France, Peter and Lydia successfully evaded one full typhoon and one tropical storm and were nearly arrested by Communist patrol boats after accidentally drifting into Red Chinese waters.

THOMAS WAS TO SPEND most of the first two years of his life in Taiwan while his father worked at the first regular paying job he'd had since leaving California in 1959. It was here too that his parents formalized their relationship and married each other on February 2, 1978. This very likely wasn't a valid marriage, for as far as anyone knows, Peter and Simonne were never divorced. Simonne in later years insisted to friends she never agreed to any divorce, and there is no evidence Peter ever sought or obtained one against her will.[4]

---

4. According to Simonne, it wasn't until she read a story in *Paris Match* about Thomas being born at sea that she realized Peter and Lydia were together again.

Peter in his autobiography mostly complained about both his job and Taiwan, but the family did make a good deal of money there. There was, however, a price to pay. The harbor of Kaohsiung, where Peter worked supervising the construction of Claude's yachts, was so polluted the family was forced to move off their boat into a rented apartment. *L'Artemis* was hauled out and stored in a shed on shore, where unfortunately she was damaged in a strong typhoon that struck the city in July 1977.

Peter did not enjoy managing Chinese workers—it made him "feel like some kind of policeman," he wrote—but he nevertheless took on an extra job at another boatyard as a technical advisor. Lydia meanwhile quickly became proficient in Mandarin Chinese and was hired as Peter's interpreter. With three salaries coming in, life in Taiwan proved so lucrative that Peter readily agreed to stay on after his initial six-month contract with Claude expired. But by the spring of 1978, he was ready to move on.

On leaving Taiwan, Peter and Lydia steered south for the Philippines. With its countless islands, remote anchorages, and warm tropical climate, it seemed an ideal cruising ground after the filthy urbanity of Kaohsiung. For Peter, who was tired of relying on Lydia to communicate with people, it was particularly attractive, as English was the official language. The family again had a difficult voyage. Twice they were harassed by an early typhoon, Atang, that passed both south and north of them as it recurved into the western Pacific, but finally *L'Artemis* arrived safely in Manila in late April.

It was in Manila that young Thomas first began to assert himself as an independent agent. The Norwegian ambassador to the Philippines, himself an avid sailor, invited Peter and family to an embassy party to celebrate the Norwegian national holiday, Constitution Day, on May 17, and Thomas put on quite a show there. Peter first spotted his son eagerly cadging extra servings of ice cream from one of the waiters and was pleased by the boy's display of initiative.

"I was amused," he later wrote, "and, at the same time, quite proud of that little boy who, though not yet two-and-a-half years old, was able to manage so well on his own. I concluded that, when he reached a suitable age to look for a bride and find a livelihood later on, he would succeed in getting the best."

Peter was not so pleased a little later when Thomas, having discovered a side room full of electrical wiring to play with, succeeded in disabling the embassy's public address system in the middle of the ambassador's speech. There was a long delay while an electrician was summoned. "The electrician found it very funny and laughed heartily while returning Thomas to us," wrote Peter. "[But] the ambassador's laugh hadn't sounded nearly as good-natured as the electrician's."

The precocious boy wasn't done yet. As soon as his father released him after the ambassador's speech, Thomas at once stripped off his clothes and jumped into the deep end of the embassy pool, though he had not yet learned to swim. Peter's description of the event again reflected a good deal of chagrin mixed with a fine stripe of pride: "Rushing to the edge, ready to jump in to save him from his foolishness, I saw two muscular swimmers pulling him to the surface. Far from exhibiting the small, scared face I had expected, Thomas was laughing and as happy as he could be."

And even as Peter was thanking his son's saviors, Thomas immediately jumped back into the pool and had to be fished out once again.

Thomas's spirit and initiative were again on display some months later after the family settled for a time in the Filipino village of Consolacion on the island of Cebu. Here Peter had found a perfect spot to finish repairing the typhoon damage L'Artemis had suffered back in Kaohsiung. This included rerigging the boat as a schooner and building a new mainmast.[5] The boat lay in a tiny landlocked anchorage, perfectly secure against any passing storm, with good access to lumber and even an electrical connection, so Peter could run power tools to speed his work along.

The boat was moored beside the shore, and the village was safe enough that Thomas was allowed to come and go as he pleased. Peter eventually noticed that Thomas went ashore and disappeared into the village at a certain time each day, as though on a schedule. On following the boy through the length of the town, he learned Thomas had made a friend of a local shopkeeper, who was serving up a free treat of cake and Coca-Cola every afternoon.

"We both felt a bit embarrassed to think of his having begged food and drinks," wrote Peter. "But we were also a bit proud of his sense of enterprise and concluded once more that he would certainly be able to manage for himself later on in life."


IN ALL, THE FAMILY SPENT ten months roaming the Philippines aboard *L'Artemis de Pytheas*, and one thing they learned was that certain places in the vast archipelago were much less friendly and secure than others. In contrast to the great welcome they received from the villagers of Consolacion, they were for example treated with much hostility at Iloilo, the main town on the island of Panay. Peter, because he had hair on his chest, had been openly mocked here as a foreign monkey by a jeering crowd of locals. Lydia was robbed at knifepoint at the market in front of witnesses who only laughed when she begged for help. Teenage boys routinely vandalized the family's dinghy and insolently boarded *L'Artemis* without permission. A local fishing boat skipper

---

5. *L'Artemis* was originally rigged as a yawl, with her mainmast forward and a smaller mizzenmast aft, at the very back of the boat behind the rudder. In a schooner rig, the larger mainmast is set behind a smaller foremast.

also negligently smashed into *L'Artemis* and refused to pay for the damage.

Given these experiences, it is surprising that Peter ignored the many warnings he received about the dangers of sailing across the Sulu Sea, which lies between the Philippines and Borneo. It was well known that pirates and Muslim Moro rebels based in the southern Philippines were active there. Indeed, back in Manila the port captain had sternly ordered Peter to stay away from the area, as the winds there were unreliable and it would be impossible to get across quickly in a sailboat without an engine.

But Peter Tangvald was used to doing what he wanted. He'd often flirted with the cusps of the typhoon season while sailing about Asia, unwilling to let the fear of storms rule his life. As for pirates, he doubted they even existed anymore. As he wrote in *At Any Cost*: "Who could seriously believe in pirate stories in the 20th century—an age of radios and coast guards most everywhere."

So it was that when Peter and his family at last departed the Philippines in mid-February of 1979, they struck out to the southwest, straight across the Sulu Sea, bound for Brunei, a small British protectorate on the northern coast of Borneo. From there they planned to sail eventually to the United States—via the Indian Ocean, the Red Sea, Europe, and the North Atlantic. Peter was excited at the prospect of returning to his adopted home country, from which he'd been absent for so long, and he looked forward to showing it to Lydia, who had never been before.

As expected, conditions during the first days of the passage were calm, with only light winds from the north and northeast. The passage thus was slow and uneventful, until Tuesday, February 20. The wind that day was again light and from the north, and by this time, after six days at sea, *L'Artemis* had covered little more than 300 miles, an average of only about 50 miles a day.

Sometime in the late morning, not long after *L'Artemis* had passed by Bancoran Island, one of myriad small islands spread out across the Sulu Sea, Peter and Lydia heard the sound of a motor approaching. They were both down below at the time, sheltering from the blazing sun. They went on deck to investigate and were surprised to see a low-slung wooden power vessel, about the same length as *L'Artemis*, that was quite close and heading straight for them. The approaching boat looked old and poorly maintained, with a motley deckhouse and about a dozen men onboard.

Lydia at once urged they should break out the shotgun Peter kept on board and fire off a warning shot to keep the strange vessel at bay. Peter immediately vetoed the idea. He hoped these were nothing but fishermen who were coming to offer fish they'd caught in exchange for cigarettes and booze. *L'Artemis* had been approached in this way several times before while cruising the Philippines. Peter and Lydia, who did not smoke or drink, had disappointed their supplicants, but the encounters had always been friendly.

Even if these weren't fishermen, Peter knew it was now too late to try to warn them away with gunfire. Because there had been no one watching on deck, and because the approaching boat had a quiet motor, it was now too close for that. There wouldn't be time to retrieve the gun before the boat was alongside.

Peter described what happened next in a log entry he wrote the following day that he later transcribed into the text of *At Any Cost*:

> Lydia didn't argue and went down below leaving me at the tiller. Shortly afterwards to my dismay, I saw her come out of the forehatch with the gun. She fired a shot from forward of the mast over the boat which was alongside us a couple of feet away. The reaction was immediate—a shot was fired at her from inside the deckhouse just

abreast of her and only about three yards away. Lydia fell into the sea immediately tainting the water red with her blood.

The man came out and sighted me with his gun. I looked into his gun which had a very big bore and expected to meet the same fate as Lydia. I wasn't scared—I just didn't care anymore and was resigned. But the shot I expected didn't come. Instead [the man] lowered the gun from his shoulder keeping [it] pointed above my head. Only then was I aware of Thomas who was clinging to my legs looking at the strange boat.

Two men then jumped aboard *L'Artemis* and dove down the forward hatch, ostensibly to loot the boat. But they took very little. Down below they grabbed about $100 US they found in a drawer that Peter pointed out through the companionway. They also grabbed two boxes of shotgun shells. Beyond this, they searched for nothing more. They scrambled out the forward hatch, picked up the shotgun that Lydia had dropped on deck, then jumped back aboard their boat.

With a quiet roar from its motor, the boat then pulled away from *L'Artemis* and headed south. To Peter it seemed the men aboard were, like him, very scared and anxious to get away.

# 4. IN NEW TERRAIN

IT IS DIFFICULT TO IMAGINE how Thomas, at age 15, must have felt during the immense transition he went through after losing his father and sister. He traveled first from Bonaire to Curaçao to Amsterdam to Barcelona, all by airplane, a fantastically rapid mode of transport he had never experienced, covering in a matter of hours vast distances that would take months to traverse by sailboat. Then he rode inland on a bus for three more hours, farther from the sea than he'd ever been before, into the high mountains of the Pyrenees, an utterly alien and uncannily elevated landscape that was now to become his home.

Andorra itself could not have been more different from what Thomas was used to. In place of the languid entropy of the tropical Caribbean, with everything a bit rundown and decayed around the edges and only a few stray patches of nicely groomed prosperity here and there, he now found himself in a universally prosperous, well-organized Western European tax haven, the Switzerland of the Iberian peninsula, with ski resorts, luxury shops, and neatly maintained stone buildings everywhere.

Might the shock of this have prompted some primordial memories to bleed into his consciousness? For Thomas had briefly lived on land once before, when his father worked building boats in Taiwan, but he could not remember this. He had once swum in a freshwater pool before taking that amusing plunge in Curaçao, in Manila at the Norwegian embassy on Constitution Day when he was a toddler, but he could not remember it. He'd even had a mother once, a genuine biological one who had loved him unconditionally, but he could not remember her. Perhaps now, in the vortex of change that consumed him, some faint ghosts of these distant experiences reached out to him.

For all the turmoil of the present moment, it was also true this was one of the great strokes of good fortune Thomas was to enjoy in his life—that his father had anointed the Allcards as his guardians. Thomas himself seems to have intuited this. Very soon after he arrived in Andorra, a woman from the American embassy in Madrid, a social worker, came to interview him. Clare Allcard was very impressed that the American government moved so quickly to aid Thomas and protect his interests, as compared to the French, his alternate national custodians, who did nothing for him.

The interview took place in the Allcards' home, a relatively modest stone chalet that clung to a nearly vertical mountainside overlooking the town of La Massana. One of the first questions the woman asked, right in front of Clare, was whether Thomas really wanted to live in this strange new place, with these strange new people.

Clare thought this rather awkward and at once offered to leave the room, so that Thomas could answer openly and freely.

But Thomas immediately interrupted her.

"No, it's fine," he declared. And he turned to the social worker: "Yes, I do want to live with them."

The social worker also asked Thomas if he knew how much money his father had spent supporting his family each month before the accident.

Thomas replied: "Three hundred dollars."

The woman, taken aback, at once corrected him: "Ah, you must mean three thousand."

And Thomas just as promptly rebutted her: "No, it was three hundred."

For Clare this was not surprising. From her long correspondence with Peter Tangvald, she knew how frugal life had been aboard

*L'Artemis.* When the Tangvald family wanted to eat bread, for example, Peter had not simply purchased bread. He instead bought sacks of raw grain at a discount and ground it to flour—or rather had his wife of the moment grind it—and from that flour bread was baked, or more often pancakes, fresh aboard his boat.

In Clare's own mind the poverty of Thomas's previous existence, and her belief that he must be undernourished, was only confirmed when she baked a Victoria sponge cake, with coffee icing and walnuts, to celebrate his arrival in Andorra. When it was done Clare cut the cake into generous slices, and Thomas immediately grabbed two. To her it seemed he was terrified this delicious food might be taken from him and he'd be left with too little to eat.


HE WAS, FROM THE BEGINNING, very much Clare's project. It was she who had urged Edward to assure Peter they would care for his children, and now, with Thomas in their home, it was Clare who assumed most of the burden of helping him put his life back together. Edward, at age 76, had had one daughter, Dona, now middle-aged, by his first wife. He had also raised with Clare a second daughter, Kate, now a young woman of 22, and he was not eager to deal with yet another child. Clare meanwhile had confessed to her own mother, after she and Edward first agreed to act as guardians to Peter's children, that she was daunted at the prospect. But still she was very willing to take on the challenge.

She was an energetic, highly intelligent woman, but calm, endowed with a good deal of common sense leavened with an extra helping of empathy. That she was so willing to care for a wounded creature such as Thomas stemmed in part from having been badly wounded herself when she was younger. At age 19, while studying as a psychiatric nurse, she'd been forcibly raped in 1965 by a stranger on Hampstead Heath in London. This experience, compounded with severe chronic pain in her arm that was misdiagnosed as psychosomatic, compounded in turn with a misdiagnosis of incipient schizophrenia, led ultimately to four suicide attempts. Clare was institutionalized against her will and over the course of two years was subjected to 26 bouts of electroshock treatment, as well as a sadistically long bout of deep narcosis therapy, during which she was kept in a drug-induced state of unconsciousness for three weeks. One consequence of all this was that her IQ, which had tested out at 155 before her ordeal began (she was a member of Mensa), was reduced by 20 points.

It was Edward who saved Clare, a fact she gratefully acknowledged through all her later years. One afternoon while sitting hopelessly in her psychiatric ward, she spotted a discarded bit of a newspaper on the floor, a section of *The Sunday Express*, and picked it up to read it. She found in it a fascinating article about a bluewater voyager who had always sailed alone but wistfully admitted he wouldn't mind having a partner to share adventures with. Clare at once wrote a fan letter, asking if she might sail with Edward once she was released from "the looney bin."

Edward, amazingly, answered Clare's letter, and they did meet and enjoyed a picnic together on the South Downs in Sussex after Clare was finally discharged in the spring of 1968. To Edward, Clare seemed perfectly normal. He did not believe in "trick cyclists," as Clare later put it, and insisted there was absolutely nothing wrong with her. For her it was a tremendous affirmation. Soon enough they were indeed having adventures together and in the latter half of 1968 trekked overland across all of Europe and Asia, from Great Britain to Singapore, via Land Rover. En route Edward was arrested (briefly) as a spy in Bulgaria after taking photos of cows; later the couple narrowly escaped an ambush by bandits near the Khyber Pass in Afghanistan. Writing of this journey long afterwards, Clare noted: "If two people spend five months living together in the close confines of a Land Rover they either murder each other or fall in love. Luckily, we fell in love."

Their daughter Kate was born in May 1969, in Auckland, New Zealand, where Edward had left his boat *Sea Wanderer* after hitting the pause button on his seemingly endless solo circumnavigation. Over the following four years Edward continued on his lonely voyage, but now with Clare and baby Kate meeting up with him in different locales. This included yet another long pause in the Seychelles, in the western Indian Ocean, where the family lived on a coconut plantation for two years in a palm-thatched hut, which Clare christened the Ant's Nest, after all the termites that infested it. After Edward finally completed his circuit of the globe in Antigua in 1973, not long after meeting up with Peter Tangvald and his teen paramour Lydia in French Guiana, he sold *Sea Wanderer*. To replace her he and Clare next bought an antique Baltic trading ketch that was large enough, 69 feet long, that the family could all live on it together.

On this last boat, *Johanne Regina*, Edward and Clare roamed the world together for 12 years, again having all sorts of adventures. As recounted by Clare in her classic cruising memoir, *A Gypsy Life*, they were nearly sunk by a French fishing boat, were raided by the Italian Mafia, attacked by the Ethiopian navy, and jailed as spies in Yemen. They finally "swallowed the anchor," as cruisers like to put it, when they moved ashore in Andorra in 1984. But for many years afterwards they still kept *Johanne* close by, three hours away in the port of Torredembara on the coast of Catalonia southwest of Barcelona.

During the remainder of that summer, after Thomas came to live with them in early August 1991, Clare took the boy down to the shore and often spent time on the boat so as to ease him more gently into his new existence. Edward himself, the inveterate mariner, once he had his hernia repaired, also spent much of his time on *Johanne*, lost in the endless chore of maintaining her. A favorite local cruising ground was the delta of the Ebro River, the largest wetland in Catalonia and one of the most significant aquatic habitats in the western Mediterranean, filled with birds, including herons, egrets, eagles, and flamingos. Edward had found a secluded hard-to-access anchorage in the heart of the nature reserve, a great spot for windsurfing where local shellfishermen in small skiffs often stopped by to share their catch. Thomas enjoyed the windsurfing and at night slept up in the bow, in the boat's forepeak, which must have recalled his childhood aboard *L'Artemis de Pytheas*, only without the locks and bars.

To further bolster Thomas as he adapted to his new life, Clare decided to buy him a bicycle. Thomas had told her of a grievous loss he suffered—of a bicycle he'd built himself and dearly loved that been stolen from him back in Puerto Rico. He was extremely proud of it. Having studied the subject, he had designed and built it as a recumbent machine, as this is the most efficient and aerodynamic type of bicycle, and on it he had often cycled long distances when on the "big island" of Puerto Rico.

To replace this Clare now bought Thomas a brand new upright bicycle, a lightweight carbon-fiber road-racer. Because she still got confused making conversions between the British pound and the two currencies then used in Andorra (the French franc and the Spanish peseta), she accidentally spent much more than she intended, and Thomas ended up with a very expensive machine. As Clare later remembered, a bit ruefully, she and Edward spent more on Thomas's bicycle than they had on a car, a used Fiat Panda, that they'd recently purchased as a 21st birthday present for their daughter Kate. Thomas however was very pleased with his new bike and was also very afraid it too would be stolen. To guard against this, he laboriously hauled it up two flights of stairs every night and slept with it in the bedroom he'd been assigned in the house in La Massana.

Supposing this also might ease Thomas's transition, Clare asked Kate to come visit for a while. Though Kate was seven years older than Thomas, Clare hoped they were close enough in age, and had enough in common as "boat kids," that they might easily relate to each other. Kate arrived from Great Britain in September—she was en route to Gibraltar to join a yacht she was to crew on—and stayed at La Massana for some time.

Thomas's first concern when Kate appeared was that she'd be upset that he was staying in what had been her bedroom. Kate however wasn't bothered in the least by this, and the two got on well together. Thomas was immediately comfortable sharing with Kate certain things he hadn't mentioned to her parents; it was through Kate, for example, that Clare and Edward, who'd been pronouncing Thomas's name in the French way, learned that he actually preferred the English pronunciation. Kate also spoke with him a bit about what had happened on Bonaire and got him to open up about Carmen's fate. For Clare this was a relief. As she described it in a letter sent in September to Elizabeth Moore, back at the consulate on Curaçao, it was "the one part of the tragedy that I felt had not been properly exorcised."

To Kate, Thomas seemed a normal teenager, in spite of his traumatic past, and not overly mature for his age. Years later she did not recall discussing the shipwreck with him, but clearly remembered that they enjoyed talking about "teenage things" together, including the sexual dynamic between young men and women. Kate claimed Thomas was astounded when she told him she'd stopped shaving her legs so as to deflect romantic interest from boys.

"That was totally beyond his comprehension," she later wrote. "I could see his mind grappling with the problem rather like trying to envision infinity. I found it very funny that he couldn't grasp the concept at all."

Kate could see too that Thomas had very traditional ideas, presumably absorbed from his father, as to gender roles. When her mother, for example, asked the two of them to hang out some laundry to dry, she could tell Thomas thought this job "was definitely beneath him."

Kate, like Clare, also noticed that Thomas ate as much as he could. He always took more food when it was offered, even if he was very full already, and particularly liked sweet things. He had a great passion, she recalled, for Nutella and ate at least a jar every week.

One thing Kate and Thomas shared was a love of the outdoors. Kate was already an accomplished outdoorswoman and would later canoe solo across much of western Canada. Thomas, of course, had practically grown up outside. One outing the two enjoyed was when they climbed together to the top of Casamanya, a popular local hiking mountain. In true boat-kid style, they did this barefoot, thoughtlessly, without really noticing or caring whether they had any shoes on.

ONCE THE SUMMER WAS OVER Thomas, to his chagrin, was menaced with the prospect of school. It was a problem that had plagued him for much of his life. Most kids who spent much time living on cruising sailboats in those days were enrolled by their parents in formal home-schooling programs, with programmed lessons and exams sent back and forth by mail, but Peter Tangvald had found this inconvenient. Instead he'd sent Thomas to whatever local school was available whenever the family was in one place for more than a few weeks. In his autobiography Peter bragged that Thomas, who had an IQ of 148, had attended classes taught in five different languages—Italian, French, Portuguese, English, and Spanish—and usually earned A's. Thomas's own description of his schooling, in a blog he later maintained online for a while, belied this sort of engagement.

"Most of my time at school," he wrote, "would be spent counting the hours till I would be released from that day's serving of mind-crushing boredom." Once he discovered "the thrills of skipping class" when he was a bit older, he spent his days instead exploring and swimming.

By Thomas's count he attended 15 different schools while growing up, to little avail. What he mostly remembered about them was being ostracized. In some cases he'd been badly bullied. He was always the outsider, the strange new kid, seemingly from another planet, who could not fit in and had no desire to. In one extreme instance he'd even been sexually molested in front of a group of boys in a school on Culebra, according to a letter his father wrote to the Allcards at the time.

Most of what he learned when he was young, Thomas always insisted, he'd gleaned from listening to what the adults around him talked about and from reading books on his own. He particularly enjoyed books on sailboat design, the more technical the better. By the time of the wreck in Bonaire he in fact believed he was finished with school, as his father the previous year, sometime after the molestation incident on Culebra, had agreed he could quit going to classes if he instead spent some time tutoring his sister Carmen.

Thomas thus could not have been pleased when Clare proposed to send him to the French Lycée Compte de Foix, the most respected school in Andorra. To her this seemed the best option, as Thomas's first language, thanks to his mother, was French. Thomas consequently took placement exams in French history and mathematics, and after the results were tallied the director of the school called Clare in for a meeting. He gravely advised that Thomas should not be placed in academic classes but should instead be enrolled in the school's vocational catering program. Clare, who knew very well that Thomas was unusually bright, refused to agree to this. Ultimately, the director allowed that Thomas might enroll in the academic program, but he would have to be put back two years with the younger 13-year-old students.

Thomas really had no interest in going to any sort of school, with any sort of kids, younger or older, but Clare made a deal with him: he would give it a try, and if after a full year of school he was unhappy with it, she would then help him study at home.


THOMAS'S VERY FIRST EXPERIENCE with school had come not long after his mother was murdered. Through a curious turn of events, it was this that led his father to the woman who was to become Thomas's first stepmother.

In the immediate aftermath of Lydia's death on February 20, 1979, Peter had continued sailing southwest out of the Sulu Sea towards Brunei, as he originally planned. He was terribly depressed and rundown and later had no memory of how he managed to both care for Thomas and navigate for a week alone through the reef-strewn waters of the treacherous Balabac Strait. He did remember that Thomas became very ill during this time, running a fever and taking little food. As soon as *L'Artemis de Pytheas* reached Brunei, on February 27, both father and son were immediately hospitalized.

Peter also soon became the focus of an intense police investigation. He was shunned by the expatriate community in Brunei after a story on this appeared in the local paper with a sensational headline: *Pirate Attack, or the (Nearly) Perfect Matrimonial Murder?* The police were well aware that pirates were active in the Sulu Sea, launching an estimated 300 attacks there each year, but they did not understand why Peter and Thomas had not also been slain by the pirates who supposedly killed Lydia. In the end, however, they accepted Peter's story and closed the case after they interviewed Thomas (outside Peter's presence) and also produced a photographic reconstruction of the attack. One shot in particular—showing where and how Peter and Thomas were standing when Lydia was shot, as seen from the pirates' perspective—answered their question. The image of two-year-old Thomas staring innocently into the camera while clinging to his father's leg was so heart-rending, the police told Peter they concluded the pirates hadn't the stomach for more killing.

As soon as he was free to leave Brunei, in April, Peter sailed on to the port of Malacca, on the west coast of Malaysia about halfway between Singapore and Kuala Lumpur. He was still badly depressed, on the verge of a breakdown he believed, and this it seems may have been one of Thomas's earliest conscious memories. In a television interview many years later, Thomas explained he had never felt bad about losing his mother, as he never knew her, but that he did feel very bad about the pain his father endured after she was killed.

Peter now had resolved to return to the West and sell his boat as soon as possible, but he had to wait several months for the monsoon season to turn so as to recross the Indian Ocean from east to west. He grew weary of people asking him about the boy's mother when he was out on the street alone with Thomas, and to avoid this he enrolled the lad in the local Salvation Army nursery school. The headmistress of the Salvation Army school system was a young Chinese woman, Ann Ho Sau Chew. She was small, barely five feet tall, but was dressed in a bright white uniform with gold epaulettes and struck Peter as a stern authoritarian. She kept the initial intake interview as brief as possible, and when she was done peremptorily summoned a servant with a bell to remove Peter and Thomas from her presence.

With Thomas in school, Peter's life fell into a tolerable routine. He was able to work on the boat during the day, preparing for the next passage; in the evenings he fed Thomas and read books to him. At night, while sleeping, he bonded with Thomas in a way he never did with any of his other children. Ever since the pirate attack, Peter had been unable to sleep in the double berth he'd shared with Lydia. He slept instead on the settee in the main saloon, with no mattress, and now Thomas insisted on sleeping with him. They slept together through each night while in Malacca, their bodies lying at a right-angle, their heads near each other, holding hands on the L-shaped bench seat.

Peter's morale received another nice boost when one day, from down below on *L'Artemis*, he heard a familiar voice with a British accent hailing the boat from on shore. This proved to be his old friend Edward Allcard, who had left *Johanne Regina* in the Seychelles with Clare and Kate aboard and had flown to Malaysia as soon as he heard what had happened to Lydia. He stayed a week with Peter, talking over the old days and what the future might bring. He brought with him a letter from Clare, addressed to Peter, in which she offered, on behalf of herself and Edward, to assume custody of Thomas and take him into their home. But Peter, as low as he felt, was not willing to let the boy go.

"[Edward's] visit passed all too quickly," he later wrote, "but even after his departure the spirit of optimism which he'd brought remained with me."

It seemed Peter's luck was turning. Several months later, in early December of that year, with the monsoon due to turn in a week or two, Peter went to the Salvation Army school and asked to see the headmistress. He explained to her that he would soon have to take Thomas out of school, as he planned to sail away from Malacca by the end of the month. He was a bit taken aback when the grim young woman asked if he had someone to go with him to help care for his boy. Peter answered no, then was even more surprised when the woman offered to sail with him herself. The one condition she set was that he had to wait 30 days so she could find someone to take her place at the school.

OF ALL THE IMPROBABLE romantic connections Peter Tangvald made during his life, this was perhaps the most inexplicable. Why would a young professional woman abruptly abandon her career and estrange herself from all her family, seemingly on a whim, to take up with an eccentric sailor, 22 years her senior, whom she barely knew? Thomas when he was older attributed this, with some pride, to his father's great "magnetism for the girls." Clare Allcard, based on letters she'd exchanged with Peter, believed Ann's initial affection was not for Peter, but for Thomas—that somehow the small blond-haired boy who'd just lost his mother had captivated her. A third factor to consider, which does not preclude either of these other explanations, is that Ann likely had buried within her a suppressed seed of wanderlust. Raised in a strict Chinese family, leading a proscribed life within narrow boundaries, still a virgin at age 32, she might have seen in her unlikely glancing exposure to Peter Tangvald and his son a fleeting chance to tread a path to a broader, more varied existence— an opportunity not to be missed.

Whatever her motives, Ann was as good as her word. A month after she made her bold declaration to Peter in her office at the school, she arrived on January 2, 1980, with a pile of luggage at a dock where *L'Artemis de Pytheas* was tied up. That same day, after Ann and her kit were loaded aboard, Peter cast off his lines and set sail to the west, bound for Sri Lanka.

Ann was to spend most of the next five years with Peter and Thomas aboard *L'Artemis*. During that time the family first wandered west across the Indian Ocean, then up the Red Sea and through the Mediterranean, then twice back and forth across the North Atlantic between Europe, South America, and the Caribbean. Peter in his autobiography described a genuine affection that grew up between him and Ann, but privately he also likened her to "a maniacal old lady." At least one cruising family who came to know them later claimed the couple often fought with each other. Meanwhile, in both his book and in private conversations and letters, Peter extolled Ann's virtues as a mate: she was orderly, efficient, an excellent cook, and a clever housewife who extracted the maximum amount of value from the least amount of money. It was for these reasons, presumably, that he later declaimed to certain friends that she had been his favorite wife.

As for Ann's relationship with Thomas, it might initially have been sympathetic, as Clare's impression of its genesis would suggest, but ultimately her attitude toward the boy became hostile. One likely turning point came early during Ann's tenure aboard *L'Artemis*, when the boat was hunkered down against the onset of the Mediterranean winter in a fishing port called Gabes on the coast of Tunisia in November of 1980. During the night of the 11th, the family was suddenly awakened by three masked men who came aboard armed with knives and clubs. They demanded money and threatened violence if the family failed to cooperate.

Peter immediately gave the thieves all the money he personally had aboard, less than $200, but they insisted there must be more. When Peter denied this, the thieves beat him until he was unconscious. They gagged and bound him, then turned to Ann. She offered to give the men all her money and jewelry if only they would leave peacefully. In response they attempted to rape her. One man with a knife stood over Peter, who by now had regained consciousness. The other two ripped off Ann's nightgown. One held her down while the other dropped his pants and tried to mount her. Ann, who weighed less than 90 pounds, fought back so ferociously the men could not consummate the deed, but they did beat her without mercy. Landing 20 to 30 blows on her face, they broke one of Ann's teeth, nearly strangled her to death, and left her badly swollen and bruised before finally retreating from the boat.

Thomas, frozen in place, now just four years old, had witnessed all this. Later, mimicking Ann's Chinese accent, he declared: "They are nasty men. I don't like them. I am glad they are gone."

It may be Ann never had any real affection for Thomas, or it may be that what affection she did have curdled and turned foul in the shame she felt after the attack. Deeply humiliated, she became badly depressed, professed that she wished to die, and started vomiting daily.

"For me her permanent bad mood is not uplifting," Peter wrote to an old friend he knew from Port Grimaud in France, "but it is certainly poor Thomas who suffers from her suffering."

Ann became physically abusive with the boy, often spanking him and lashing out at him. In one instance, when the family was moored at Falmouth, England, in the fall of 1981, Peter left the pair on the boat while he rowed to shore in the dinghy to run errands. Once ashore he heard Ann screaming at Thomas—and Thomas crying out in return. He immediately rowed back and found the boy sobbing and bleeding from the wounds Ann had inflicted. In the face of such evidence, Peter did move to protect his son and at once banished Ann from the boat. She flew back to Malaysia, on a ticket paid for by Peter's old partner Simonne, and stayed away for some time, perhaps for as long as six months.

Thomas certainly did not miss her. As Peter related in a letter, as soon as the boy understood Ann had left, he stared up intently and said: "Papa, I think we should sail back to a warmer harbor and there find a new Mama for me. One who is not always cross at me and who does not spank me all the time."

And Peter noted: "It is certain that she hardly loves him, and he feels it."

But eventually Peter relented, the couple somehow reconciled, and Ann returned to the boat. And in other less dramatic instances it seems Peter was also sometimes more openly complicit in mistreating Thomas. Clare Allcard, for example, after Thomas came to live in Andorra, learned one detail of his early childhood that truly disturbed her. She and Thomas were discussing Carmen, and Thomas mentioned he thought his little sister had always cried too much. Clare noted that she'd heard from Edward, after he visited *L'Artemis de Pytheas* in Malacca, that Thomas when he was much younger had also cried a bit.

Thomas at once protested: "But I hardly ever cried!" He went on to describe the one exception he remembered, which was when his father and Ann used to go out at night—they would leave him locked up in the forepeak, all alone on the boat. "Then," he confessed, "I screamed until they finally returned."

Clare later wrote: "That was the day that I began to despise Peter Tangvald."

PETER AND ANN WERE MARRIED sometime in early May 1982 at the Church of Sagene in Oslo, Norway. From the beginning Ann had realized she was not cut out for ocean sailing. She was often seasick when the boat was underway, she had no real interest in or aptitude for the physical process of sailing, and she pressed Peter on the subject of selling the boat and moving ashore. Peter, who had entertained this notion himself immediately after Lydia's murder, was at least partly open to the idea. The question was: where might they swallow the anchor?

Norway seemed like one logical answer. At some point after Ann rejoined *L'Artemis* in England, Peter managed to borrow a car from a friend and the reunited family set out in this together on a ferry bound for Peter's original homeland. They were not always well received, nor were they prepared for the climate. One old sailing friend of Peter's lent the family a boat to stay on for a few days, a famous old ketch named *Stavanger*, immediately after they landed in Norway. This was in April 1982, and Ann was horrified one morning when she stuck her head out the companionway hatch to confront her first snowstorm. Peter hadn't the heart to tell her that these conditions, with temperatures barely below freezing, were by Norwegian standards rather mild. After so many years in the tropics, he really didn't enjoy them either.

Peter's family was a more serious puzzle. He and Ann with Thomas in tow visited different relatives and were treated politely, but relations in some cases were strained. The exception perhaps was Thomas, who was pleased to find younger Tangvalds to play with. The irony was these were the offspring of his older half-siblings, the issue of Peter's first marriage—not Thomas's cousins, but his nephews and nieces.

The one closest in age to Thomas was his half-nephew Gjermund, the son of Peter's daughter Janike and her husband Erik Sæterbakken. Gjermund years later became close to Thomas and recalled with amusement their first attempt at playing together. They sat in a pile of sand together with Gjermund's collection of toy cars, which he offered to share. Thomas by now often played with Lego blocks, his favorite toy, and according to one of his half-siblings could build "the most fascinating and imaginative figures" with them. But he likely had never seen such things as toy cars before.

"He just took them one by one by one, until I had none, and he wouldn't give them back," remembered Gjermund. "It was not playing at all. There was something else going on."

Peter evidently was hoping the long hiatus in his relations with his three oldest children might end now that they were adults. Reidun, their mother, had never prejudiced them against him, but her second husband, Rasmus Hansson, an architect, had willingly served as a father in Peter's place. He had adopted all three children, and they had taken his name, a process to which Peter had never objected. While growing up the children were well aware that Peter was their biological father. Their mother showed them photos of him, sometimes they read about him in newspapers and magazines, and they may have harbored some romantic notions regarding the life he led. But neither Peter, nor their Tangvald grandparents, ever reached out to them as family. Peter's younger daughter, Jessica, was the hardest against him. She remembered later that during this visit she mentioned to her father, whom she'd only met briefly once before, that she was concerned about Thomas's peripatetic upbringing afloat. She worried about Thomas's education and wondered whether he was being properly socialized. Per, as she knew him, became mad at her and excoriated her for pestering him over such "details."

The other two, Gjermund's mother Janike and Peter's oldest child, his son Jørgen, felt more open toward their father. Jørgen was the most sympathetic. He found an apartment for Peter, Ann, and Thomas to stay in and also arranged for a friend of his, a priest, to marry Peter and Ann. Janike, on the other hand, was truly torn. Her husband Erik was very interested in Peter. Their son Gjermund later recalled: "The way my father looked at him and talked to him, I immediately understood this was a special man." Ultimately, though Janike felt no animus toward her father, she also felt an obligation of loyalty toward her mother.[1]

The confusion and ambivalence regarding Peter's Norwegian family was evident at the wedding in Oslo. There were only two

---

1. Both Jørgen and Janike later changed their last names to Tangvald, despite protests from Reidun. Jessica earlier had changed her name to her mother's maiden name, Kathle.

guests, Jørgen and Erik, who attended the ceremony and reception. "Even the minister was a bit embarrassed to see his church so empty," Peter wrote in *At Any Cost*. He privately complained that his Norwegian family and friends were prejudiced against Ann because she was Asian, a claim his older children strongly deny. It seems Peter never acknowledged these awkward relations might have been rooted in his own failures as a father.

Peter and Ann retreated from Norway back to England in their borrowed car soon after their wedding. Two months later they decided to resume their wandering and set sail for the tropics. By October the family had crossed the Atlantic and dropped anchor at Cayenne, in French Guiana, where *L'Artemis* had first been launched nine years earlier. The couple again toyed with the idea of settling down, as old friends of Peter's offered to stake him in starting up a boatyard, but Ann was haunted by thoughts of the two previous wives Peter had been with there.

In a few weeks they moved on again to the West Indies. During the latter part of that winter, early in 1983 while *L'Artemis* was still in the Caribbean, Ann learned she was pregnant. Some who knew her during this time remembered how happy she seemed then compared to the dark, often angry woman she had been before. Her daughter Carmen was born that fall, on October 14, 1983, thousands of miles to the east in the port town of Faro, on the southern coast of Portugal—not on the boat, but in a hospital.

Thomas, however he felt about Carmen when he was older, apparently welcomed her arrival. Seven months later Peter proudly wrote to a friend that "Thomas adores his little sister and plays with her all day long in his cabin from where we can hear laughter at any time."

Ann's last voyage aboard *L'Artemis de Pytheas* began on December 31, 1984. Having spent a fine summer cruising the Portuguese Algarve and the southwest coast of Spain, the family had sailed south late that fall to the Canary Islands. From there, on the last day of the year, they set out from Santa Cruz de Tenerife, bound west for the island of Grenada in the West Indies, on what would be Peter Tangvald's seventh and last transatlantic passage. The ever-persistent tradewinds were blowing fresh and clean from the east and sped the family on their way.

By the morning of January 26, 1985, *L'Artemis* had almost reached Grenada. After breakfast Ann went up to do the laundry, which consisted mostly of soiled diapers, in a bucket on deck. Despite having lived on the boat for years now, she still understood nothing about how it worked and thoughtlessly hung the diapers out to dry on one of the control lines that led from the self-steering windvane on the boat's transom to the boat's tiller. The weight on the line restricted its motion and caused the boat to swerve off course, pointing it further downwind.

Peter was in the forepeak at the time with the two children. He at once sensed the boat was bearing away off course and rushed up on deck. By the time he reached the cockpit, the boat was already sailing by the lee, with the wind blowing on the wrong side of the mainsail. In a panic he jumped for the tiller to disengage the windvane, but it was too late. The mainsail jibed all standing, swinging all the way across the back of the boat, from one side to the other, in one thunderous, calamitous instant. The heavy wooden boom at the bottom of the sail struck Ann cleanly as it came across and sent her flying overboard far from the boat.[2]

Having heard the awful crash, Thomas too rushed up on deck. He and his father scanned the waves all around them, searching for Ann, but saw nothing.

---

2. To avoid accidents like this while sailing downwind, many sailors rig a line known as a preventer to hold a mainsail boom in place in the event the mainsail is backwinded. It is not clear from his account in *At Any Cost* whether Peter had done this. It may be there was a preventer on the boom, but that it broke.

Peter sailed *L'Artemis* around in circles for six hours, until finally Thomas spotted something in the water. It proved to be the bucket Ann had been doing laundry in, a sure sign they were in the area where she had gone overboard. But still there was no other sign of her, and still they kept on searching.

Many years later in an interview, Thomas described the denouement: "She did not know how to swim, plus she very well might have been knocked unconscious, or maybe even killed, just in the first instant when the boom hit her. But of course you try... you hope. Then when it started getting dark there was no more hope, so we carried on sailing to Grenada."

Thomas when he was older never fully acknowledged how badly Ann had treated him. He often described her as having been strict with him, but he never openly allowed that this might have risen to the level of abuse. It may be that he had blocked such episodes entirely from his mind, or perhaps he was simply reluctant to confess them to others. In the case of his nephew Gjermund, paradoxically, he in later years created the impression that he might actually have felt some fondness for her.

The one brief anecdote regarding Ann that Thomas committed to writing, in his blog, is more or less a parable. He recounted how one of his daily chores when he was seven and the family was in Faro, Portugal, around the time Carmen was born, was to walk from the boat to the local bakery to buy bread.

"One day I came back with the wrong change," he wrote, "and my Chinese stepmother sternly advised me to return at once to the bakery and reclaim the missing change. Luckily I was able to convince them to correct the matter, but ever since then I am always careful to check my change."

CLARE KNEW NOTHING ABOUT Thomas's family in Norway prior to his arrival in Andorra. Neither she nor Edward, who had known Peter for 34 years, had any idea he'd had three children prior to Thomas. They soon established contact, however, as the clan's patriarch, Peter's uncle Lyder Tangvald, the younger brother of his father Thor, wrote to Edward a few weeks after the wreck, asking after Thomas. Lyder had learned of the tragedy through a newspaper article and at once made inquiries to the Norwegian foreign office and the authorities on Bonaire.

Though she wondered why Peter had not arranged for his own family to care for his children in the event of his death, Clare was pleased there was an extended family for Thomas to connect with. She soon started planning a trip for Thomas to Norway so he could visit with them. Thomas did this twice during his time in Andorra, flying to Norway for two weeks in the summers of 1992 and '93, and both times was welcomed with open arms by all three of his half siblings and their six children.

During his visit in 1992, Thomas particularly enjoyed spending time with the nephews who were closest to him in age. With Gjermund he had something of a ribald experience. They went out to parties together, and Thomas asked Gjermund to teach him enough Norwegian so that he could introduce himself to girls. Gjermund played a joke on Thomas and without his knowledge taught him the crudest, foulest pick-up lines he could think of. When Thomas tried them out, girls were not impressed, but Gjermund was greatly amused. Though miffed when he figured out what was going on, Thomas soon was laughing at himself and later took great pride in being able to perfectly recite the lines Gjermund had taught him.

He had a much more intellectual encounter with the son of his half-sister Jessica, Ola, who was three years older than him. They stayed up late into the night talking together about the subjects that most interested each of them—math and physics for Thomas, and philosophy for Ola. Ola later remembered he was struck not only by their physical resemblance, but also by how much they thought alike.

During Thomas's 1993 visit to Norway, he had a chance to form a deeper, more somber bond with his extended family, as his father's uncle Lyder died while he was there. Thomas joined with the others in attending Lyder's funeral and in mourning the passing of this last member of his grandfather Thor's generation.[3]

Clare meanwhile also put Thomas in touch with someone else who might be considered family in the larger sense: Peter's fourth wife Simonne. She was very keen to connect with Thomas, for she saw in him something no one else did, a surrogate for the child she never had with Peter. Simonne had never recovered from her relationship with Peter Tangvald and had prayed always they might someday get together again. She had hovered around the periphery of his life, staying friendly with him, offering assistance whenever she could. She lived in a house in Trans-en-Provence, in the south of France, which she maintained as a shrine to Peter. It was filled with belongings of his he had no space for on his boat, and over the years he had stopped by now and then, picking things up and dropping them off. One of these was the Moto Guzzi motorcycle on which Peter had taken Lydia for that purportedly fateful ride back in French Guiana.[4]

With Peter now gone, Thomas was the last tendril of his father that Simonne had to cling to. She had met Thomas just once when he was younger, when Peter brought him to visit in Trans-en-Provence in 1982. Her affection for the boy was most certainly sharpened by a secret she later shared with Clare and

---

3. Lyder Tangvald, unlike his brother Thor, had maintained contact with Peter's older children.

4. Peter kept the motorcycle in storage at Simonne's until sometime in 1982, when he moved it onto the boat. He later sold it in Puerto Rico in 1987. To store the bike on the boat he completely disassembled it and carefully stowed away all the separate pieces. To use the bike he took all the pieces ashore and reassembled them.

Thomas—that she once had conceived a child by Peter, and he had convinced her to abort it. According to one secondhand source, Simonne explained to Thomas this had been done in the crudest way possible, literally with a coat-hanger, onboard *L'Artemis*.

Trans-en-Provence was not too far from Andorra, a little over six hours by car, so it was relatively easy for the Allcards and Thomas to visit back and forth with Simonne. Clare later recalled that Simonne and Thomas got on very well together. As a retired gymnastics teacher, Simonne was gratified when Thomas started taking gymnastics lessons not long after moving to Andorra. She also enjoyed presenting him with books and objects that had belonged to his father, and Thomas in turn, now living in an English-speaking household, especially enjoyed being able to communicate with Simonne fluently in French.

Simonne's love for Thomas was effusive and maternally unconditional. Even before he came to Andorra, she had taken out a life insurance policy and named Thomas as its sole beneficiary. Her affection for the boy even survived what proved to be the crushing blow to her enduring obsession with his father. Peter's English-language autobiography, *At Any Cost*, was published just a few months after Thomas came to Andorra, and Simonne put off reading it for some time. She assumed she would find it upsetting, and sure enough, when she finally did read it she was furious. It was full of lies! It misrepresented how she and Peter came to marry and how he'd betrayed her with Lydia, it made no mention of how she'd filled in for Lydia during the passage around Iberia, or how she'd paid to send Ann away, and several other things besides.

Simonne, in response to this final betrayal, acted decisively. She threw away or destroyed all of Peter's possessions that she had cherished and stored for him, then she sold the house in Trans-en-Provence and moved to a small flat on the waterfront in Marseilles. The only thing she kept was an old painting, a portrait of Jean

Bernadotte, the French general who became king of Norway and Sweden in 1818. This had come to Peter through his family and was presumed to be quite valuable. Now Simonne resolved she would keep this painting in trust for Thomas, and would bestow it upon him when he was older.

# 5. AN EDUCATION CONSUMMATED

FOR THE MOST PART it must have seemed to Thomas as he was growing up that the life he led and the world he lived in was the school he attended. For a mind such as his, everything he perceived presented learning opportunities. From a relatively early age he developed an abiding interest in fluid dynamics, the science describing the flow of both liquids and gasses, and this did not spring from any well of abstraction within him. It rose instead from a keen desire to understand what was happening around him.

At sea while on passage Thomas's cabin up in the bow of his father's boat always experienced the most severe motion. "Upwind in strong weather," he later remembered, "I would be nearly weightless as the bow began its descent, and then at the bottom of the motion, crushed into my bunk and against the side of the boat." Sailing downwind, he recalled, the motion was gentler. There was no violent pitching, just the slow rise of the stern as waves approached and a cyclical pattern of the boat rolling from side to side. "I would lie down on the saloon settees," he wrote, "and press my ear against the wood and listen to the water sloshing around in the water tanks and the bubbles rushing along under the hull."

Until about age 10, Thomas was never allowed on deck while *L'Artemis* was under sail. He spent hours at a time standing in the companionway, poking his head out and looking around. He noted the sails overhead and their position relative to the direction of the wind. He studied intently the action of the waves all around him while letting his mind ponder "all manner of things great and small."

At night, when he wasn't sleeping and hadn't been locked into his cabin, Thomas manned his post in the companionway and marveled at the stars overhead. Those used to living on shore anywhere near human habitations cannot imagine how velvety black the sky can be at night far out at sea, nor how brightly the stars shine within that velvet, nor how many stars are visible. Though he had seen this countless times, Thomas was always amazed by the view. He studied the star charts his father kept aboard and memorized all the constellations. On cloudy nights he tested himself by seeing how quickly he could identify different stars when only a few were visible. During both the day and the night he kept track of the arcs of the sun and the moon, noting where they rose and set and how high they climbed. When he was a bit older he studied his father's books on celestial navigation, built himself a crude sextant, and figured out how to use it. His father, though initially dismissive of his effort, was properly impressed by the accuracy of his position plots.

For the first couple of days on a passage Thomas was sometimes seasick, particularly if *L'Artemis* had been in harbor for a long time, but once this passed he could focus on things in detail down below in the boat's cabin without feeling ill. He enjoyed playing with Legos, and drawing, and he particularly liked to read. When he was about nine years old he began devouring his father's books on boatbuilding and naval architecture, the bibles that unlocked for him the secrets of how the boat he lived on actually worked and how it interacted with the wind and the sea.

He also was very fond of reading comic books. When he was younger he particularly enjoyed the Belgian character Gaston Lagaffe, as well as such classics as Tintin and Asterix. When he was older he discovered Corto Maltese, drawn by the Italian artist Hugo Pratt. Maltese was "a rogue with a heart of gold," a self-described gentleman of fortune, the son of a British sailor and a

Spanish gypsy who was both a prostitute and a witch. He lived as an itinerant sailor, a sort of laconic Lone Ranger of the seven seas who had all sorts of adventures in the early part of the 20th century in different parts of the globe, taking up with all sorts of real-life historical figures, such as the American outlaw Butch Cassidy, writers such as Jack London, Herman Hesse, and James Joyce, and political figures like Rasputin, Enver Pasha, and Josef Stalin. Corto, for Thomas, became something of a fictional role model, just as his father was a factual one.

Much of Thomas's childhood, of course, was not spent at sea, but in port—still afloat, but with land in sight. He always remembered the thrill of making a landfall at the end of a passage. The loom of the lights on shore, sometimes visible from as far out as 50 or 60 miles if it was a city they were sailing into, and the smell of it, car exhaust and refuse for a city, damp soil and rotting vegetation if it were somewhere more remote.

"With my keen eyesight," he wrote, "I would not only be almost always the first to see land, but also the first to pick out the outermost approach buoys. Then the features become more and more distinct, landmarks then houses, masts in the harbor, then cars and finally people can be seen. And the calm! After days of never-ending jostling around, the boat's motion becomes surreally serene."

For Thomas what was most exciting about arriving in any new harbor were the new people to be encountered there. He was an inherently social creature, and through all his childhood the focal points of the society he circulated in were the ports and anchorages where cruising sailboats routinely gathered. Most of the people he met lived just as he did, aboard boats on the water, and for a number of years he believed this was how most humans lived. He was a bit surprised when he eventually deduced there were many more people, a stupendously vast number of them, who lived on land. On arriving in any new harbor, Thomas always loved to "go meeting," as he called it. He would row around a new anchorage in the boat's dinghy and introduce himself to any other cruising sailors he found loitering about on the decks of their boats. He later boasted: "I was an expert at judging which boats were most likely to have other children aboard."

Even when he was still quite young Thomas was particularly interested in befriending girls his age. At age six, for example, while *L'Artemis* was cruising in the French West Indies in early 1983, while Ann was still aboard, he developed a strong crush on another boat kid, a Dutch girl named Agnita Twigt, who lived with her parents and younger sister aboard a smaller 33-foot sailboat. For Agnita, who was just a few months younger than Thomas, the feeling was mutual. Years later she still thought of Thomas as her first boyfriend and recalled how they played "boat" together, pretending he was the father and she the mother: "We had a lot of fantasies about building our own ship, so we drew a lot of pictures of how we would design our boat and where we would sail."

A few years after this, it seemed to another cruising couple who encountered the Tangvalds, again in the French West Indies, after Ann was lost, that Thomas had a talent for capturing the attention of young girls. Tom and Ros Cunliffe were then cruising full-time with their six-year-old daughter Hannah on their antique wooden pilot cutter *Hirta*. As they later remembered it, Peter came by and dropped off Thomas, then age eight, for an impromptu tea party with Hannah and another girl, Sarah, visiting from another boat. Thomas had brought a jigsaw puzzle that he presented to Hannah as a gift.

"When Ros went up to tell him it was time to leave," Tom recalled, "they weren't playing with the jigsaw, they were all on our bunk. Thomas was sitting on top of the bed, telling them some tale, and the girls were lying on their stomachs, totally engrossed!"

Inevitably all such friends were lost once anchors were hoisted and sails were set for another ocean passage.

"Leaving a harbor would be a rather sad affair for me," Thomas later wrote, "leaving friends and sometimes little girlfriends behind in the dim faintly grey landmasses astern."

NO ONE WAS TOO SURPRISED when it turned out that Thomas was not happy attending the French lycée in Andorra. The school's program was quite regimented, not at all open to fluid experiential learning styles, and it didn't help that Thomas was set back two years at the start. In what now seems a parody of scholastic discipline, he was more than once set the onerous task of writing out repeated pledges of mindless obedience. "Je doit me mettre en rang" (or "I must stand in line") read one of these, scrawled in neat handwriting dozens and dozens of times across numerous tightly ruled pages. But what most galled him, he complained to Clare Allcard, was that the instructors sometimes had no idea what they were talking about. He cited examples of an art teacher who drew perspectives incorrectly on the chalkboard, and a geography instructor who didn't know which way the Gulf Stream flowed.

When Clare spoke with Thomas's instructors after his first term at the school, she found only the science teacher had any appreciation for the boy's intellect.

"Ah, he has rubies, that one," exclaimed the man enthusiastically. "I sometimes feel like a television the way the students stare at me with lifeless eyes. But Thomas, he is constantly watching and listening."

By the following term the math teacher, who had previously been quite critical of Thomas, had also come around. But for Thomas by then, the writing, as it were, was on the wall.

He did have a few friends at school. One was a classmate, a British girl named Sarah Hanrahan Talty, whom Thomas quickly became romantically interested in. He often rode over to her house on his new bicycle and spent time there hanging out with her. At one point he drew her a picture, a pair of eyes and some flowers, and she showed this to her mother.

"My mum said: 'You do realize that's you, don't you?'" recalled Sarah. "And that's where I freaked out a bit. I just got scared, so I kind of pushed him away."

She was, after all, two years younger than Thomas, just 13 at the time. All she really knew about him was that he was an orphan, and she later regretted how she rebuffed him.

Thomas's best friend in Andorra was another British expatriate, a Chinese Brit from Hong Kong, Stephen Macdonald, who also attended the lycée, but was not in Thomas's class. Like Sarah, Steve was a good bit younger than Thomas, the son of a woman from a mainland Chinese refugee family and a British police officer who once raced automobiles. While studying his father's books aboard *L'Artemis*, Thomas had designed and built many model sailboats— at least 30 by his count—to test and refine his ideas, and he was happy to find that Steve had a very similar hobby, building model radio-controlled gliding airplanes.

Steve had what he later described as "a very fundamental knowledge" of aerodynamics, while Thomas had a more technical understanding of both aero- and hydrodynamics, gleaned from his reading and his own model-boat building. It must have been a huge relief for Thomas to find an alternative outlet for his keen interest in the science of sailing, and for Steve it was exciting to learn more about the science of flying, and of sailing, through Thomas. During the summer months the two boys designed and flew gliders together in the Andorran mountains, where conditions in certain places were sometimes ideal, with strong thermal air currents to keep their planes aloft. They flew them also down on the Spanish coast, when Steve stayed with Thomas as a guest of the Allcards' aboard *Johanne*. In the latter case, Steve recalled, as there were no thermals to play down on the shore, he and Thomas flung their planes aloft with an elastic catapult they built. They then sent them into screaming dives and banked them into long, sweeping turns with their wing tips skimming along within a foot of the ground. The challenge was to see how far they could stretch out those low turns before landing their planes as close to their feet as possible.

This willingness to dance on the edge of things, to release some adrenalin and court a bit of mishap, was something the two boys shared. It was more pronounced in Thomas, but Steve was a willing acolyte. "This was a very interesting time for me," Steve later recalled, "because [Thomas] certainly opened my mind to what could be attempted provided you keep a modicum of self-control."

During one visit to *Johanne*, for example, Thomas challenged Steve to join him in climbing to the top of the boat's mainmast, a height of about 60 feet, and to then descend hand over hand via the wire forestay running from the masthead out to the end of the boat's bowsprit. For Thomas, who had been climbing around in sailboat rigging for much of his life, this was an almost routine trick. For Steve it was more taxing. He climbed the mast and was about halfway down the forestay when he realized he was "in a little bit deeper" than he expected. He did survive the stunt, but afterwards found his hands were badly blistered and needed bandaging.

Another adventure involved an enormous boom crane that towered high over a construction site a short distance up the road from the Allcards' home. Steve was staying over one night, and Thomas "casually mentioned" he'd taken to climbing the crane and asked if Steve would like to walk up with him and give it a go. As Steve remembered it, Thomas went barefoot, as he claimed his feet had better grip that way, and also calmly walked out to the end of the boom once they got to the top. Steve meanwhile kept his shoes on, and while he did climb all the way up the crane, he elected not to venture out on to the horizontal boom.

Some weeks later Thomas also announced he had recently scaled a light mast atop the roof of a nearby discotheque and had disconnected its array of flashing laser lights. Clare and Edward had been complaining about these lights, and Thomas resented their interfering with his view of the night sky. Characteristically, he set out to solve the problem in a very direct manner. Steve recalled that Thomas seemed pleased as he described the chaos and shouting that broke out around the disco beneath him after he extinguished the lights.

"I was very impressed," said Steve, "but I did not want to climb up that mast, I have to admit."

When it came to skiing the two boys were on more equal footing. Steve had joined a local ski club soon after his family first moved to Andorra and later became an expert ski instructor and coach. Thomas had no prior experience at all. During the Andorran winter, when all the local ski resorts came alive with visitors and conditions precluded flying gliders, this became their preferred weekend activity. Thomas, however, was never interested in the nuances of control; he was interested only in raw speed.

"We would spend the days just going straight down the slope from top to bottom, rotating around the same lift every time," Steve recalled. "Turns were absolutely prohibited. We were just going as fast as possible in the most aerodynamic position."

Steve and Thomas never wore glasses or goggles while streaking down the slopes in breakneck fashion, and this made things more difficult, particularly when it was snowing. Thomas's proposed solution was that they should tape together a pair of toilet paper tubes, one for each eye, and wear these instead of goggles. The differential in pressure between the air inside the tubes and the air outside would be enough, he claimed, to keep snow from blowing into their eyes.

This sort of bizarre "non-standard" reasoning was what most impressed Steve about Thomas. Led on by Thomas and his unconventional ideas, Steve took to traipsing about town in bare feet, learned to recite the obscene Norwegian pick-up lines that Thomas had learned from Gjermund, and once with Thomas attempted to climb a mountain, unsuccessfully, in the dark of night, all to the chagrin of his parents.

"As an impressionable teen I was looking at [Thomas] with my eyes wide open," Steve later recalled. "Often I could not believe what I was hearing, but he always made absolute sense."

AS SHE HAD PROMISED Clare let Thomas drop out of school after he completed his one unhappy year in bondage. But the goal of his alternative home-study program, she insisted, would be for him to sit for the five O-level exams he would need to pass in order to apply to attend a university in Great Britain.

Clare personally supervised Thomas's first year of at-home study, putting in four hours a day with him, five days a week. They worked through a Worldwide Educational Services correspondence course in the five O-level subjects they figured would be easiest for Thomas to pass—physics and math, plus the languages he was fluent in: English, Spanish, and French. This effort was in addition to Clare's cooking special vegetarian meals for Thomas, as like his father he refused to eat meat, and the mindless chauffeur duty any parent of a non-driving teen is destined to suffer through. Clare regularly drove Thomas to extracurricular gymnastics and art classes, then waited patiently for him to finish his courses before driving him home again. It irked her that Thomas, in typical modern teen fashion, never thanked her for any of these services. With a shrug she later recalled how Thomas would say nothing and only slammed the car door behind him as he loped off into the gym for one of his appointments. This sort of attitude irked Edward even more, schooled as he was in Old World notions of polite conduct, and jealous also of the enormous drain on Clare's attention.

Viewed from Thomas's perspective, it may have been he genuinely felt no gratitude. Since coming to Andorra he'd been subjected to much more direct and prolonged regimentation in his day-to-day life than he had ever before experienced. Thomas may not have actively resented this, but it most probably took some tolerating, and Clare was attuned to this. She always appreciated that Thomas had led a largely independent existence before coming to her—living on his own boat, earning his own money—and she anguished over how best to prepare him for the future now that his prior existence had been destroyed.

During his first year studying at home Thomas was quite certain he did not want to attend university, in Great Britain or anywhere else. What he most wanted, as he made clear to Clare and Edward from the moment they assumed custody of him, was to get back to the sea and to boats as soon as possible. To that end he conceived an ambition to find work as a yacht rigger, and Clare, to her credit, did everything she could to nurture and help fulfill that ambition. Tapping her and Edward's connections within the yachting community, she wrote various letters seeking an apprenticeship for him, focusing primarily on the south coast of England, where he would have Clare's mother and family close by, and the south of France, where he'd be close to both the Allcards and Simonne. One likely prospect was a rigging shop Clare found in Antibes, just 45 minutes from Simonne, who was ecstatic at the prospect of having Thomas working and living so close to her.

"I would like this to happen!" Simonne wrote enthusiastically to Clare and volunteered to go to Antibes herself to lobby directly on Thomas's behalf.

But none of these efforts were immediately fruitful, and Thomas's desire to work as a simple rigger was ultimately undermined by his own intellectual curiosity. He had a very genuine thirst for knowledge and could not ignore opportunities to satiate it. One key figure in this regard was Donovan Madden, another British expatriate then living in Andorra, who agreed when asked by Clare to serve as Thomas's physics and math tutor.

There was a lot in Don Madden for Thomas to relate to. Of West African descent on his father's side, Don had been raised by nuns from age six in a London orphanage. He left the orphanage and started working full time at age 15, first as a low-paid "bricky" hauling stacks of bricks around construction sites, then later as an electrician's "mate." He subsequently found a job at the Woolwich Royal Arsenal, where he was soon recognized as being unusually intelligent and was sent off for more schooling. He eventually became a physicist and worked for many years with the European Space Agency on communications satellites (he was once selected as the ESA's Scientist of the Year) before finally retiring to Andorra.

Thomas and Don worked together twice a week to fill in gaps in Thomas's knowledge, starting with simple mathematical equations and moving on eventually, over the course of 18 months, to mid-level calculus and physics. More importantly, Don encouraged and titillated Thomas's curiosity, and the two often wandered far off topic in their discussions. They talked at length of the physics and mathematics of sailing and flying, but also of skateboards equipped with sails, of the flow of air through an Australian didgeridoo, and other subjects.

Thomas was particularly intrigued with the concept of perpetual motion, and together he and Don posited a hypothetical model in which this ideal might be achieved: a hole dug clear through the moon. You drop an object down the hole, and it falls through to the other side. There's no atmosphere on the moon, thus no air resistance, so the object is accelerated by gravity as it falls toward the center of the moon, then decelerates once past it, traveling the same distance away from the center as it had toward it, then is drawn in again toward the center, ad infinitum.

"He loved it," Don recalled. "He loved the idea, and toyed with it, and thought about it endlessly."

Don appreciated the breadth of Thomas's intellect as well as anyone, and a recommendation he later wrote described it concisely. In spite of having "near-zero formal education history," Don noted: "[Thomas] is very intelligent, has exceptionally good learning capacity, and is unusually adept at grasping novel concepts. He possesses innate analytical powers, and revels in conducting independent 'thought experiments.' He also insists that 'facts' be adequately demonstrated or verified before he is content to accept them."

AT THE END OF THOMAS'S ONE YEAR of independent study, he and Clare traveled to England together in June 1993 so that he could sit for his O-level exams. They stayed with Clare's mother in Newick, a village in Sussex about an hour's drive from the test site, at a local school in Hove, just outside Brighton.

Clare had time to kill while Thomas was taking tests and ended up cruising the shelves of a local used bookstore during the first day of exams. She had previously given Thomas a copy of Stephen Hawking's breakthrough bestseller, *A Brief History of Time*, and he had eagerly devoured it in a single night. Thinking he might be interested in learning more about Hawking, she purchased for him a biography she found of the famous Cambridge University cosmologist. She also snagged a copy of *The Man Who Knew Infinity*, Robert Kanigel's biography of the great Hindu math prodigy Srinivasa Ramanujan, the first Indian ever elected a Fellow of Trinity College at Cambridge.

In between taking tests Thomas inhaled these two books as quickly as he had the first. The morning after he finished them, as Clare was driving him down to Hove from Newick for more exams, he asked out of the blue: "So what do I have to do to go to university?"

Clare clutched the car's steering wheel and took a deep breath. Mustn't mess this up, she thought to herself, and decided it might be best to try some reverse psychology.

"Oh, Thomas, you don't want to do that," she answered. "You'll have to take at least three A-level exams, and it will take two years to prepare for them."

Thomas thought about that for a moment, then declared: "I'll do it in one."

Clare was thrilled, though was careful not to show it. Thomas's desire to accelerate his A-level exam timeline also left her with a neat problem to solve. If Thomas were to sit for A-levels in just one year's time, they needed to get him provisionally accepted at a university somewhere almost immediately, within the remaining two weeks of their stay in Britain.

A bit of research in a local library revealed there were just three British universities with serious programs in fluid dynamics. Though she didn't yet have Thomas's O-level test results (he got four A's and a B) to help tout his abilities, Clare immediately wrote what she later described as "manipulative sob-story letters" to the admissions offices at each school—Southampton, Cambridge, and Leeds.

They traveled first to Southampton, but neither Clare nor Thomas were very impressed with what they found there. Next came Cambridge, where the admissions don proved to be a psychologist who was intrigued by Thomas's unusual background. He had his office prepare a personalized questionnaire for Thomas that accounted for that background and also arranged for an interview with the school's top fluid-dynamics professor.

Thomas's straightforward, almost diffident answers to some of the written questions he fielded from Cambridge recall the laconic attitude of his comic-book hero Corto Maltese. For example, one query was perfectly anodyne: "Why should we take you rather than any other candidate?"—a clear invitation to engage in a bit of personal salesmanship. In response Thomas wrote: "I don't know what the other candidates are like, so I can't really say. I just do my best and hope you will judge me as being eligible."

After touring the Cambridge campus, Thomas spent an hour in deep conversation with the fluid-dynamics professor. Immediately afterwards he was offered a place in the following year's entering class, provided he scored at least one A and two B's on his three A-level exams.

Clare was over the moon. She'd always believed Thomas was a genius, and now that genius had been recognized! Her young ward, without even filing a formal application, had been invited to attend one of the world's most renowned universities, the home of both Hawking and Ramanujan, with what was recognized as the premier mathematics department in all of Western Europe. And this time she could not contain herself.

"Wow! Thomas, that's amazing!" she exclaimed as they drove away from the school.

But Thomas's reply was immediately dismissive. "I couldn't possibly go there," he said. "Didn't you see? All the signs that said 'Keep Off the Grass'? I can't go to a place like that."

Thomas was similarly well received at the University of Leeds and after an interview was also offered a spot there, contingent only on his scoring one B and a minimum passing grade of E on two of his three A-level exams.

Returning to Andorra in something like triumph, Thomas set out that fall to prepare for rigorous tests in mathematics, advanced mathematics, and physics in half the normally allotted time. He worked again through the WES home-study program, but now entirely on his own, with no supervision from Clare, though he did have weekly sessions with a new math tutor, John Crozier, another bright Andorran Brit who had once written the math exams given out to students at Cambridge. Thomas on his own initiative sat down promptly at 8:30 each morning to start studying and didn't get up again until the afternoon, at which point he'd head off to gymnastics classes, or to art classes, or up into the mountains to ski or fly gliders with Steve. And he made rapid progress, earning top scores on mock A-level tests after studying for only a fraction of the time most students did.

Clare meanwhile had to figure out how to pay for Thomas's university education. Had he been a British citizen Thomas could have attended school for free, through government grants, but as a foreigner he was entitled to no public assistance. Clare wrote over 100 letters seeking private scholarships or grants, with little luck, until finally an old sailing connection came through. A fellow named John Campbell, who once crewed for Clare and Edward aboard *Johanne Regina* and helped sail her across the Mediterranean, now happened to be working as skipper of a fancy motor-yacht owned by Richard Giordano, chairman of the board of the energy conglomerate British Gas. John persuaded his boss to consider Thomas for a company sponsorship, and ultimately Thomas won a very generous grant. British Gas agreed to pay his full tuition (£6,630 per annum) and to also provide a stipend of £7,000 a year to cover room and board and living expenses, more than twice what a public grant would have yielded. In return Thomas would have to spend summers working for the company.

There was now almost nothing to prevent Thomas from attending university, and he and Clare returned confidently to Sussex the following June so he could sit for his A-level exams. Thomas had just turned 18 the month before, and Clare as a special birthday treat paid for him to take lessons in piloting proper full-size gliders at the East Sussex Gliding Club. For Thomas, with his many hours of flying model gliders, this must have been a dream come true, and Clare later remembered that the instructor was very impressed by his ability.

Sometime later, however, when Thomas's test results came back in the mail to Andorra, there was one thing Clare found puzzling. Thomas as expected had earned top marks in two subjects, scoring A's on both his math and physics exams, but the result for his third exam, in "further" mathematics, was marked down mysteriously as N. Clare at the time had no idea what this meant, but she later learned it signified Thomas had not taken the test. This, she realized with a smile, had been his insurance policy—by only taking two of the exams he disqualified himself from attending Cambridge and so short-circuited any effort she might make to persuade him to enroll at the more prestigious school.

THOMAS ENTERED THE UNIVERSITY OF LEEDS just a few months later, in October 1994. He completed his studies there in June 1997, having largely met the requirements for a Bachelor of Science degree in fluid dynamics and advanced mathematics. Characteristically, however, so as to avoid the distinction of graduating "with honours," he didn't show up for two of his final exams. He also didn't attend graduation and technically never received his degree.

As is so often the case, Thomas's formal course of study was in any event the least formative aspect of his undergraduate experience. As an inherently social person raised in socially limited circumstances, Thomas was very happy to at last find himself in a place where he was surrounded by lots of intelligent, like-minded people his own age. And here, finally, his unusual background was more an asset rather than a liability. Having evaded all the conformity imposed on students during a conventional primary and secondary education, Thomas stood out as something of an icon to other university students now questioning all the conformity they'd endured when they were younger.

During his first year at Leeds, Thomas lived at Bodington Hall, the school's largest dormitory complex, in a single room in Seton House. He quickly became good friends with his neighbor in the room next door, Dan Barton, who had enrolled in the university's French program. The two young men bonded immediately over their ability to communicate fluently in this language, and Thomas's social life promptly metastasized from there.

He had always been something of an exhibitionist. Clare Allcard, for example, often recalled one episode when a concert was given on the waterfront in Torredembara, with *Johanne Regina* in her berth on the quay as a scenic backdrop. Thomas, to Edward's dismay, disrupted and stole the show by clambering up the mainmast and monkeying about in the rig behind the orchestra. Now he had an entire university as a captive audience and soon established himself as a singular figure on campus. He strode about mostly barefoot, in mismatched ill-fitting clothes that conceded nothing to fashion, with long kinky-curly locks that now reached down to his shoulders. With Dan Barton as an accomplice, he built a pair of stilts and quickly mastered them, stalking about everywhere six feet off the ground on long 2x4 pine peg-legs. He took up juggling and ladder-walking after making friends with a fellow student named Colin, who was an incipient acrobat. He bought himself a didgeridoo and sat out under a willow tree at night on the Bodington Hall grounds teaching himself how to play it. He scavenged a bit of sewer pipe from a construction site, hauled it back to his room, skinned one end with packing tape, and made a drum of it. He taught himself also how to free-climb the outside of Seton House, a height of some 40 feet, so he could sneak in and out of his room at will. And in his room he listened to the most extreme techno music he could find—loud, raucous, rhythmic, and violent—as he could not countenance anything mainstream or popular.

"He was just so well-known across the whole of the university," Dan later recalled. "Everybody loved him. They thought he was amazing, because he was so friendly, so open, so warm, so interesting. He made friends with everybody. Every encounter was a possibility."

And for many of the friends Thomas made, getting to know him was a revelation, a surprising window into alternative modes of thinking.

"I wish I was eloquent enough to describe the enormous range of ideas, inventions, and original ways of seeing the world that Tom had," one undergraduate friend, Chris Briggs, later wrote.

"It was he, more than anyone or anything, who prompted me to look around and try to experience the world in a different way," wrote another. "As far as Tom was concerned, right and wrong, real and imaginary, even up and down, were matters for debate and challenge."

Thomas in his first term at school also quickly found himself a girlfriend, one Kathryn Young. She had dark brunette hair cut in a saucy bob, wire-rim glasses, an open smile, and a background in sailboats, thanks to her dad, who had often taken her out on weekends and holidays on a 25-foot cruiser named *Daisy*. Dan

Barton was also interested in Kathy and resented Thomas's success with her, but it was, Dan remembered, the sole instance in all the time he knew Thomas that he was ever upset with him.

Ultimately, Thomas's relationship with Kathy was not long-lived. In one of his earliest letters home to Clare and Edward, he described her as "a tremendous person" and happily proclaimed: "We get on perfectly." Soon after the end of the first term, however, he announced in another letter to Andorra that she had broken things off. "I thought I could share something with her," he wrote, "teach her what I know, but she's so defensive she couldn't handle that."

Tellingly, he added: "In fact, the whole business of men and women getting together seems just as difficult here as anywhere else. Actually, it's by far the most difficult thing about university."

But Kathy still was to some degree haunted by the relationship. She and Thomas remained friendly and exchanged letters and e-mails for some time after university. "I feel very regretful about how I split up with Thomas," she later wrote. "Looking back, I must have been an independent-minded young woman who didn't really show as much empathy as I should have done. In later years, I always worried [about] how much I might have hurt him."

More than the opportunity to court young ladies, what was for Thomas most transformative about university life was his exposure to mind-altering substances. It is a common enough tale, young people from sheltered backgrounds learning to enjoy some undergraduate debauchery after leaving home, but in Thomas's case the shift in perspective was dramatic. His father had raised him strictly in this regard. Proper living meant no meat, no cigarettes, no alcohol, no intoxicants of any kind, and Thomas during his short life had always adhered to this credo.

"He came to the university a total puritan," Dan Barton recalled. "He was massively into gymnastics, health, and veganism.

He was like a proper ingénue. Voltaire's *L'Ingénu*. That was Thomas. An amazing intellect with no formal schooling, a child of nature, deposited in modern society."

The puritan in Thomas may have played a part in Kathy's breaking up with him. He wrote to Clare and Edward describing the aftermath of the end-of-term Seton House formal dinner, noting he couldn't participate, as he wanted to study, and complaining: "[T]he party in my corridor evolved into total mayhem with my neighbours spraying ketchup & shaving cream all over their room and in the corridor and urinating on the carpets… there were about 25 people in Dan's room (other neighbor) all at once sniffing poppers and 'absolutely out their faces' as they say here. Kathy drank too and was sick till 0100—I got angry with her and I think it's fairly well understood that she's not to do that again!"

It seems likely this was something Kathy might have become "defensive" about.

But Thomas's holier-than-thou attitude quickly evaporated. By second term he was indulging with the others, although not in alcohol, and became particularly interested in psychotropic substances like marijuana and psilocybin mushrooms. He developed an interest in botany and began growing these plants in his dorm room.

"He was fascinated by botany," Dan Barton later noted. "Rather than just growing it, he was examining it scientifically."

And as Thomas prepared to start his second year at Leeds, he shared some of what he'd learned in a letter to his buddy Steve back in Andorra, offering advice on how to grow pot. This was intercepted by Steve's dad John Macdonald, the ex-cop, who complained vociferously to Clare Allcard. Clare in turn sent a scorching letter to Thomas.

"John has said for a long time that he considers you to be a bad influence on Stephen. Before, I've always defended you," she wrote. "How can I do that now that you are trying to involve him, a schoolboy, in something illegal?" Though she understood Thomas's wanting "to experiment like everyone else," she couldn't help adding: "It seems weird to me that someone who treats their body as a sacred citadel should treat their mind like a laboratory animal."

Thomas responded contritely, at once apologizing for getting Stephen into trouble, but he also carefully explained and defended his change in perspective:

> I have realized that my past firm anti-drug views were not compatible with the rest of my personal attitude to life, and I now hold that one of my most fundamental rights is to be able to consume whatever naturally occurring substances I wish to. As you know, I put a lot of thought into what I eat and I continue to do so. I only consume what I consider to be beneficial to myself. I could continue for many pages on this topic, but all I need add now is that so far, my personal experience tells me I have [made] the right choice.

And to a large extent Thomas's drug use at university was indeed deliberate and purposeful and complemented a great deal of extracurricular reading he was doing. Dan Barton remembered he and Thomas were very into Carlos Castaneda's books on the Mexican shaman Don Juan, Robert Pirsig's *Zen and the Art of Motorcycle Maintenance*, Michel Tournier's *Vendredi ou les Limbes du Pacifique*, and other countercultural literary touchstones. Another good friend of Thomas's, Dan Axon, an art student, recalled these times fondly and insisted: "We were always very intellectual about it—we tried whatever was going but we used the experience well—we would use the altered state to philosophize, explore, create."

Thomas's experiments were also wide-ranging. Beyond pot and mushrooms he also sampled a good bit of LSD, very probably a few other drugs, and at one point tried smoking brown heroin "a fair few times," though he later insisted "that was never, and would never be, a problem."

Inevitably these adventures did involve a degree of "hedonism," as Dan Barton came to describe it. Thomas in his letters home to Clare and Edward was relatively frank about all this and quite casually mentioned many long nights spent out at raves, nightclubs, and underground acid houses.

Dan Axon later recalled: "We would go [out] to hear wildly abstract and obscure electronic music and dance all night. I always remember how lost in the music Tom would become and how freely he would move, devoid of any inhibition—we were all in 'another dimension' but Tom was truly in his own dimension. I can recall those images vividly even now, 20 years on, seeing Tom lost in techno music, skewered by laser beams and dressed and dancing in his own unique style."

THOUGH THOMAS MOSTLY ENJOYED his life at university, it created in him a certain tension he had probably never experienced before. Living on a boat when he was younger, he had been used to a slow unfolding of day-to-day existence. Priorities were simple, revolving mostly around provisioning and maintaining the boat; hard deadlines were few and far between and normally only involved natural seasonal transitions; leisure activities consisted mostly of watersports—windsurfing, swimming, and snorkeling. Now in his new life, with classes to keep up with during the day and a consuming social whirl to get lost in at night, Thomas often felt pressed for time, a very modern predicament.

Though he had been disciplined studying at home in Andorra, he'd never seriously attended classes and lectures before, particularly in such technical subjects, and this in itself took some getting used to. He struggled a bit academically early on at Leeds, failing one class and merely passing three others in his first term, though he tried to downplay this.

"I'll try to be a bit more consistent this semester," he wrote soon afterward. "I now know that, basically, don't take notes = poor grade. Simple, really."

Moving forward, even as he found his feet and gained confidence academically, Thomas's social life became increasingly intense. He had much less time for physical exercise and noted more than once that he thought university was unhealthy. He told the Allcards in one letter of how he collapsed at a nightclub, from flu and fatigue, after weeks of sleeping poorly. "University is a contrast," he wrote, "between sober, formal, impersonal lectures, tutorials, studying, etc. and mad social doings at night. Sleep? Forget it."

To better regulate his time as he studied for exams at the end of his first year at school, Thomas for a few weeks transformed himself into a nocturnal creature. He shifted his regular sleeping time by an hour a day until finally his body clock was the opposite of everyone else's. This way he could study at night while others were out partying.

"It was so weird," recalled Dan Barton. "Some of us would be coming back from clubs at three in the morning and he'd be: 'Hey man, how's it going?' He'd just be awake. And then sleeping in the day."

During his second and third years at Leeds, Thomas lived in houses rented off campus with groups of seven or eight friends, and this immersed him in a close-quarters social dynamic that was quite different from what he'd known living in Andorra or on his father's boat. For a young man so thoroughly schooled in onboard economy and austerity, the profligacy of modern life sometimes seemed almost insulting. In his letters to the Allcards, Thomas marveled at how much electricity and water his housemates wasted, at the number of TVs they owned and how they often sat watching the same show on different sets in their separate rooms, how removed from nature they were, and "how much freedom people willingly throw away for comfort."

"Not only do I abhor extravagance and waste," he later wrote, "but we split the bills so I had to pay for their idiocies."

As popular as Thomas was at school, an attractive figure of unconventional fun and adventure, those who knew him well acknowledged he also had a dark side. In the house he shared during his third and final year at school, the ubiquitous lure of television became a friction point. First he announced to his housemates he would not pay his share of the cable bill for the communal house TV, and that he'd prefer not to have a TV at all "as then we'd have conversation instead of blank staring at the god box."

To drive the point home, Thomas ultimately appropriated and sold off the house TV. Certain housemates were ambivalent about this, but others were outraged.

As Dan Barton recalled: "People were like: 'OK, Tom, you've crossed the line, man. You've stolen from us.' I think things ended pretty badly."

Even worse, Thomas almost burned the house down.

He began having what some described as "black-outs." The cause was unclear. It might have been a simple lack of sleep; there was also a suggestion it might be related to his use of heroin. Or it might have been something else entirely.

What happened was he passed out in his room, hard asleep,

with a candle burning atop an enclosure he was growing mushrooms in, which sat in turn atop one of his stereo loudspeakers. When Thomas awoke, the speaker, now "a puddle of mouldering plastic," was fully aflame less than a foot from his head. "Had my head not been so near the flames," he later wrote, "I would never have woken up."

The inside of the room was pitch black with smoke, so dark it made no difference at all when Thomas switched on the lights. He scrambled to find the door latch, then finally burst out of the room. The fire brigade was alerted. The fire fortunately was extinguished. Thomas was briefly hospitalized due to smoke inhalation, and again his housemates were not amused.

"Well, my room is all fixed up now and better than it was with new furniture, carpets and wallpaper," Thomas later wrote to Clare's mother, Ro Thompson, "but I realize that I've had yet another very lucky escape."

What was also unclear was whether, and to what extent, any of Thomas's friends at university at the time correlated his darker moments with the traumatic experiences he'd suffered through when he was younger. In his much more limited social circle in Andorra, Thomas had never shared many details of his past. Most people, his good friend Steve Macdonald among them, understood that he'd been orphaned in a shipwreck before coming to Andorra, but they knew little if anything beyond that. At university Thomas had shared more of his story, telling not only of the shipwreck, but of the mother and stepmother he'd lost before losing his father and sister.

"He didn't do it very much," remembered Dan Barton, "because it was actually painful. But yeah, he told us about it."

Though some of Thomas's friends suggested he should perhaps seek help and find a therapist to talk to, a notion he most likely would have rejected out of hand, there were none who really pressed the point. For more than a few, no doubt, the dramatic tale of Thomas's early life was simply another notch on his belt, one of the many things that made him such an intriguing character.

"Tom was funny, a rebel who mocked society and its petty foibles," Dan Barton wrote many years later in an e-mail to Clare Allcard. "He empowered us all through his stance and rejection of rules. Now, 20 years on, those memories are laced with sadness. When I imagine how he was really feeling—his sense of isolation, his loneliness—I yearn for the opportunity to go back and put my older mind in my younger body. How differently I might have responded to him… I now believe that he wore his rebellion and anger as a disguise to mask his pain."

# 6. AFLOAT AGAIN

IF THOMAS EVER HARBORED any shred of a notion that he might follow a conventional career path after leaving university, it was quickly exploded once he started his summer job with British Gas. During both the summers he worked for the energy conglomerate, in 1995 and '96, he was dispatched to its research center in Loughborough, in Leicestershire, near the center of England. He was treated well, working a flexible schedule of 37 hours a week that allowed him to sleep in if he liked, and was housed at company expense in very comfortable accommodations. During his first summer he lived in a company-owned house populated largely by transient executives and happily fed himself "scrounging their bins for thrown away food." His second summer was spent in a "pretty smart" hotel where he marveled to find himself eating breakfast and dinner every day in a nice restaurant.

But the work itself was, for Thomas, exceedingly dull. He appreciated that it gave him a chance to learn to use computers, but otherwise found it entirely pointless. The first summer was spent grinding out routine spreadsheets and reports; the second found him in "combustion science," calculating hypothetical mortality rates on offshore oil rigs that would enable the company to comply with certain new government regulations.

"[W]hat I've learned is that an office job is absolutely horrible," he later wrote to Clare and Edward. "Without the slightest exaggeration, I'd say about one in twenty of the people at work looked healthy. The rest ranged from just being fat to looking positively ill."

What Thomas ultimately saw in his relationship with British Gas was not a path to a secure job after school, but a means of obtaining what he termed his "post-university dream ship." In his first term at Leeds, he quickly realized he needed far less than the £7,000 a year that British Gas was giving him for living expenses and at once started mailing excess checks to Andorra for Clare to deposit in his bank account there. At some point during his second year at university, to augment these funds, he also decided to become a drug dealer.

Thomas ran a highly specialized operation and in certain circles in London became known simply as "the Flash." He dealt solely in LSD, a highly psychotropic non-addictive substance, physically discrete and easy to conceal in quantity, for which he had recently developed an appreciation. It seems he made just one big wholesale purchase of the highest quality acid he could find, most likely in Amsterdam, then sold it off in batches on a series of quick trips to London.

Thomas years later described his business and its two guiding principles to his nephew Gjermund. Rule one was "in and out" with no time wasted—into London to make an exchange, then right back out again. Rule two was he never fronted product on credit; every deal was strictly cash on the barrel. He was, according to Gjermund, "the most famous LSD salesman in London for a period of time."

But it was a brief career. Thomas had no interest in making money for its own sake and quit dealing as soon as he had enough to buy a boat he was confident he could sail away from Britain in. And this was, not surprisingly, an exceedingly modest boat. He purchased it in August 1996, during his second summer working for British Gas, from a fellow named Reggie, in the River Blackwater on the north side of the Thames estuary east of London. She was a traditional Itchen Ferry cutter named *Melody*, built with oak frames, teak hull planking, and a pine deck. She carried a modern Bermudan mainsail, presented a long full keel to the water beneath her, and was ballasted with lead—half of it fixed in her keel, the rest loose in her bilge. She was in most respects very similar to *Dorothea*, his father's second bluewater cruising boat, the one Peter Tangvald had sailed away from Britain on in 1959, and then ultimately clear around the world. Thomas's boat, however, was much smaller, a full 10 feet shorter—just 22 feet long on deck.

Her price was £5,000. Thomas paid £3,500 up front, then soon afterwards extracted £1,500 from his account in Andorra to satisfy the balance.

Thomas's nautical prejudices were entirely the product of sailing with his father, and like his father before him, Thomas would always favor traditional boats equipped with minimal technology. The two major modifications he felt were needed to make *Melody* truly seaworthy, not coincidentally, were the same modifications Peter had made to *Dorothea* nearly 40 years earlier—he thought her engine should be removed and her cockpit decked over. Thomas spent a weekend shortly after the sale going over the boat's particulars with Reggie and happened to mention his plans regarding the cockpit.

"[H]e seemed to be concerned about my carpentry skills," Thomas wrote to Clare and Edward soon afterwards, "as he kept suggesting loads of alternatives, including mak[ing] a waterproof apron that fits over the cockpit and around my waist, like a kayak!"

In mid-September, not long before the start of his third and final year at university, Thomas set out to sail *Melody* north up the east coast of England. His route would take him first about 200 nautical miles up the coast from the Thames estuary to the Humber River, another large tidal estuary, the largest and most daunting in Britain in terms of the volume of water that flows through it. From the main core of the Humber he could access two lesser rivers, first the Ouse, then the Aire, which would take him another 50 miles inland to Leeds. It would be the first voyage of any significant distance that Thomas had ever undertaken on his own.

For the first bit of the trip he was joined by Dan Barton, "who made a very good crew," Thomas noted, "despite knowing nothing about sailing." Battling contrary wind it took them four days to sail a relatively short straight-line distance, about 40 miles, from the mouth of the River Thames to Ipswich, a short ways up the River Orwell, where Dan had to leave the boat to catch a train home.

Thomas carried on alone from Ipswich and encountered all sorts of difficulties. His prejudice against *Melody*'s engine was soon confirmed, as it failed to run reliably. This led to the boat's battery repeatedly running flat, which in turn left Thomas with no lights to show at night due to a lack of electrical power. He spent many anxious dark hours watching out for ships along the heavily trafficked coast and at one point just barely averted getting run down by a freighter by persistently shining a flashlight on his mainsail.

For a full week he was weatherbound at Southwold, not too far north of Ipswich, hiding out from gale-force winds. Feeling pressed for time by then, he left Southwold earlier than he should have, with the wind still blowing too hard from the wrong direction, and struggled to make it through the narrow channel and steep breakers at the harbor entrance. He faced more challenges when he finally reached the Humber River over two days later.

First Thomas had trouble simply finding the Humber and had to ask for directions from a passing fishing boat, as his compass had seized up. He had even more trouble entering the river. Arriving at nightfall with both the ebb tide and the river's current raging against him, it took him two full hours just to sail across the main channel. Then he got caught in steep breaking waves near shore behind Spurn Head, a spot where he'd hoped to anchor and catch some sleep. Moving back into deeper, smoother water in the main body of the river, he could make no progress against the outgoing tide, even though he was now sailing ahead full speed at 6 knots. Eventually he was rescued from this predicament by a pilot boat, which towed him into the town of Grimsby on the river's south shore and left him tied up in an insecure cul-de-sac with steep quay walls on three sides. Thomas had to stay up all through the rest of that night, fending the boat off to keep it from smashing into the high stone surfaces that surrounded him.

The next day, on a fair incoming tide, he sailed much further up the river. That night he finally enjoyed a good sleep at anchor, but the following day he was accosted by the local coast guard after he intentionally grounded *Melody* on the low tide so as to clean her bottom. Once he was afloat again, they towed him to a marina in the small town of Brough, west of the city of Hull on the Humber's north shore. Here Thomas got *Melody*'s engine repaired. He also took her mast down, preparatory to taking her further inland under low bridges, and soon set off again.

He didn't get far before the engine promptly quit again. With his mast down on deck he couldn't sail, so Thomas anchored the boat. He then jumped overboard, swam to shore through the brown icy-cold water, and hiked back to the marina to arrange a tow. Meanwhile someone had spotted him in the water and alerted the coast guard, who immediately scrambled a helicopter to rescue him. Thomas fortunately reached the marina in time to call off the helicopter, but he did have to submit to being towed back to Brough, once again, by a coast guard launch.

He was annoyed when he later found both local and national newspapers were carrying "an absurdly sensationalistic report" of the "dramatic rescue of [a] stranded sailor" and of a Leeds

University student's "amazing bid for survival." As Thomas asserted soon afterward in a letter to the Allcards: "[I]n both cases I didn't even want the coastguard."

But he was not at all sanguine about the experience.

"[C]oming into the Humber was pretty frightening," he admitted. "In fact, I don't think I've ever been that scared for that long ever. Several people including the coastguard have told me that the Humber is the second most dangerous river in the world—after the Orinico. I think they may well be right."

FROM THE MOMENT he acquired *Melody* the tenor of Thomas's existence changed. Having a boat again certainly altered his perspective on university life. His animus toward the communal TV in the house he shared with friends during his third year at school was in fact born during his trying passage up the coast. In the same letter to the Allcards in which he described his dramatic arrival in the Humber, he concluded by mentioning he'd watched far too much television while working for British Gas over the summer, "becoming virtually hooked on certain programs."

"I think my sailing trip brought me to a new level of awareness," he wrote and declared his intention to withhold funding from the house TV in the coming school year, concluding: "[T]his year I'll be far too busy to join in any TV worship."

And he was. Though he had to leave *Melody* in Brough to attend his first lectures at school, Thomas soon returned and brought the boat the last 50 miles along the Ouse and Aire Rivers to Leeds, where he installed her near the center of the city at Granary Wharf, just a few miles from where he lived. His letters back to Andorra increasingly included news of the boat, with carefully detailed drawings of proposed changes, complete with exact dimensions. In return the Allcards sent on spare boat gear they thought Thomas might find useful—an extra staysail, a compass, tools, a sextant, charts, and many other goodies.

Meanwhile, in addition to working on *Melody* whenever he could, Thomas was still carrying a full course load. To a layperson, the subjects he studied certainly seem impressive: transformational geometry, special relativity, numerical solutions to partial differential equations, and so on. His most challenging work was a special project on time-dependent diffusive flows of variable viscosity fluids. And the load only became heavier after he accidentally set his room on fire. Much of the work on his special project was destroyed in the conflagration, and he was hard pressed to reconstruct it from memory.

All in all, Thomas's third year at Leeds was by far his most stressful. The whole of it, he wrote, was "spent under a dark cloud" and by its end he had grown critical of the university society he once reveled in. He looked forward to getting away from "those arrogant people with all their flash clothes and snobbery" and to having a chance to "just be as I please." He was particularly scathing regarding the dating scene and complained that "95% of the women here are interested only in how rich their man is going to be."

Even now, before he'd ever set out for anywhere, Thomas understood he wasn't likely to find a woman who would happily join him "in a wooden shell on the oceans."

AS TO THE QUESTION of where exactly he should set out for, it seems certain the destination Thomas always had in mind was Puerto Rico. It was here primarily that the last years of his life with his father had played out. It was where he'd come of age, in a series of anchorages that ranged from Culebra in the Spanish Virgin Islands to the east, to Salinas on the south shore of the main island, to Boquerón and Puerto Real on its western coast. Of all the places he'd visited in the fluid geography of his upbringing, Puerto Rico had come closest to seeming like a fixed point, and in the time before he lost his father he had made many friends there, both on shore and afloat.

One of these was an American hippie-cum-sailor, Elmer Van Pelt, known simply as Elm, who lived aboard an eccentric 33-foot skipjack, a type of boat traditionally used for oyster dredging on Chesapeake Bay, that he called *Nevermind*. He was based primarily at Boquerón, in the large open bay there, an idyllic untouristed spot that was rimmed with white sand beaches and backed by quiet dry hills. Elm eventually became something of an alternative father to Thomas and later recalled how he first met the Tangvald family. Peter Tangvald, with young Thomas and baby Carmen aboard, had bowled into the bay at Boquerón in early June 1985, little more than four months after Ann had been lost overboard.

"It was amazing! He came in here all broken-hearted over the death of his wife, with two kids to care for," Elm remembered. "A few months later he came back happy as a clam with a 14-year-old girl as his mate."

And it was true—just as he had after losing Lydia, Peter Tangvald quickly found himself a new partner to replace Ann, though his seventh and last wife wasn't quite *that* young.

FLORENCE MERTENS WAS IN FACT all of 18 years of age when she first met Peter Tangvald, then age 60, during the summer of 1985, at Great Bridge, Virginia, on the Intracoastal Waterway, not too far south of Norfolk. She was Belgian, raised primarily in Canada, and at the time was sailing with her father, Jacques Mertens, aboard his boat, *Emilie*, a modern 41-footer with a foam-cored fiberglass hull. Jacques and the Tangvald family, as is the way with bluewater cruisers, had crossed paths before, on the

Guadiana River between Spain and Portugal during the previous summer, not long after Carmen was born.

Florence was a slender, willowy girl with a shy smile and long dirty-blonde hair. She was keenly interested in sailing and often joined her dad on his boat during school vacations. Her parents had divorced when she was about 10. At age 16, she'd purchased a sailboat of her own, a small fiberglass Cal 21, in Nassau while sailing with Jacques down in the Bahamas. Together they had sailed north in tandem until they reached New York, where Florence managed to sell her boat for three times what she paid for it. Now she and Jacques were again heading down the U.S. East Coast, bound once more for the Bahamas, and she was hoping she might repeat the trick. Peter meanwhile was also sailing south, having spent some small part of that summer in Chesapeake Bay, where, for a while at least, still depressed from the loss of Ann, he'd entertained the notion of selling *L'Artemis de Pytheas* and perhaps moving ashore with Thomas and Carmen.

What most impressed Florence about the Tangvald family was their engineless boat. In the realm of East Coast yachting, relying on sail alone to transit the Intracoastal Waterway, a series of heavily trafficked interconnected canals and small rivers studded with lifting bridges, is almost unthinkable. The wind is fickle, the current can be strong in places, and the water everywhere is unforgivingly shallow. The schedule of bridge openings is just as unforgiving and often demands that vessels stay on station, waiting in place, for as long as 30 minutes. For a sailor with no engine this is somewhat akin to a dancer holding a pirouette, on the tips of one's toes, indefinitely.

Florence figured she could learn a great deal sailing on *L'Artemis* and volunteered during that first meeting at Great Bridge to join Peter as a nanny to the two children, at least as far as Beaufort, North Carolina, where most southbound cruising sailboats exit the

ICW and take to open water again. Peter declined, but Florence repeated her offer several days later when the two boats, *Emilie* and *L'Artemis*, met again down in Beaufort. This time she proposed to stay on as far as Florida, where she could easily rejoin her father, who had started a business there. Peter again demurred, noting he could not abide cigarette smoke on his boat, but relented when Florence promptly volunteered to quit smoking for the duration.

The duration proved longer than anticipated. There was some potential for romance here and Peter Tangvald, ever an opportunist, was happy to promote it. Florence, a young aspiring sailor with a sharp sense of adventure, was willing to succumb. So Florence wrote a "Dear Dad" letter to Jacques, skipped the rendezvous in Florida, and sailed with Peter straight to the Caribbean. They were married on September 25, 1985, by a judge in San Juan, Puerto Rico. There were no guests, and the sole witness was a janitor they'd found in the courthouse hallway.

As Florence later recalled, her relationship with Thomas, then age nine, was initially positive and open. "He was talking non-stop," she remembered. "He finally had someone to talk to, and I paid attention to his stories."

But she was quickly overwhelmed. The positive feelings between Florence and Thomas "faded away" and eventually, she believed, he came to resent her. Her responsibilities as the wife of Peter Tangvald, feeding a family on the slimmest of budgets and minding the toddler Carmen, only increased after she gave birth to a child of her own little more than a year later. Peter's sixth and last offspring, another daughter, Virginia (named after the place where he and Florence first met), was born aboard *L'Artemis* in the bay at Boquerón on October 11, 1986—on the same berth where Thomas had been born 10 years earlier.

Elm Van Pelt, on his boat *Nevermind*, rafted alongside while his partner, Miriam Ramos, a nurse, acted as midwife to Florence.

Elm kept Thomas and Carmen aboard *Nevermind* until the baby was ready to come, then brought them over to *L'Artemis* to witness the birth. He remembered that Carmen cried out "Put it back!" when Virginia appeared. According to Florence, she also yelled "Not another one!" when the placenta was expelled. Thomas, as Peter later recounted proudly in his autobiography, was the one who cut the umbilical cord.

The Tangvald family was based primarily in Boquerón from December 1985 until the spring of 1987, a period of fleeting stability that Thomas must have enjoyed. During this time he became fast friends with another boat kid his age, Nathan Perer, who lived with his single mom, Felicia Cohen, and a younger sister, Delilah, on a 35-foot steel-hulled sailboat named *Shiane* that was anchored close to *L'Artemis*. Both Thomas and Carmen spent a great deal of time aboard *Shiane*. Thomas and his buddy Nathan, when they weren't hanging out afloat, wandered far and wide together, exploring the small town on shore, its beaches, and the surrounding hills and cow pastures.

Both Nathan and Thomas became close to Elm Van Pelt and spent many hours with him aboard *Nevermind*. Elm had recently lost access to his own son in a bitter divorce and poured that displaced paternal energy into the two boys. Nathan remembered that *Nevermind* seemed "like a beautiful treehouse," with a cedar cabin that Elm had rubbed down with cinnamon oil.

"We'd sit there with this really cool hippie who was making paintings and playing guitar and telling us awesome stories about all the shit he did back in the '60s," he recalled. "I remember just loving every minute of it. Me and Thomas both felt that way."

Peter Tangvald was also quite content during this time. In letters to one old friend in France, he described his life with Florence as an eternal honeymoon and bragged about her youth, her cooking, and her "absolutely perfect body." To Edward Allcard he crowed

CHARLES J. DOANE

about their age difference, 43 years, noting with pride this was even greater than the difference in Edward's and Clare's ages.

For Florence, however, her new life was a struggle, far from the adventure she'd envisioned. In addition to caring for the infant Virginia and for Carmen, she worked a part-time job on shore to help make ends meet and scrambled to find enough food to feed the family. Thomas and Carmen were able to augment their diets cadging snacks aboard *Shiane*, but Florence's weight eventually dropped from about 130 pounds to 104. Elm later recalled having dinner aboard *L'Artemis* one night and being served nothing but a soup that had just three carrots in it. Florence also increasingly resented Peter's chauvinistic attitude, his abdication of any responsibility for domestic chores, and his insistence on controlling the details of her existence.

"Simple pleasures like going out for an ice cream was absolutely out of reach and a jug of fresh milk was a rare luxury," she later wrote. "But somehow Peter believed this was the price to pay for some sort of elusive freedom. When I look back I strongly question this whole notion of 'freedom' and what it is worth."

By April 1987 the family had shifted base to Culebra and here encountered another cruising sailor, Nigel Calder, who later became a successful marine technical writer. Nigel and his wife Terrie were having a hard time caring for their toddler daughter, Pippin, who often cried while they were sailing. Nigel anxiously asked Peter how he managed when his young children cried. Peter proudly showed off the jail cell in the bow of *L'Artemis* and explained: "I just put them in there and let them cry themselves to sleep."

Nigel remembered Peter had happily proclaimed he'd like to have still more children, but that Florence stood behind him "looking pale and washed up" and mutely shook her head "no."

Nigel also later recalled that young Carmen was suffering from an eye infection at the time, but that Peter, ever careful with his money, refused to buy the antibiotic medicine required to treat it. In the end some other cruisers who were then anchored in the harbor took up a collection and bought the medicine for Carmen instead.

In the fall of that year the Tangvald family hoisted anchor and again shifted base, from Puerto Rico to Florida, ostensibly so Florence could be closer to her parents. They drifted from the Florida panhandle in the north, where Peter found the weather too cold, to Naples on the west coast, where liveaboard sailors were not welcome, and landed finally in the Florida Keys. After a few months there, Florence decided at last she'd had enough.

As Peter later told the story, he suffered his terrible heart attack the moment Florence announced she was leaving him. But Florence's story is more nuanced. *L'Artemis* was anchored at Big Pine Key, and Florence had gone ashore with Virginia and got a ride to Key West to buy firewood. On the way there and back she realized she couldn't bring herself to return to the boat. She wrote a note to this effect, had it delivered to Peter, and moved in with a friend she had made on shore. A couple of days later Peter found her ashore at Big Pine and begged her to come back to him.

"Someone passed by on their bicycle and rang their bell," Florence recalled. "He was so tense he jumped and had a heart attack. I called an ambulance and they took him away."

Florence took care of the children while Peter was in the hospital, and weeks later, after he was released, he eventually convinced her to move back aboard *L'Artemis*. But in June 1988 she took Virginia and Carmen to visit her mother in Canada, again decided she couldn't return to the boat, and sent Carmen back on her own. Peter was devastated by what he saw as Florence's betrayal and, in terms of his health, was never really whole again.[1]

---

1. In spite of the fact that she did send Carmen back to Peter, he soon developed a paranoid fear that Florence was plotting to kidnap the girl. Florence did have a strong connection with Carmen and was devastated when she learned of her death.

FOR THOMAS, IT WAS the third time in his life he'd seen his father lose a wife, and it seems he processed and interpreted this as he had before, in terms of the pain and anguish he observed in his father. In a long letter to Clare and Edward, Peter later described how Thomas, now age 12, had consoled him and bolstered his spirits by urging him to put Florida behind them and set sail back to the West Indies. The boy was worried his father might die if they didn't return to sea and promised, if the worst happened, he was capable of handling the boat on his own.

"I will always love him, if for no other reason," Peter wrote in a self-pitying tone. "Everybody else, including the doctors, wants me to sit at the doorstep of the hospital waiting to die."

Still *L'Artemis*'s voyage back to Puerto Rico that summer, in the middle of hurricane season, was probably ill-advised. The boat, Peter admitted, was in poor condition and the last weather chart he saw before leaving the Keys showed four tropical waves, each a potential storm, marching west across the Atlantic toward the Caribbean.

In other respects, Thomas's relationship with his father was by now significantly altered. Both before and after Florence's departure, there was a distance between them that was only growing larger as Thomas matured. Many who knew them at the time remarked on this.

Among these was Elm, who was properly impressed that Peter had sailed back from Florida, at the height of hurricane season, so soon after a heart attack, with only his 12-year-old son as crew.

"Peter was a Viking!" he later declared. "You might not like him, but you had to respect him."

Elm also saw that Peter was quite strict with Thomas and that father and son often didn't get along too well. There were no open arguments, but the relationship was taut and burdened. Elm recalled that Peter increasingly disapproved of the "Puerto Rican street rat" friends Thomas was making on shore. And though Thomas was growing more and more interested in music, Peter allowed no playing of music on his boat. He also prohibited Thomas from taking art lessons from Elm after he found that Thomas, at his own insistence, was learning to draw monsters rather than human figures. Elm let Thomas spend nights aboard *Nevermind* whenever he wanted, which was not infrequently. He also often found a way, with a gentle twinkle in his eye and a bit of wry humor, to prod Thomas into questioning a few of the edicts his father was so fond of handing down.

Thomas's buddy Nathan's appraisal of the situation was a bit more blunt. "His dad was kind of a pain in the ass," he recalled. "He was a Type-A male and had to have shit his way. If it wasn't his way, it wasn't any way at all."

Steve Macek, another cruising sailor who also knew the family, was even blunter: "Plain and simple," he later declared. "Peter Tangvald was a Nazi."

But Morgan MacDonald, yet another Caribbean cruiser who had more than once crossed paths with the Tangvalds, had a more balanced view. Of Peter he recalled: "He was a minimalist who drove himself extremely hard, set very high standards for himself, and also set those for his children."

For Thomas, as for any teenager, part of the process of developing an identity apart from his parent was to develop ambitions of his own. Morgan remembered that Thomas around this time told him he wanted to be the youngest person to sail around the world alone and shared with him an original design model of a boat he'd conceived and wanted to build himself so that he could accomplish this goal. Morgan, a trained naval architect who had designed yachts himself, took this quite seriously, critiqued the design, and discussed it with Thomas in some detail.

"I remember being impressed by his knowledge, maturity, and ambition at the time," he later wrote.

The irony was that as Peter's health deteriorated over the next two years—through another heart attack, painful kidney stones, and ongoing angina attacks—he more than ever needed Thomas's help to manage and maintain *L'Artemis*.

In one dramatic instance, sailing down the south coast of Puerto Rico in a strong following breeze in late February 1990, *L'Artemis*'s temporary rig[2] was badly damaged in an accidental jibe. Peter and Thomas worked together for an hour to get the boat sailing again, then were promptly boarded by the U.S. Coast Guard, who in those days were often searching boats at random, pursuant to their "Zero Tolerance" drug interdiction policy. The stress of this led Peter into an angina attack, which he managed to hide from the Coast Guard officers, fearing they would commandeer the boat if they thought he needed medical attention. As soon as they departed he collapsed on deck, and it was up to Thomas, then age 14, to bring *L'Artemis* to safety.

Thomas sailed the boat on his own down the remainder of the south coast, then around Puerto Rico's southwest corner at Cabo Rojo. Following his father's directions, he anchored outside Puerto Real, just north of Boquerón, as it wasn't possible with the boat's damaged rig to tack quickly back and forth against the wind

---

2. Throughout all the time he sailed aboard *L'Artemis de Pytheas*, Peter Tangvald was constantly changing her sailplan. There were at least five major variations over the years—three different yawl rigs, a schooner rig, and a cutter rig (a single mast with two headsails), which was what she carried when she was destroyed in 1991. Within these major variations there were also countless minor variations, including a brief experiment with an unusual square "raffee" sail that could be hoisted when sailing downwind. At this time Peter was preparing to re-rig the boat once again and was sailing with a temporary mainmast. He also had changed out the boat's original centerboard for a more hydrodynamic but more unwieldy daggerboard. All these changes required a great deal of carpentry work.

through the narrow channel into the harbor. Once the boat was secured, Thomas then paddled ashore one-and-a-half miles on his surfboard[3] and arranged with friends to have *L'Artemis* towed into port.

As Peter's abilities decayed and Thomas yearned for more independence, Peter also was becoming an increasingly controversial figure. Behind his back other cruising sailors often discussed the spreading rumor that he had heartlessly murdered two of his wives, Lydia and Ann, while at sea. Some now openly shunned him. And on shore Puerto Rican social-services workers became increasingly concerned about the austere conditions in which he was raising his children. They began monitoring the Tangvald family, conducting interviews and inspecting the boat.

Peter resented this and scoffed at the notion his children were deprived because "they get no pocket-money, sleep without mattresses, don't take a bath every day and live in small cubbyholes with no windows." He grew worried they might be taken from him and kept the boat ready to sail on short notice just in case. As he wrote to the Allcards at the time: "So what if we all prefer to sleep on Chinese bamboo mats and don't care about electricity? I can't understand that in the fanciest restaurants candle lights are great, but for me it is a sign of living in a slum."

IT WAS LATER IN 1990, in October, that Thomas at last physically removed himself from his father and sister by buying his own boat, *Spartan*, in Culebra. She was a very odd craft, a narrow unballasted scow with a shallow flat bottom, leeboards on both sides, and square ends, little more than an oversized sailing dinghy with a rotting deck and a tiny cabinhouse tacked on. Thomas had

---

3. This was the same surfboard that saved Thomas's life when *L'Artemis* was wrecked on Bonaire the following year. Nathan Perer had given it to Thomas earlier in Boquerón, when he saw Thomas had no way to get ashore on his own save swimming.

earned the $200 he paid for her earlier that summer doing varnish work on a fancy vintage yacht that had belonged to Herbert von Karajan, the famous conductor of the Berlin Philharmonic orchestra. This was in Curaçao, where *L'Artemis* and the Tangvalds spent two months hiding out from hurricanes that season.

Thomas's purchasing *Spartan* took his father entirely by surprise. Peter had planned to stay only a couple of days at Culebra, to pick up mail en route from Curaçao to Florida, where he looked forward to meeting prospective female crew who had answered a classified ad he placed in *Cruising World*, a popular American sailing magazine. He was also beginning to formulate plans to eventually sail *L'Artemis* back to Europe. But Thomas's sudden *fait accompli* presented him with a dilemma. As he explained to the Allcards in different letters, he "had not the heart" to either "abandon [Thomas] here just 14 years old" or to simply take *Spartan* away from him.

Though he was certainly annoyed, Peter's tone in describing what Thomas had done was mostly one of pride. As he had many years earlier in the Philippines, at the Norwegian embassy party in Manila, and later following the toddling Thomas through the Filipino village of Consolacion to his secret treat rendezvous, Peter respected Thomas's audacious self-interested behavior and recognized in it something of himself. But he also realized that without Thomas aboard to help him, he'd again have to alter *L'Artemis*'s rig to make her easier to sail.

Though Peter was willing to abandon his nebulous itinerary to accommodate Thomas, he was not content to just sit in place. Soon after Thomas purchased *Spartan*, Peter helped the boy sail the small, somewhat dilapidated craft 20 miles downwind from Culebra to Isletta. This was a small island marina just off Fajardo, the main town on Puerto Rico's east coast, where Thomas could more easily access materials he needed to fix his boat up. Peter then retreated to Culebra and lived there with Carmen. He returned to Fajardo occasionally by ferry, and at least once sailed back on *L'Artemis* to check on Thomas. But after a few months he tired of this. Eager for a change of scenery, he hoisted anchor and sailed further east to the U.S. Virgin Islands.

All told Thomas lived on his own for almost six months anchored off Fajardo, earning money by working on boats at the Isletta marina and working on his own boat in his spare time. Paul Berry, a 34-year-old singlehanded cruiser who was a friend of the Tangvald family, remembered spending time with him there. "He was sure he was doing the right thing," he later wrote. "He wasn't angry with his father, he just sort of felt he had outgrown him." Paul recalled Thomas had a notebook full of equations he often studied, talked of taking a high-school equivalency GED exam, and was always eager to discuss boat design and hydrodynamics.

For almost half the time he was in Fajardo, Thomas had no contact at all with his father, as Peter and Carmen were anchored 50 miles east at Great Cruz Bay, just south of Cruz Bay, the main town on the island of St. John. One sailor who spent a lot of time with Peter and Carmen here was Gary "Fatty" Goodlander, an author and lifelong cruiser, a self-styled "ink-slinging sea gypsy," then living with his wife Carolyn and their 9-year-old daughter Roma on a 38-foot boat named *Wild Card*. Fatty was well aware of Peter's reputation and had great respect for him, but over time became increasingly concerned about his health and state of mind. Peter, he learned, couldn't even raise the mainsail on *L'Artemis* without help, had trouble walking over the steep hill into town, and sometimes seemed overly paranoid and nervous.

"I perceived him as a horse that was in a barn burning, and he had to get out," he recalled. "I got a really strong jolt, like… whoa… this guy is having difficulties here."

And like many others who'd gotten to know her, Fatty also grew extremely attached to Carmen, who became close friends with Roma and was often aboard *Wild Card*. The more time he spent with Peter, the more Fatty worried about the little girl's safety. He even tentatively discussed with an attorney the logistics of taking Carmen away from Peter, but he realized any such effort would not result in Carmen permanently moving aboard *Wild Card*.

"I kept saying this to Carolyn," Fatty remembered. "This is a disaster waiting to happen."

At some point around the middle of April 1991, Peter sailed back to Puerto Rico with Carmen and extracted Thomas from Fajardo. With *Spartan* in tow, he made one more circuit of the south coast—first to Salinas, where he was briefly hospitalized again with heart trouble. Then to Boquerón, where Nathan's mom Felicia begged him to leave Carmen with her. Peter countered by asking Felicia if she would join them on the upcoming passage to Bonaire, to help care for Carmen, but she declined.

"I never liked Peter. He was just too mean," she later remarked in explaining why she turned down this invitation.

And then back once more to Culebra. From there in July, and against all advice, towing Thomas and *Spartan* behind him, Peter Tangvald set out on his last passage, his ill-fated voyage to Bonaire.

THE BOAT THOMAS NOW FOUND himself master of, six years later in Great Britain, was exactly the same length on deck, 22 feet, as his previous boat. But *Melody* was infinitely more seaworthy than *Spartan*. Where *Spartan* had the crudest of hull forms and was little more than a shallow, flat, hard-cornered box, *Melody* had a much more seakindly shape. Her flowing curves yielded to passing waves rather than resisting them. Her deep hull and long keel, weighted with dense lead, magnified her stability and helped steady her on her course. She was also much more robustly constructed, but still she was old, and there was work to be done.

Thomas's departure from Leeds aboard *Melody* was somewhat clandestine. For one thing, there were certain obligations he had to worry about. Due to the fire that had destroyed his bedroom, he either owed his landlord the cost of repairs, or he owed his housemates their confiscated security deposits. He wasn't quite sure which, and he didn't really want to find out. He was also fretting over whether he was required to work another summer for British Gas, a prospect he could not abide. Now that he had a boat, spending another summer at a desk "would have been hell," he later wrote.

Thomas had told everyone he planned to sail east out the Humber again, then down the east coast of England and on to Spain, or perhaps the south of France, in a series of short jumps. He had supposed this was his best course of action, for in southern Europe, in a much warmer climate, he could more comfortably prepare *Melody* for a transatlantic passage back to the Caribbean. One of his university friends, who according to Thomas had become chronically depressed, was eager to come along, but Thomas wasn't keen on the notion of sailing with this person.

In the end, at some point in early July 1997, having finished his classes and skipped two of his final exams, Thomas slipped quietly away to the west, alone, down the Leeds-Liverpool Canal.

By shifting all the loose ballast in *Melody's* bilge forward to the bow, Thomas had found he could lift the heel of the boat's keel just enough to allow her to negotiate the canal's three-and-a-half foot controlling depth. The boat's mast was still down on deck, so she could still squeeze under bridges. The one major modification Thomas had made thus far was removing the engine, so instead of motoring down the canal he had to scull. This was an obscure mode of propulsion he'd learned from his father, who often had sculled *L'Artemis* in and out of harbors on windless days. It consists of waving one long oar in a controlled motion in the water behind a boat, so that its blade twists back and forth something like the tail of a fish. With sustained effort, on a heavy ballasted boat like *Melody*, it was possible to achieve speeds of one or two miles an hour.

Much of the traffic on the canal, which stretches some 120 miles across the countryside of northern England through 91 locks, consisted of tourists in chartered holiday barges. In separate letters to the Allcards and to his old friend Elm, Thomas complained that many of these people had little or no boat-handling experience and on three different occasions had run into him. His progress was slow, on average just five miles a day, and at one point he was held up for days waiting for one hired barge to be refloated after its novice skipper managed to sink it in a canal lock.

Thomas was not in a hurry, however, and on the whole found the experience "very relaxing and enjoyable," a welcome decompression after the anxiety of his last year at university. To Elm he noted: "[T]he landscape is quite idyllic. Odd really, since the whole landscape has been modified by man. Three thousand years ago this was all forest. Now it's 99% grasslands, 1% trees, the whole thing cut up by thousands of manmade stone walls to keep all the domesticated animals from roaming freely. Yet it looks good."

Thomas needed still more patience to escape from the canal. By early August he'd reached the end of the canal's Rufford Branch and had to wait a couple of weeks for a peak high tide that allowed him to lock into the River Douglas at Tarleton, about 16 miles north of Liverpool. Several miles earlier at a town called Wigan, where the canal dropped abruptly 250 feet in altitude through the foothills of the Pennine Mountains, he'd had to negotiate 25 locks, one right after the other, all in one day.

"I think I've pretty much reached saturation with locks!" he wrote to Elm. "I'M FEDUP! I'M FEDUP WIS AL DIS KRAP!"

Thomas spent the end of that summer, almost two months, in the River Douglas. First he saw to re-stepping *Melody*'s mast with the help of the owner of an old fishing trawler that had a strong derrick hoist on deck. Then he holed up in a small creek just off the river. He worked on the boat, perfecting her interior, painting her, patching holes and gaps that had been left by the engine's removal, then had to wait some time again for another peak tide to get out the mouth of the river.

By now it was luxuriantly hot, and Thomas reveled in this, as it reminded him of Puerto Rico. He gorged himself on plums and pears he found growing in trees along the side of the lane that ran between his creek and the nearby village of Longton. To get on and off the boat, surrounded as it was by boggy marsh, he ran a line from the top of the mast and secured the other end with a stake some distance away in firm ground. By climbing the mast and traversing the line hand over hand, and vice versa, he could come and go as he pleased without getting all wet and muddy.

Finally, as the summer began to wane away, the water in the creek and river mouth was at last high enough for *Melody* to take wing. Thomas sculled the last mile or so down the Douglas and arrived on the deeper, wider River Ribble. Here he hoisted sail for the first time since the previous fall, when he'd entered the River Humber on the other side of Britain.

As *Melody* leaned to the wind in her rig, and as the water chuckled past under her transom as she picked up speed, Thomas smiled. It was his first time sailing his new boat without the burden of an engine and the drag of a propeller, and he felt the difference immediately. She was faster, more nimble, and he felt rather pleased with himself as he sailed out the mouth of the Ribble into the open water of the Irish Sea.

# 7. A VOYAGE OF HIS OWN

THE YOUNG MAN WHO EMERGED as a solo sailor on the west coast of Britain in the fall of 1997 had evolved a good deal in the three years that had passed since he first enrolled at the University of Leeds. Certain particulars were unchanged. Thomas still, for example, had odd, overly large feet with very widespread toes, the result, some had presumed, of a childhood spent gripping ropes with them. And he still usually preferred to go barefoot, even in the cool, often damp British climate, both because he had trouble finding shoes that fit him and because he always felt more sure-footed that way. While sailing on *Melody*, for example, as he explained to Clare and Edward Allcard in one letter, he sometimes did wear shoes to help keep his feet warm, but would take them off before going forward to the spray-drenched deck to handle sails, both to keep the shoes dry and to bolster his confidence.

Thomas's attire was also much the same as before; he wore purely functional, usually secondhand cast-off clothing, with no thought given to appearances. But one physical attribute that was very different now was his hairstyle. Clare Allcard would later wonder if Thomas had ever cut his hair in all the time that she knew him. When she first took him in, his hair had been quite short, but he had suffered no haircuts during his years in Andorra, and by the time he left for Leeds it had grown out into a thick cloud of tight blond curls, almost like an Afro. He had since let his naturally curly hair mat up into clumps and now wore these in long unruly dreadlocks. Edward had disapproved of this, as would have Thomas's father, had he still been alive. When Clare probed Thomas on the subject, he explained, tongue partly in cheek no doubt, that he liked to wear his hair this way as a social filter, to keep "the boring people" at bay.

It was an answer that illumined what was perhaps the biggest change in Thomas. The naïve ingénue, the free-thinking child of nature who had so easily charmed and captivated his fellow students during his first year at Leeds, had grown harder, more critical, and at times a bit cynical in his attitude toward others. He was more judgmental than before, even arrogant on occasion, both because he perceived he was much more intelligent than most people he met, and because his background and upbringing put him so at odds with the often thoughtless materialism of Western culture.

But Thomas was self-aware. Prodded gently in letters he received from Clare, he could see this harshness in himself and regretted it.

"There is far too much hatred, fear and intolerance in my heart," he wrote. "It is like a dark crust that needs shedding. One can either hate the world or love it, it is a choice for a conscious being. I would prefer to love it but change takes time and persistent application of will."

And he added, more concisely: "I have to learn to let go and become more easygoing."

What had also evolved in Thomas as a result of his education was an enhanced ecological and political awareness. His opinions and instincts were now more thoroughly informed, and his critical mind had learned to dissect and examine not only individuals and groups he encountered, but the whole of civilization. Humanity's fate seemed to him now as inexorable as a mathematical equation. Years before this was commonly accepted by many laypeople, he saw climate change and the warming of the planet's atmosphere and oceans due to human activity as an existential dilemma. He worried about the accelerating extinction of other species of animals. And he saw clearly, and persistently, where the root of the problem lay: there were simply too many people. Humanity, thanks to its technology, had slipped loose from natural constraints on population.

"[W]e've now greatly overshot the mark," he wrote in one letter, "and the forces that tend to limit our numbers are increasing rapidly. We are actually undermining the stability of the entire biological system that is life on earth."

Thomas saw, too, that the only rational way to manage the problem was through increased political control.

"We could in fact probably fit ten times as many humans on this planet," he wrote, "but only if we were all immensely thoughtful in our actions and if there was a system of absolute control in place, but would that be good?"

Thomas actually doubted that humanity could easily summon the will or discipline to abandon the pleasures of unbridled consumption, or that the corporate economy could ever shift its focus off of short-term gains. But he saw also that societal and governmental control of individual lives was increasing regardless, and this is what most concerned him personally. More than anything, like his father before him, Thomas wished to be left alone to do as he pleased, and he was very willing to accept material privation as the price for maintaining his freedom.

"Big things are happening," he insisted, "and I intend to stay well clear of it all."

Concomitant with this sharpening of his personal beliefs, Thomas felt himself reconnecting to the natural world as he spent more time living aboard *Melody*, like a torn and damaged tendon reknitting itself to the solid bone of its purpose. Increasingly, instead of putting calendar dates on his letters to the Allcards and others, he simply wrote out the name of the month and beside it sketched an image of the current phase of the moon, a more relevant representation of his temporal status. And as he had as a boy standing agog in the companionway of his father's boat, "in awe at the spectacle of the world," he watched closely the gyrations of the heavens above him.

In one letter to the Allcards, illustrated with a detailed semi-spherical astronomical diagram, Thomas wrote in some detail of his discovery that the full moon set near the time of the winter solstice as far north of west as the sun set south of west. He realized these positions must be reversed at the summer solstice.

"So in winter the full moon appears high in the sky," he exulted, "the sun low and in summer vice versa. Hence the apparent brightness of moonlight in winter."

And he chastised himself: "I feel a fool for not noticing earlier."

Thomas's renewed interest in such matters and the increasing availability of untrammeled information on the Internet, easily accessed in public libraries, led him into some unusual esoterica. He wondered about the "Orion Mystery" and whether the pyramids at Giza in Egypt were in fact positioned so as to represent the stars of Orion's belt, with their sizes relative to the stars' magnitudes. He read that the primitive Dogon tribe in Africa had somehow divined that the star Sirius was orbiting a dark companion star before this was discovered by modern astronomers. He was curious about underwater pyramids that supposedly had been discovered off the coast of Japan. He was particularly concerned about reports that the American CIA had already designed a transponder chip that could be implanted in humans.

"Just think," he exclaimed, "I.D., electronic money and security monitoring system all rolled into one—how convenient! It will happen, it's just a question of influencing a voting majority into thinking it's beneficial. Democracy? Nice idea, in practice a dictatorship through brainwashed & distorted popular opinion."

Thomas professed, however, to a certain sanguinity in the

face of the threats he perceived to society and his own personal independence.

"It's pointless to get into a furious rage, especially about things one can do little about," he wrote. "The best is to just calmly observe."

BY NOVEMBER OF THAT YEAR Thomas had moored *Melody* to trees overhanging a slate shingle beach in a small cove a short distance up the River Camel on the north coast of Cornwall, between the towns of Padstow and Wadebridge, and was preparing to spend the winter there. He'd arrived on the Camel via a somewhat circuitous route, as on leaving the Ribble above Liverpool he'd first sailed northwest out to the Isle of Man, a self-governing tax haven that stood alone at the north end of the Irish Sea. He had some business there, assuming custody of a small offshore bank account he'd inherited from his father, and enjoyed the stupendous view from the high Manx hills from which he could see England, Ireland, Scotland, and Wales. Following a tip from a fellow cruiser in a small wooden yacht like his own, he also earned some money picking wild mushrooms.

From the Isle of Man Thomas sailed south first to Fishguard, in Wales, then set out for Cornwall at the southwestern end of England. He soon got caught in some strong weather, with rising wind and seas he described as "fairly ridiculous." While fixing porridge for breakfast his first morning out of Fishguard, he was interrupted by the unnerving sound of the inner forestay ripping its chainplate off the bow of the boat. He found too that *Melody*'s hull, when pressed in such conditions, leaked badly somewhere up forward. "It's like seeing the tide come in on the beach," he wrote and had to work pumping out the boat every 20 minutes to keep the water in the bilge under control.

It was clear Thomas had a good deal more work to do before *Melody* would be sound enough to chance a long ocean passage to the Caribbean. The tidal range on the Camel was large enough, a bit over 11 feet, that it was relatively easy to get the boat out of the water to work on her hull. By nudging *Melody* close to shore on a high tide, Thomas could carefully tie her off as the tide drained away so she'd stand upright on the firm shingle clear of the water throughout the following low tide. Or he could let her dry out lying prone on one side or the other. Soon he was sketching detailed diagrams of *Melody*'s hull construction to share with Edward for advice on how to locate and staunch the worrisome leak.

Thomas also turned his mind to the problem of heat and set to work converting first a fire extinguisher and later an old bus muffler he'd found on shore into a small wood-burning stove. He fashioned a chimney pipe for the stove by neatly riveting together a series of empty bean cans. On first arriving in southern England, he'd been encouraged by the relative rise in air temperature— instead of having to wear five sweaters to stay warm, he joked, he now needed only three. But as the winter bore down on him the joke seemed less amusing, not only because of the cold, but also because of the lack of light.

"The days are so short," he fretted. "I sleep twelve hours a day and there's still four hours of dark. I wake up before dawn to make best use of daylight."

Later that same winter he also wrote: "The days go so fast; the sun almost looks like a strobe light!"

It did not take long for Thomas to realize his presence on the river was not entirely welcome. First there was the problem of the local harbormaster, who was empowered to extract fees from those anchoring within his jurisdiction. Thomas had to play a small game of cat-and-mouse with this fellow, occasionally shifting *Melody* from cove to cove along the riverbank to avoid the tax.

The farmers whose land abutted the river were also nervous about Thomas. He was tying off his boat to their trees, they complained, and to cope with them Thomas alternated between diplomacy and stealth—sometimes presenting them with gifts of whiskey or helping out with chores to placate them, sometimes sneaking across their property as he came and went.

"[T]he way I'm living is effectively illegal," he noted with some pride. "Although there's no explicit law banning how I live (yet!) there is the possibility of certain people doing whatever they like with me. I'm slowly realizing that I'm an illegal person doing illegal things, having illegal thoughts."

But Thomas was not alone and had at least one immediate ally in his life on the river. Robert Corke, more popularly known as Boogie, was in fact the very first person he met in Cornwall. He was, like Thomas, something of a "boat bum," a fellow in his forties who lived hand-to-mouth on the shores of the Camel as he worked at fixing up an antique 36-foot French crabber. Thomas had anchored next to Boogie's boat when he first came to the river, fresh from the Isle of Man, and, as Boogie remembered it, was so famished he helped himself to a big chocolate bar Boogie had left out unguarded.

Boogie was a generous and gregarious soul, well educated, outgoing with a taste for conversation, and he and Thomas quickly became fast friends. Over the months to come they would spend a good deal of time together. Boogie fondly remembered them swapping stories and smoking a bit of hashish over a fire on the beach "as frost formed on our shoulders and backs." Inevitably they also aided each other through the chores and small misadventures that punctuate a life afloat.

Thomas, in letters to the Allcards, told of a lost (ultimately destroyed) dinghy he helped Boogie chase down and of boat transfers they made together from cove to cove at night along the riverbank. Years later Boogie recalled with particular enthusiasm, and a bit of lingering amazement, a day he once spent with Thomas pulling the mast out of *Melody* so Thomas could rebuild the maststep beneath it. Together they brought *Melody* a short distance up the river to a high bridge just west of Wadebridge and anchored her fore and aft right beneath it.

"Thomas refused to pay for a crane to lift his mast out," Boogie explained. "Instead he climbed across this enormous bridge, then dropped a rope and tackle down, and we lifted the mast up with that. It showed the kind of mentality he had."

It was through Boogie too that Thomas first made a meaningful connection with the larger society on shore. Boogie was well received in certain homes nearby, a local character welcomed around a table for his congenial company and lively conversation, and on one day less than a month after Thomas arrived on the Camel, three such friends came down together to the riverbank to search for him. One of these was a 43-year-old divorcée named Jean Buchanan.

As Thomas later remembered the encounter: "I'd little human contact since uni and I suddenly realized I'd become a flippin' weirdo!"

Jean, however, was not put off.

"Thomas I discovered just around a few rocks," she later wrote. "His head was poking out of his cabin piled high with dreads. A gentle voice greeted me. Something instantly drew me to him, the chemistry strong. It was cold and I realized he needed help, although Thomas would never ask for help."


AFTER THEY CAME TO KNOW each other better, Thomas confessed to Jean that she was his first lover, but she never really believed this. She likewise was a bit surprised he had any romantic interest in her in the first place. Once Thomas had been introduced around the neighborhood "he was certainly noticed by some very lovely young gals," Jean observed, and it took her a while to realize, as he came repeatedly to visit her, that she in fact was the one he was attracted to. She tried at first to ignore him, "but he was quite persistent," she later wrote.

It was a liaison as unusual as any that Thomas's father had fallen into, although in the opposite direction age-wise. And there seems no reason to believe that Thomas would have lied to Jean about having lost his virginity to her. His relations with and feelings about the opposite gender had definitely been conflicted up to this point. On the one hand he was clearly biologically attracted to females and had been actively courting them since childhood, an urge his father's example could only have encouraged. He still remembered all the names of the girls with whom he'd formed special friendships as a young boy, in harbors around the world, and the pang of loss he felt each time his father had hoisted anchor and sailed away.

On the other hand, as Clare Allcard had surmised in the moment she first met him, Thomas fundamentally distrusted women. He'd been abused by Ann, and Florence (though he likely never saw her as a mother figure) had simply disappeared, leaving his father in a state of very palpable distress. Later it was Kathy, his one girlfriend at university for at least a short time, who'd been the one to suddenly break off their inchoate relationship. His cynical view of young women's materialist mating goals had presumably inhibited his forming other relationships.

Clare's kind treatment of Thomas no doubt helped to smother any sprouting seeds of misogyny within him. Simonne, who always maintained a very active interest in Thomas and like Clare came eventually to visit him in Cornwall, had also offered nothing but untrammeled maternal affection. All of which might serve as at least a partial explanation of Thomas's attraction to Jean and his willingness to ultimately trust her. She was certainly attractive— slim and lithe, with straight long brunette hair cut in bangs over a pair of lively eyes, a slightly upturned nose, and a wide engaging smile. She was alluring enough to attract the interest of a 21-year-old male, but she was, undeniably, a much older woman and also a mother, with a 12-year-old son, Ryan, to care for.

Thomas himself was a very yin-yang proposition viewed from a female perspective. He had, like his father, a certain base magnetism and appeal, as evidenced apparently in the fact that Kathy was still writing to both him and the Allcards hoping to somehow maintain a connection. He was physically attractive in an elemental sense— with piercing blue-green eyes, strikingly handsome features, and a well-proportioned, very fit physique—but he was also objectively somewhat repulsive. He bathed infrequently, brushed his teeth with clay, boasted a dramatic love-it-or-leave-it hairstyle, dressed thoughtlessly in odd bits of mismatched clothing, and now lived like a medieval peasant on a tiny boat with no amenities. In the cabin he called home he couldn't even stand upright and spent much of his time squatting on his haunches with his usually bare feet splayed flat on the floor. When he hurt himself, he licked his wounds like a dog to heal them. He cooked on a tiny Primus burner and heated his boat with fallen tree limbs and bits of driftwood he gathered along the shore. He relieved himself in a bucket and subsisted mostly on rice, potatoes, porridge, and a kidney-bean mash seasoned with any vegetables or spices he could lay hands on.

Jean had enough of a nautical background to have some sense of where Thomas was coming from. Raised in a family of sailors in Bristol, at the northern root of the Cornish peninsula, she had once worked as a sailmaker in the United States, had sailed briefly in the Caribbean, and had voyaged as crew in strenuous conditions across the North Atlantic from west to east before getting married and giving birth to Ryan. But she was not blind to Thomas's idiosyncrasies. She could see the pride and arrogance in him and a certain social disconnectedness. He was very guarded and perpetually wary of other people until they proved themselves trustworthy and was often a bit awkward, with an inability, remarked on by others who knew him well, to read body language and common social cues. Clare Allcard had always attributed this to Thomas's having been isolated and locked up alone in the bow of his father's boat when he was very young; a few others would later assume he suffered from some species of high-order autism.

Jean too was exposed to a bit of Thomas's darker side as their relationship developed. She later remembered one instance when he suddenly, for no apparent reason, became quite angry with Ryan when they were all sailing together on *Melody*. She was also a bit shocked when he once became very jealous and violently punched a male friend of hers. Ultimately though the bond she forged with Thomas was profound.

"I loved him unconditionally," she later wrote, "and was very protective towards him."

Circumstantially they were in similar places in their lives. Thomas was in a state of transition, attempting to move from his life as a university student back to a life afloat in the Caribbean and was working to fix up *Melody* to facilitate this. Jean, who had divorced only a few years earlier, was meanwhile still transitioning into a new life as a single mother and was working to bolster her finances by renovating a beautiful structure known as the Old Chapel, in the nearby village of Chapel Amble. Each willingly aided the other as they strived toward their goals, but as Jean saw it, they also shared something more essential. She, like Thomas, had suffered in her childhood and had been "ruined from an early age," in ways she is loath to publicize, and thus felt a certain kinship with him.

"Like me he was always in survival mode," she recalled, "battling with insecurity."

THOMAS'S CONNECTION WITH JEAN helped to civilize his life in Cornwall. Jean was living in the Old Chapel as she fixed it up, not too far from where Thomas was keeping *Melody* on the river, and it provided him with a comfortable and convenient base of operations. He could sleep here in a proper bed when he wanted, he could bathe and eat here, there was space to stretch out sails he wanted to work on, and it was easy enough to move back and forth between chapel and boat on the fancy bicycle he'd cherished and carried with him ever since receiving it from the Allcards in Andorra six years earlier.[1] Jean even managed to persuade Thomas to wear shoes more often, after a friend of hers produced an old pair of size-12 boots that fit his oddly shaped feet reasonably well.

Thomas spent almost two and half years, three winters and two summers, based in Cornwall, an interlude no doubt protracted both by his affection for Jean and the quality of his life there. Through Jean he accessed a much wider local social circle, and though some of her friends were put off by his aloof and uncompromising manner, Thomas could rise to an occasion when he wanted. He warmly described to the Allcards, for example, one outing where he and Jean attended a reception for a local film production maven who had just married. Thomas reveled in the preparations and rigged himself out in an Italian silk jacket with a fancy waistcoat. He also spent some time lolling about on Jean's bed, advising her as she tried on "her sexiest gear," a process he described as "great fun." He marveled at the size of the crowd at the reception, almost a

---

1. Thomas had taken this bicycle with him to university but painted it a ghastly color to make it less attractive to thieves.

thousand people, and at the fantastic band flown in from Senegal, and the constellation of TV and film celebrities in attendance.

"I felt a right swanky bastard," he boasted, "with Jean towing me round by the hand."

Thomas also got along well with Jean's son Ryan. Tellingly, what Ryan later remembered about more common neighborhood dinner parties he, his mother, and Thomas attended was that Thomas often preferred hanging out with him and his teenage friends rather than the adults. Boogie Corke, who attended similar gatherings with Thomas, later noted that Thomas would sometimes "retreat into himself, silent and immobile" in social situations and was "far happier with people in more singular doses."

At home Ryan and Thomas played with Legos together, a flashback to Thomas's own childhood, and Ryan marveled at the elaborate contraptions Thomas designed and created. Thomas also introduced Ryan to his old hobby of model boats and showed him some models he'd made aboard *Melody*. Ryan was amazed by these and the very base materials from which they were constructed: hull parts were carefully shaped cast-off bits of foam laminated in micro-thin coats of epoxy; properly paneled sails were cut and shaped out of old plastic shopping bags. Their designs were just as fantastic as Thomas's Lego creations, like "crazy spaceships," Ryan remembered, with self-adjusting moving parts that kept the models hydrofoiling at ever-increasing speeds until finally they self-destructed.

And it was thanks to Ryan that Thomas got his first chance to play with some 3D boat-design software. Ryan had received this from his grandfather but couldn't quite figure it out. Thomas took to it instantly and at once started designing on Ryan's computer the "dream boat" he boasted he would build and live aboard one day.

"He explained all about why he designed it the way he had,"

Ryan recalled. "How he'd done this to reduce that, and so on. It was really cool. I didn't know what he was talking about half the time, but you could tell he was really into it."

One of the congenial aspects of Thomas's life with Jean was that it revolved so immediately around sailing. During both his summers in the area he was able to earn money working for Jean's brother Keith, who ran a sailing school and boatyard on St. Mary's, the main island out in the Isles of Scilly, some 25 miles off the southwestern tip of Cornwall. For Thomas this was a long daysail or overnight sail away, about 40 miles southwest of the entrance to the Camel. Here he could work on his own boat much more efficiently, and the Scillies, a tide-scoured outlier with many hidden rocks and shoals that had claimed more than 500 wrecks over the centuries, were themselves a charming if challenging cruising ground. Thomas and Jean, sometimes with Ryan aboard, spent a good deal of time roaming the islands together in *Melody*, enjoying the casual, sometimes episodic pleasures of summer sailing in England's outermost archipelago.

Cruising aside, Thomas also made a big impression in the local racing scene. The racing, as is often the case in British yachting, was biased in favor of traditional boats, so Thomas felt comfortable and was eager to participate. Though he had no racing experience, he was a highly skilled sailor with instincts honed literally from birth. "All the basics," he later wrote, "I learnt by osmosis; complete immersion." He had no memories of being taught anything, as it "hardly required belaboring."

For two years running, in August of 1998 and '99, Thomas succeeded in winning the biggest local event, the Round the Island Race, organized by the Scillonian Sailing Club, with a course that ran around St. Mary's then over to the neighboring island of St. Agnes. His only serious competitor was his boss, Keith Buchanan, who sailed a beautiful, meticulously maintained 23-foot antique gaff cutter, originally built during the 1920s, named *Bee*.

Ryan later speculated that his uncle Keith, who had dominated local racing for years and knew the local waters like the back of his hand, might have been a bit chagrined that he'd lost out to a newcomer like Thomas.[2] Thomas for his part discounted his victories, as they were awarded on corrected time and in both cases Keith had actually finished ahead of him[3]. What he was proud of was that the difference between them was smaller the second time. He also was bemused by the fact that the club commodore, after his second victory, only reluctantly surrendered the club's splendid trophy, a perpetual cup worth £3,500 to be held by each winner until the next year's race, as certain club members were worried it might not be safe aboard *Melody*.

There was some cause for this, as Thomas's life afloat in the waters of southwest England was also marked by some less than victorious moments. Local sailors had clucked their tongues over the lack of safety gear aboard *Melody*—she carried no engine, no liferaft, no radio transmitter. Ryan's dad, Nick Nethercot, himself a sailor and otherwise on good terms with Thomas, had prohibited Ryan at least once from sailing between the Scillies and Cornwall on *Melody* for just these reasons. And in one dramatic instance Thomas, with Jean aboard, had been caught out on *Melody* in dangerous circumstances in Porth Cressa Bay directly in front of Hugh Town, the main town of both St. Mary's and all the Isles of Scilly.

Porth Cressa is the southern arm of the sea that embraces the narrow isthmus on which Hugh Town stands and is less protected than the northern arm, St. Mary's Pool, which forms the town's

---

2. Keith Buchanan did not respond to repeated requests regarding his recollections of Thomas. His sister Jean, however, does not believe that he was jealous of Thomas's victories in the Round the Island Race.

3. This has long been a controversial issue in yacht racing. When sailboats of different designs and construction race against each other, as is most commonly the case, various rating systems are applied to equalize them, with time penalties assessed against boats deemed to be inherently faster. The vices and virtues of different systems are often hotly debated among racing sailors.

main harbor. Perfectly safe and convenient when the wind and seas are running from the north, Porth Cressa springs shut like a trap when trends shift to the south and the very open water of the North Atlantic. Even a strong offshore swell from the south, stirred up by some distant Atlantic gale, can cause problems as it stacks into breaking waves in the bay's shallow waters, most particularly when cutting against an outgoing tide.

Thomas, with no radio to immediately monitor weather forecasts, had anchored here during a short cruise with Jean and was surprised during the night when the wind shifted south and increased to gale force. Legions of steep breaking waves about five feet high were soon marching straight into the bay. In describing the event to the Allcards, Thomas afterward was mostly sanguine and treated it as a technical lesson learned: that it was better to anchor on rope instead of chain in such conditions, as rope has much more give to it. But at the time, as Jean remembered it, Thomas was stone-cold petrified, and it is hard to imagine this crisis did not provoke in him memories of that awful night on the windward coast of Bonaire.

"I noticed he was shaking all over," she later wrote. "He told me to jump for it, as he thought the boat would smash up on the beach. I was shocked by this shaking, definitely not the norm for Thomas, and thought adrenalin would have kicked in."

With no engine Thomas and Jean could not simply motor out of the bay and had zero chance of sailing out against the howling wind. Jean felt jumping overboard would be fatal and instead resolutely shone a flashlight into the windows of the houses lined along the shore, not so far away. Eventually someone alerted her brother Keith, who roared out in an inflatable boat to tow *Melody* to safety, "in the nick of time," as Jean put it.

Thomas also managed to get into a few scrapes while simply working on his boat. On at least two occasions, with *Melody* tied off straight upright out of the water on hard shingle beaches in the

River Camel, he managed to drop the poor girl violently flat onto her side after mismanaging the lines supporting her. The second time he was on deck as the boat crashed over on to the ground, and he got a bad rope burn as a line he was trying to control suddenly zipped out of his hand and off the cleat he'd turned it round.

In another instance, he badly gouged himself and severed tendons in his arm with a sharp chisel while doing some carpentry on the boat. This again was something Thomas downplayed to the Allcards, saying he had done it "in the daftest way possible," but it was also a bit shocking to Jean. She rushed Thomas to the hospital, very much against his will, as he was "terrified of not being in control, and being under the supervision of doctors in a large hospital was for him a nightmare."

Thomas was operated on, but soon afterward he yanked the drip from his arm and insisted on leaving the hospital, even as his doctor stood by cursing at him.

His biggest misadventure, where he came closest to losing *Melody*, was on the water during a solo transit from the Scillies back to the Camel. This was in the fall of 1998, and Thomas had aboard "a full cargo" of beach stones that Jean had collected during the summer's cruising. Thomas left the Scillies in the afternoon to be sure of reaching the entrance of the Camel, which is constricted by the darkly named Doom Bar, on a flood tide the following morning. The wind was fresh from the northwest, and as *Melody* shot out from the northern end of the Scillies toward Cornwall, Thomas later wrote, "it got so rough I several times had solid water on the f'[ore]deck."

By 3 a.m. in the dark of the following morning, he was off Trevose Head, a bit over five miles west of the Camel entrance. To keep from arriving before daybreak, Thomas decided to heave to for a few hours on alternate tacks, with the wind coming from either side of the boat in turns, so as to hold his place. In between tacking *Melody* back and forth, looking out for traffic, and sometimes pumping the bilge dry (the boat was still leaking up forward), he allowed himself to doze off.

"I woke up to a bump," he later wrote, "and leaped outside—I was on the beach!"

And quite lucky to be on it, as it turned out. In the dregs of the morning as he slept, Thomas realized, *Melody* must have passed very close to a craggy offshore islet, Gulland Rock, then was driven onto a small sandy beach in Mother Ivy's Bay "with black slabs of rock literally fifty yards to either side." It was one of only two such beaches lying amid the rocks and below the cliffs that studded the four miles of shoreline from Trevose Head to the river entrance.

It was now bright daylight, and Thomas confessed to falling at first into a panic. The sea was strong enough that the boat was being flipped from side to side as the waves piled up and broke on the beach. Thomas first tried to push her off all by himself, a pointless exercise, then waved to bystanders on the cliff overhead to come help him, which likely would have been just as pointless. Soon enough—something he hadn't thought of—the coast guard launched their lifeboat from a boathouse at the far end of the beach. They got a line on *Melody*, pulled her off the beach, and towed her up the Camel to Padstow.

Thomas was grateful, but he was also "disagreeably surprised" when he saw a video crew recording his entrance into the harbor.[4]

It is of course not unheard of for solo sailors to fall asleep while sailing. Whenever one sails any distance alone, getting some

---

4. There was at least one other instance in which the Padstow lifeboat came out to assist Thomas. In a letter to the Allcards, Thomas recounted an incident in which the lifeboat responded to several reports of a vessel in distress and came out after dark to find Thomas on *Melody* patiently sculling his way into the River Camel in windless conditions. After further searching the lifeboat crew concluded *Melody* was the boat that prompted the reports, and they retreated without bothering Thomas. According to Boogie, there was also an instance where the lifeboat crew towed Thomas against his will into Padstow after he anchored *Melody* off the entrance of the Camel. Thomas however left no record of any such incident, so it may be that Boogie misremembered this. Coast guard crews manning lifeboats in the United Kingdom and Ireland work as volunteers under the auspices of the Royal National Lifeboat Institution, a public charity.

sleep without putting one's vessel in danger is a puzzle that is not always easily solved. The closer one is to shore, the more serious the consequences of dozing off for too long, and in this sense, at least, Thomas's failure was not unusual.

But Jean remembered other times Thomas had dozed off in odd situations while she was sailing with him. He seemed almost a feral animal, "curled up in a fetal position" for hours sometimes on the hard cabin floor, and could be "very hard to wake up." She later wondered if he had some sort of "a sleeping disorder."

And to Thomas himself, significantly, the manner of his falling asleep in this instance also seemed out of the ordinary.

"What puzzles me is why I fell asleep," he wrote to the Allcards. In his previous adventures, sailing *Melody* up the east coast and into the treacherous River Humber, and later entering the Camel for the first time, he'd sailed for days alone, dozing "controllably," as he put it. Eager for an explanation as to why he'd lost control this time, he accepted Jean's reassuring suggestion that it might have been because he was feeling a bit seasick. This was objectively plausible, as sleepiness for most people is a threshold symptom of seasickness.

"I certainly had a very narrow escape," he concluded. "I put it down to having prayed to all the invented gods while sailing."

THOMAS WAS SO VERY DETERMINED to return to the Caribbean he apparently never for a moment considered abandoning this goal to stay with Jean. This was his first constructive romantic relationship, something he'd been striving toward on one level or another since childhood, and was not easily sacrificed. Yet he and Jean had understood from the beginning that they must eventually part ways.

Thomas had worked very hard to prepare for his departure. He had, he hoped, finally solved the problem of the leak up forward in *Melody's* bow. He had replaced the boat's maststep with a much harder wood, a piece of afzelia he'd received as a gift from Keith, and also redesigned it so as to spread the compression load from the mast over a wider part of the hull's structure. He had also finally decked over the cockpit, had further simplified the boat's interior, had rebuilt the rudder, and repaired a few parts of the boat where he'd found rot in the wood.

Thomas had worked carefully, but also frugally. To create a tiller extension, for example, so that he could steer the boat from the companionway hatch without climbing out of the cabin, he had simply cut down an appropriately sized tree branch, trimmed off the lesser branches and twigs, and lashed it to the end of the tiller. To save on paint he had repainted just one side of *Melody's* hull, the side that would routinely face the heat of the sun as she sailed west across the Atlantic. To create more ballast, as he'd noticed *Melody* was floating high in the water since her engine was removed, he had spent many hours melting down bits of scrap lead he gathered. He poured the molten lead into molds he created out of beer cans and short lengths of old roof gutters so as to form proper-shaped pigs that would fit neatly into the boat's bilges.

His final preparations were quite casual. To provision the boat, Boogie recalled, Thomas brought her up the river on an early morning flood tide to a public dock at Wadebridge. He walked to the grocery store and came back with about £40 worth of food and a few gallons of water. Boogie urged he would certainly need more water, "but he assured me it would rain and that was that."

As for navigation, Thomas had borrowed from Boogie a chart of the Western Approaches to southern England and had traced out all the relevant bits on pieces of paper, enough to get him clear of the Cornish peninsula and the Scillies. For a passage chart of the North Atlantic he had a page from a world atlas. As for the Caribbean and the approaches to Puerto Rico, Thomas was confident he would remember it all well enough when he got there.

Once he had his provisions aboard, Thomas waited for the tide to turn. Then he said his goodbyes, cast off his lines, hoisted sail, and headed down the river one last time to open water. For both Thomas and Jean this seemed an extraordinarily tragic moment. He assured her it was the saddest day of his life, and later wrote to the Allcards: "We fit together so well that I'm sure had chronology and situation been different we'd have been mated for good."

After Thomas left the dock, Jean jumped in her car and raced to Brea Hill, a 200-foot-high mound on the eastern shore of the Camel overlooking the wide river entrance. *Melody* passed below outbound with her sails pulling hard, and Jean saw Thomas had scrawled across them "I LOVE YOU" in huge letters.

It was, she wrote later that day, "the most beautiful yet the saddest sight I will experience for a long time!" And she added: "My tears could have easily carried *Melody* across the big pond."

This was on April 6, 2000. Thomas had the wind behind him as he sailed southwest away from Cornwall, and it grew fresher as he and *Melody* made their way across the mouth of the English Channel and passed 200 miles west of Finistère, the northwestern tip of France. Here he found the largest waves he would encounter through all of his 47-day voyage. He remembered one in particular he estimated was over 25 feet high: "It came at me like a monstrous eyeless almost reptilian scaled beast, the water swelling up to accommodate its submarine advance."

The boat shot up the wave's face as though carried on a powerful elevator, then the wave broke "in a mad gush of spume" all across the deck amidships.

"By that point the boat was going almost into orbit," Thomas wrote afterwards to the Allcards, "just swept along weightlessly in the frothing mass for a moment before sighing down the back of the wave. Had it exploded round the stern I might not be telling you about it now."

He slept very little in these strong conditions during those first two days, jumping at every loud noise and fretting about his loose ballast, those beautiful lead pigs he had cast and lain so carefully in *Melody*'s bilge.

"600 Kg of lead tumbling out of the bilge onto the [interior] side [of the boat] would not even give me time to grab a jerrycan before I'm swimming," he noted.

But these were fast days, during which *Melody* covered much ground—160 miles the first day and 140 the second, very good numbers for a traditional craft just 22 feet long. This got Thomas across the Bay of Biscay, but he then suffered through two short gales that spawned 40-knot winds blowing straight against him as he passed west of Spain and Portugal. The motion was terrible, so violent it sent the companionway hatch smashing back and forth, and again there was one particular wave Thomas remembered well.

"[T]he boat must have come almost entirely out of the water," he wrote, "since it came down with such a crashing thud I was absolutely astounded that the side of the boat didn't split open."

On the day between the gales, as his becalmed boat sloshed back and forth in leftover swell with no wind in her sails to steady her, Thomas saw a distant shape on the horizon that soon became a very large tanker. And it was headed straight for him. He had no engine, so he could not motor out of its path. He had no radio transceiver, so he could not attempt to communicate with it. All he could do was hope the crew standing watch on the bridge would notice him and his tiny boat.

This evidently did not happen, as the huge ship passed so close to *Melody* she was sucked into its hull. She bounced off the side of it, then spun about in her own length as she passed through the turbulence cast up by the massive propellers beneath the ship's stern. Thomas, looking up, grateful his boat was still intact, could see the tanker's name emblazoned there: *IRIAN*.

After the second gale it all came much easier. The wind became lighter and *Melody* was much slower, covering not even 60 miles each day. On the 16th day Thomas sailed past the Canary Islands, off the northwest coast of Africa, and finally turned west straight across the North Atlantic. Here the tradewinds found him, blowing steadily from the northeast across his starboard quarter, and for ten straight days Thomas made no changes to the set of *Melody*'s sails. This was the kind of sailing every bluewater cruiser dreams of, with seemingly perpetual fair winds and following seas. On days like these all the hard days that came before are forgotten, and living afloat, cocooned on a boat in the middle of an enormous ocean, engenders a state of ceaseless exaltation.

During the last two weeks, however, Thomas had to work harder as the trades slowly died away. There were periods of glassy calm, punctuated intermittently with windy rain squalls. To keep the boat moving as well as possible, Thomas now had to frequently handle his sails—taking in reefs, letting them out again, changing headsails—and he often had to steer by hand through the tricky bits where the wind was shiftiest.

And through it all the air kept getting warmer as *Melody* dove deeper into the tropics and slowly drew closer to the Caribbean. The sun passing straight overhead each afternoon made the grey wood on her deck burning hot to the touch. Inside her tiny cabin it felt like a sauna.

"What bliss to be sweating all over again," Thomas exulted.

Thirty days after he'd last seen land in the Canary Islands, some 2,000 miles to the east, Thomas at last spotted the tiny island of Sombrero, a rocky uninhabited outpost with a tall lighthouse on it, about 30 miles northwest of the British island of Anguilla. Here the wind grew a bit stronger and blew more steadily, whisking Thomas along toward his final destination.

During the following day, as the calendar rolled over into May 23, his 24th birthday, he passed south of first the British and then the U.S. Virgin Islands. He smiled as the strong, distinctive rhythms of island tunes pumped out of the AM-FM radio receiver in his boom box. By the time he reached the Spanish Virgins and Culebra it was after dark. As he rounded Punta del Soldado, the southern tip of Culebra, he could hear waves breaking on shore and the myriad chattering of frogs and insects reaching out to him from the dark hills. The air was full of the smell of the place: "Hot moist earth and putrefying vegetation. I almost cried with joy."

By 10:30 that evening Thomas had cast anchor in Bahia Sardinas on Culebra's west coast, just off the main town of Dewey. He had at last found his way back to where he'd started, before he lost his father and sister.

"I always knew I'd come back here," he wrote. "I just didn't think it would take so long."

This might well have been the happiest day of his life. It was certainly, he asserted, the best birthday he'd ever had.

# 8. DOWN THE RABBIT HOLE

ISLA DE CULEBRA, AS IT IS KNOWN in Spanish, was then one of the great semi-secret spots of Caribbean sailing and tourism. Poised about halfway between the main island of Puerto Rico to the west and the heavily developed island of St. Thomas to the east, it is relatively small, just six miles long and less than three miles across at its widest, with a population of less than 2,000 souls. In contrast to eastern Puerto Rico, dominated by the high, lush rainforest of El Yunque, Culebra is quite arid, with few large trees and no natural watercourses. It does, however, boast one of the best protected harbors in the Caribbean, a large enclosed bay called Ensenada Honda, a great turquoise pool ringed by skirts of green mangrove and low scrub-covered hills. The one town on the island, Dewey, no bigger than a village, straddles a narrow isthmus between the western root of the bay and the open ocean on the island's southern shore. The island also has some excellent beaches, including, on the west end of its northern shore, Playa Flamenco, which is today hailed by the cognoscenti as one of the finest beaches on earth.

At the turn of the 20th century, soon after the United States plucked Puerto Rico as a prize in the Spanish-American War, the U.S. Navy, attracted by both its beaches and its excellent harbor, assumed control of most of Culebra. They used the island and a few surrounding islets to practice bombardments and amphibious landings, most intensively during World War II, and left behind as evidence of this some ruined gun emplacements and also two rusting hulks of M4 Sherman tanks, now finely adorned with graffiti, at the west end of Playa Flamenco. After intense local protests, the Navy finally departed in 1975. During the 1980s, when Peter Tangvald so often anchored here, and even as late as 2000, when Thomas returned, the island remained relatively undeveloped. It was a popular day-trip destination for wealthy Puerto Ricans with boats over holiday weekends, but otherwise saw little mainstream tourism.

Thomas's re-arrival on the island as a young adult, in a boat of his own, proved a critical turning point in his life. It was a significant achievement. Even his renowned father, who had started his own ocean-sailing career much later in life, with more resources at his disposal, had never sailed so far on a non-stop ocean passage, singlehanded, on such a small boat.

But Thomas had never really planned past this point. He had been focused on this one goal for so long he had failed to clearly conceive of goals beyond it. Yet there was one part of him after he reached Culebra that immediately turned to matters any serious bluewater sailor would prioritize: the status of his vessel and the maintenance and improvements it needed to carry him on to further landfalls. In his increasingly infrequent letters to the Allcards, Thomas described the work he was performing on *Melody*. He wanted to reconfigure her rig and had taken her mast down; he'd taken off her wooden bowsprit and was preparing to install a new one in stainless steel; he'd hauled her out and was refinishing her bottom.

And he readily confessed to a sentiment any dedicated ocean sailor could wholeheartedly relate to: "Yea, I get slightly depressed if the boat is not ready to go, hence the desperation to get it finished."

But another part of Thomas was happily captivated by the familiarity of his surroundings. At long last he had arrived in a place where many people already knew who he was, somewhere that felt something like home. The small community of Culebra marveled at his return, some were openly incredulous, and he reveled in routinely speaking Spanish again.

"The best thing about Puerto Rico," he declared, "is that I can be totally honest with my words."

Before he dismantled his boat's rig and hauled her out of the water, Thomas embarked on something like a victory lap, sailing the full length of Puerto Rican waters, from Culebra to Boquerón and Puerto Real and back, stopping at old harbors on the south coast of the main island that he remembered along the way. And a few friends from his younger days eagerly volunteered to sail with him. At least one of these was an old "street rat" buddy of the sort his father had always disdained, a fellow named Ramses, who "looks like a Moor and could be a boxer," Thomas noted, and had recently been released from prison.

And of course there were women to tempt him. In Puerto Real he met an old girlfriend, Suhail, which "rekindled a strong flame," but she now was in a committed relationship and had a six-year-old boy to care for. Once back in Culebra, after his tour down the coast, Thomas found a new flame to nourish and fell into an intense whirlwind romance with an "extremely beautiful" 18-year-old Puerto Rican girl, Maria Eliza, known as Marí.

"I was a fool," he wrote, "and fell much more in love than I thought I was allowing myself to."

Unfortunately, this lasted only a little longer than two weeks. The young couple, in their initial rush of blind enthusiasm, had spoken of marriage, and Thomas precipitously purchased the materials to build a rowing dory, a proper tender for *Melody*, to facilitate their life afloat together. But on the last day of September 2000 Marí abruptly broke off the relationship, as she was daunted, quite sensibly, by the prospect of actually residing in such a tiny primitive boat.

Thomas was devastated. Though he had seemingly negotiated the tragedies of his childhood with calm reserve, he was emotionally quite vulnerable when it came to romance. In his sorrow over losing Marí he soon succumbed to yet another temptation that presented itself. To the Allcards, who were used to receiving a steady stream of letters from Thomas, it must have seemed that he had simply disappeared. They had only two letters from him after his arrival in Culebra, the last posted in early October, and then for several months, on into the summer of the following year, they heard nothing. Finally, in mid-July of 2001, Clare placed a phone call to two cruising sailors, Ulla and Christian Fischer, by then living ashore in France, whom she'd met in Bonaire when she and Edward were there in 1991 retrieving Thomas. They in turn put her in touch with two other sailors who helped to run a regional high-frequency radio net for Caribbean cruisers. People like this could quickly spread the word and hopefully gather news of a missing sailor.

One of these radio-net controllers, Bruce Goble, who was then actually based on Culebra, responded promptly to Clare's e-mailed plea for help.

"Yes, Thomas is here in Culebra," he wrote. "There is no easy way to say it but he is very involved with drugs. We have tried to help him but he is very strong willed, as you well know. The police have him under constant surveillance, he has been beat up in Fajardo by other druggies, but is all right. Cuts and bruises."

The drug in question was crack cocaine. Thomas had fallen prey to "the pipe," which presumably was something his old street-rat friends introduced him to. This is a demanding habit, as crack is highly addictive, and its effects are quite short-lived, so that the need to obtain more can become a very pressing problem. According to what he later told certain people he was close to, Thomas during this time, approximately 10 months, did maintain some semblance of principle. He refused to spend any money he had inherited from his father to support his habit, nor did he ever steal anything from anyone. But he did, harkening back to his university days as "the Flash" in London, start dealing crack in order to maintain his own supply. He obtained his product on the main island of Puerto Rico, most likely in San Juan, traveling back and forth by ferry via Fajardo, and sold it into the small, insular market of Culebra, where everybody knew everybody else's business. Inevitably, the local police did become aware of his activity, but, infuriatingly for them, could never actually catch him at it.

But just as he allowed himself to fall into this awful pit, Thomas also promptly mustered the willpower to pull himself back out of it. Clare Allcard would later remark on this, that Thomas had enormous strength of mind. She recalled he had a bad nervous habit of chewing his fingernails when he first came to her, but that he stopped the very instant he decided to give it up. It helped in this case that he also had a new paramour, or perhaps two, to inspire him. When Thomas finally wrote again to the Allcards, in early August 2001, in response presumably to a letter Clare had written after hearing from Bruce Goble, he did not mention he'd been dealing crack but otherwise was quite honest.

"I've recently acquired two girlfriends," he explained, "one American present and one German back home and to return in a month. This has taken me out of months of over indulgence in smoking crack which began when Marí left and has had me in a rotting rut ever since. The police hate me and hate my hip-length dreadlocks more and what really bothers them is they still haven't managed to find anything they can arrest me for."

ONE UNFORTUNATE CONSEQUENCE of Thomas's dalliance with crack cocaine was that he ended up neglecting

*Melody*. After the brief bout of intensive maintenance he treated her to on first arriving in Culebra, he took no trouble over her during much of the following year. Bruce Goble, by the time he wrote his e-mail to Clare in late July 2001, described the boat as being "almost beyond repair" and thought it "a miracle" that Thomas had sailed her across the Atlantic. Thomas, in his August letter to the Allcards, confessed that *Melody* was "not finished" and was at that time tied up to the town dock in Dewey with a "big black friend" living aboard to prevent his "enemies" from sinking her.

Thomas, it seemed, was bound to personify the old naval adage that both men and ships must rot in port. After quitting crack he did eventually start working on *Melody* again, but by then much of her keel and part of her hull had been colonized by the dreaded teredo worm, technically a species of saltwater clam that is very adept at boring through wood.[1] Ultimately, in spite of great efforts, Thomas could not save her, and though he did for a time still live aboard the boat, he never sailed her again.

It did not help that Thomas also could not restrain himself from acquiring more boats that likewise required much maintenance. The first of these, which Thomas purchased in the summer of 2001, was *Bonanza*, a Puerto Rican "nativo" sloop. This was a specialized type of local racing boat descended from the traditional fishing boats Puerto Ricans had sailed off the island's east coast in the days before engines became prevalent. They are quite distinctive looking, with very low freeboard aft (originally to aid in hauling fish and traps aboard) and a sweeping sheerline that runs up to a high, dramatically pitched bow. They have steeply raked masts and long raked keels, and in racing mode carry enormous amounts of

---

1. The primary reason *Melody* was infested by teredo worms was because Thomas had not covered her hull below the waterline with antifouling paint. He disliked this sort of paint, both because it was toxic and very expensive, and had hoped instead to keep the boat's bottom clean by frequently wiping it down.

sail, with very tall rigs and mainsail booms that are in some cases a good deal longer than the hull itself. Ever since he was a boy Thomas had admired these vessels intently, and at age 13 he spent much time learning all he could about them from one Angel "Don Gelo" Raphael, then recognized as the master of all nativo builders.

*Bonanza* was a bit longer than *Melody*, 24 feet, and quite old, built in 1939. Thomas was very proud of her and described her as "a jaw-dropping machine." But he soon learned, as he sailed her hard to St. Thomas and back pursuing his new German girlfriend, that she leaked very badly and, just like *Melody*, needed a lot of work. We don't know what happened to *Bonanza*, or the German girlfriend, but presumably both were soon lost somehow.

Thomas continued to collect more boats and during the years he spent on Culebra assembled a large floating menagerie. Some of these boats he owned, some were borrowed, one he rented for a time, and some he minded for friends. At its peak the menagerie numbered nine boats, including two tenders, and consisted mostly of inoperable orphaned sailboats, floating hulks that in certain cases required much looking after. His strongest, least worrisome craft was an old 26-foot aluminum lifeboat (not a sailboat) that he lived on for a while and later converted to a floating workshop. His favorite was another nativo sloop he purchased in late 2002, a so-called "mini nativo" just 17 feet long, named *Buenadaga*. This was a boat in which he could actually go sailing. He made a bit of money with her, giving sailing lessons and taking tourists out on day trips, and he also had some success racing her.

Another unfortunate consequence of Thomas's descent into cocaine was that it left him with a strong taste for alcohol, particularly that most sailorly of libations, rum. Until this time, in spite of having indulged in various other substances during and after university, he had closely adhered to his father's teetotaling regimen. Boogie Corke, for example, his buddy from the River Camel, well remembered that Thomas had always firmly declined his repeated invitations to join him in a pint of ale at the local pub, except on just one occasion, when, as Boogie put it, "he refused to enjoy it."

But as a crack addict Thomas learned that alcohol did have certain sedative virtues. "Crack makes one so absurdly strung out that one needs something to ease one's frayed nerves," he wrote several years later. "In my case that something was rum. Got the job done, but unfortunately got out of hand."

The last, perhaps most troublesome consequence of Thomas's crack habit, most particularly his crack dealing, was that it fixed the attention of the police permanently upon him. One would think law enforcement in a community as small as Culebra must be quite limited, but in fact there were a surprising number of agencies working in the area, all with marine elements that anyone on a boat needed to keep an eye out for. These included the Puerto Rican FURA (Fuerzas Unidas de Rapida Acción), a rapid-response unit that coordinated with federal U.S. law enforcement; the federal Department of Planning and Natural Resources, which enforced environmental laws in Puerto Rico and the U.S. Virgin Islands; U.S. Customs and Border Protection; and the U.S. Coast Guard.

But Thomas's biggest problem was with the small local police force on Culebra, and one officer in particular, whom he habitually referred to as "Monsieur Gestapo." The police harassed him often, and at one point, after he started leaving a boat and some gear on a small islet, Cayo Pirata, just off Dewey at the north end of Ensenada Honda, they wrote him up for trespassing. The islet was in fact a long neglected public park, and Thomas had done a good deal of work to improve it, clearing trails and removing several bags of litter. In retaliation he compiled an eight-page list of police "persecutions" he had endured and traveled to San Juan, on the main island, to present this to the head of internal affairs at the main police office.

"He was quite interested and wanted me to officially press charges," Thomas wrote to the Allcards.

But in the end Thomas's acute and growing sense of paranoia prevented him from taking such action. As he put it: "A couple of bulletholes in my head would be an easy way for Monsieur Gestapo to get rid of an unpleasant case, now wouldn't it?"


IN OCTOBER 2001 THOMAS finally met a different sort of woman, one who was genuinely interested in his unusual aquatic lifestyle. Stephanie Labonville was about six years older than Thomas—a wiry brunette, outspoken, a bit profane, with a no-nonsense attitude. She was from Canada, where she'd earned degrees in psychology and nursing, and had once worked as a nurse but found it did not suit her. When she first met Thomas, she'd been working as a dog trainer and specialty baker in Toronto and had come to Culebra essentially as a tourist, thinking that if she found somewhere she liked in the Caribbean she might move there. As she later explained, she had grown very tired of the cold weather in Canada.

Stephanie happened upon Thomas living aboard *Melody* on the town dock in Dewey, struck up a conversation with him, and one thing quickly led to another. She thought Thomas very attractive—"He was much too handsome for his own good," would eventually become a favorite pronouncement of hers—and she soon announced she would go back to Canada, get her stuff, then return to Culebra to move in with him. Thomas very likely did not believe this but said little if anything to dissuade her.

In early November, about a month after they first met, Stephanie reappeared on Culebra with a small pile of luggage and three dogs—a large Rottweiler named Bailey and two young Jack Russell terriers named Ziggy and Zippy. Thomas at the time was not on the island, as he had gone off on a passage to South America with a local sailing student of his, Pablo, on an old rat-infested 26-foot fiberglass sailboat Pablo had recently purchased. The goal of the voyage was to deliver a troublesome transient acquaintance named Donny to Venezuela so that Donny could marry a woman he knew there. All sorts of things went wrong. The crew quarreled, the boat leaked badly, was twice run aground on reefs, and ultimately was confiscated by the Venezuelan authorities. Thomas was effectively deported from Venezuela and was probably pleasantly surprised to find Stephanie waiting for him when he returned to Culebra.

The couple lived together on *Melody* with the three dogs, first on the town dock, then soon afterwards across the bay on another dock on Cayo Pirata, where they enjoyed more privacy. Later they moved on to other boats in Thomas's growing menagerie. But they were not particularly well suited to one another. Thomas, for one thing, did not like dogs and was annoyed at all the dog hair that gathered inside their cramped living quarters. He particularly disliked one of the small terriers, Zippy, a reputedly manic animal, and on one occasion heaved her overboard after she fell from the deck through an open hatch on top of him.

"I was actually very concerned that he was going to kill Zippy," Stephanie later explained, "so I ended up giving her away to a friend of mine."

As much as she cared for animals, Stephanie was not at all maternal, nor was she very domestic. She had made an affirmative decision to not bear children and had little interest in catering to or mothering a grown man. Thomas, meanwhile, following his father's example, expected Stephanie to cook for him and manage his household, such as it was.

"That did not go well with me," Stephanie later observed. "I'm not going to say I changed him in any way, but we figured out a way to make it work where he got fed and his needs were taken care of and I didn't feel like strangling him all the time."

Nor was Thomas sexually faithful to Stephanie. Having somewhat belatedly become active in this department, he had by this time become adept at the art of seduction. As he later noted wryly: "If only I could time travel and give my younger self a lesson or two."

In their first year together Thomas twice cheated on Stephanie, and she most certainly did not appreciate it.

She issued a warning: "I told him if you are out screwing around with other women, and you come home and bring me a disease, you better sleep with one eye open, because I will kill you in your sleep." She also left Thomas for a while and moved onto another boat, but ultimately came back to him.

More than anything, it seemed what held Thomas and Stephanie together was the life afloat. Thomas was grateful to finally have a woman to share it with on a full-time basis, and Stephanie was pleased to have found a very qualified nautical mentor. She had once been a lifeguard in Toronto and had learned to row proficiently, but she had only a passing familiarity with sailing. Ultimately, she credited Thomas with teaching her how to do it properly. She had enormous respect for his ability, which she described as "absolutely brilliant." Thomas taught Stephanie how to scull a boat, an esoteric skill she was quite proud to have acquired. He also designed and built for her (at her expense) a supremely fast and efficient rowing dory, a proper pulling boat, so she could more easily commute to shore from whatever boat they were living on.

For Stephanie her time with Thomas proved to be formative. Though they ultimately broke up in 2005 after almost four years together, Stephanie soon went on to acquire a sailing vessel of her own, a traditional 30-foot wooden cutter named *Tally Ho* of which Thomas wholeheartedly approved. For many years afterward she sailed the Caribbean and U.S. East Coast on this boat as an independent bluewater cruiser in her own right.

Not that the life afloat with Thomas on Culebra was necessarily simple or easy. It certainly would have been simpler, and much easier, if he and Stephanie, and the dogs, had but one boat to live on and care for, like normal liveaboard sailors. The logistics of living afloat while maintaining a working life ashore—as well as maintaining multiple other boats, some of them derelict or nearly so, in multiple locations—were often quite complicated.

After first moving from the town dock out a short distance to Cayo Pirata, Stephanie and Thomas ultimately chose to live out at anchor at a place called Dakity, at the southeastern corner of the Ensenada Honda, just behind the barrier reef that protects the great bay from the wind-driven waves of the open sea. It was a beautiful spot, one of the finest anchorages in all the Caribbean, isolated and open, but with flat water and the relentless tradewind blowing through to cut down the heat of the sun, with a fantastic reef to snorkel on right nearby. But it was a good distance from town, about two miles, with no immediate road access behind the anchorage. Thomas hustled, doing various things to make money—working random construction and boat jobs, giving sailing lessons, hosting day charters for tourists. His steadiest gig for a time was at the Kokomo Hotel right in the heart of Dewey, first doing odd jobs and later managing the property. Stephanie also worked at the hotel as a housekeeper, then later worked at a pizza place in town. These commitments entailed much aquatic commuting—rowing, sculling, or sailing, rain or shine, all or most of the way down to Dewey.

Stephanie later recalled: "For me to get to work it was about 40 minutes of rowing and 20 minutes of walking, twice a day. So I was in pretty good shape."

With all the boats to care for as well, things could sometimes get hectic. The boats needing the most attention were usually kept at anchor at Dakity. Thomas and Stephanie by then were living on a hulk named *Aquila*, which had no ballast keel and leaked badly. *Aquila* was larger and more comfortable than *Melody*, which was for a time barely kept afloat nearby with a solar-powered bilge pump running 24/7 and a pair of large plastic barrels strapped to her sides.

During this period Jean Buchanan, her son Ryan, and a girlfriend of Ryan's all came to visit from Cornwall for a couple of weeks, for what turned out to be a happy and amicable reunion. The honored guests were given yet another hulk of their own to stay aboard out at Dakity, about 50 yards from where Thomas and Stephanie were anchored. Ryan later remembered having a great time on Culebra, but he was struck by an odd chore that Thomas assigned to him.

"He pulled out a pack of chewing gum," Ryan recalled, "and he said, 'Just start chewing on this.' He just kept feeding me gum to chew, and he was doing the same. Then we jumped in the water and dove under the boat, and I was his chewing gum supplier. He was taking it off me and patching all the holes up with big clumps of chewing gum. And I thought: this is what is keeping us afloat! And we'd have to do it again a few days later."

With some boats out at Dakity and others at Cayo Pirata or temporarily on the town dock, Thomas usually had his hands full. He also often had at least one boat hauled out on shore for yard work, a much more complicated process than in Cornwall, as tides in the Caribbean are not big enough to dry out any but the tiniest boats.[2] Things got particularly frantic whenever a hurricane threatened the island, as all the boats then had to be driven up into the mangroves along the shore and secured there for safekeeping. After the threat passed they were then redeployed across the bay, as

---

2. There was on Culebra at the time a Travelift, a large machine specially designed to move boats in and out of the water, but this normally was not operational. Thomas struggled to find other ways to haul out and launch his boats, usually on trailers. In one instance he had to hire a barge and crane from Fajardo to come put *Melody* back into the water after he had her out to work on her hull.

it was too hot in the windless mangrove thickets to work on them there.

As Stephanie later described it: "It was like putting out fires. We were always just going from one boat to another to keep them from sinking."

WHEN HE FIRST GOT TOGETHER with Stephanie, Thomas had only recently quit smoking crack cocaine, and she did all she could to encourage his abstinence. As she later recalled, Thomas at this stage would not decline a taste of cocaine if it was offered to him, but he had definitely stopped seeking it out. She noticed too he was drinking heavily and later described him as a "highly functioning" alcoholic. Stephanie was much less inclined to discourage this tendency, as she herself liked to drink, did not see that drinking was immediately harming or incapacitating Thomas, and did not feel it was her place to condemn or attempt to modify behavior that did not directly impact her.

"I don't know if I ever saw him drunk," she later explained. "Maybe once. But he was definitely drinking first thing in the morning to the end of the day. He paced himself out, but was never drunk."

What concerned Stephanie much more was a phenomenon she and Thomas came to refer to as "the flops" or "flopping out." This may have been related to earlier instances in Thomas's life—his passing out in the airport in Amsterdam after the wreck in Bonaire, the black-outs that led to his room catching fire his third year at university, perhaps even the sleeping fit that put *Melody* on the beach in Cornwall—but now the symptoms were much more dramatic and pronounced. Extreme episodes could go on for as long as two weeks, with Thomas passed out sleeping for up to 20 hours a day, unable to be roused, eating almost nothing, and suffering from waking dreams, cold sweats, and severe amnesia when he was awake.

"He would be incoherent, falling asleep," recalled Stephanie. "He looked like he was on heroin, when in fact he had not been drinking, had not been doing anything."

"Obviously psychological stuff happening," Thomas wrote to the Allcards. "I've had intermittent bouts of extreme fatigue, sudden and total amnesia, and over emotionality (nervous depression?)."

It seems likely these incidents were provoked by stress, most particularly stress related to Thomas's legal problems. First, less than a year after Stephanie moved in with him, there were scheduled court appearances on the trespassing charge, one of which Thomas missed because he had "flopped out." This failure to appear resulted in his being briefly jailed on Culebra, engendering more stress and evidently more flops. The specious trespassing charge was ultimately thrown out, but not long afterward, in August 2002, Thomas was arrested on new charges. The police had found nine cannabis plants growing in pots on Cayo Pirata and assumed they must belong to Thomas. Once again Thomas was jailed, this time for three days in the penitentiary on the main island of Puerto Rico, before Stephanie managed to bail him out.[3] This charge was also promptly thrown out by the first judge that heard it, but again, in May 2003, Thomas was summarily arrested on some pretext related to the marijuana charge he thought had already been dismissed.

"My feet & hands were shackled together," Thomas wrote. "I was shoved into the car, driven straight to the airport, strip-searched, then flown in their police plane straight to San Juan, then

---

3. Thomas by this time had given up smoking pot, refused to have anything to do with it due to his fear of the police, and would not allow it on any of the boats he was responsible for. Stephanie later claimed she had no idea who was tending the plants on Cayo Pirata, but others assert the plants belonged to her and were a major bone of contention between her and Thomas.

to admissions in the penitentiary to anxiously await for Stephanie to come & pay my bond."

Through all of this, Thomas's bouts of flopping out faded and resumed in close enough concert with the ebb and flow of his legal misadventures that he himself acknowledged there must be a connection. In one letter to the Allcards, written in April 2003, just before he was arrested again, he noted the police had been leaving him alone for a while, that his "narcolepsy/amnesia" had eased, and he was "even more certain that the persecution was responsible for those stress induced collapses."

Besides having to bail Thomas out of jail, Stephanie struggled to somehow care for him while he was incapacitated. With a steady job to work on shore, it was challenging.

"This could go on for days at a time," she explained. "I was always scared when I had to leave, because I knew if something happened it was entirely possible he would not regain consciousness. I was always worried he would wander off. Sometimes I would be at work and somebody would come to me and say: hey, he's sleeping in the plaza. And I'd run out of work and go check, and he'd look like he had just fallen over. Or people would bring him back to the dinghy, and I'd find him asleep in the dinghy."

Stephanie urged Thomas to seclude himself on the boat when he was flopping out. Mostly this was for his own safety. During one episode he crashed an outboard-powered dinghy on some rocks and had no memory of it. But Stephanie was also worried that people in town, including the police, would get "the wrong idea" and would assume that Thomas was simply "shitfaced" on drugs or drink.

Stephanie also insisted that he see a doctor at the local clinic. She suggested to Thomas he might be suffering from something like post-traumatic stress disorder (PTSD), a notion he strongly resisted, but to propitiate Stephanie he did report to the clinic.

There he received a prescription for vitamin B1 and Librium, an anti-anxiety medication, from a doctor he described to the Allcards as a psychiatrist. Thomas eventually filled the prescription and may well have taken several of the vitamin pills, but as far as Stephanie knew he never took more than one or two of the Librium tablets.

Meanwhile, some people in town were indeed getting the wrong idea about Thomas. Since the triumph of his arrival on the island, his reputation had steadily eroded. To some older, more conservative Puerto Ricans his appearance itself—the dreadlocks and shabby clothing—seemed disrespectful. His drug dealing had been an open secret, and now he was in and out of jail and sometimes appearing in public "completely zoned out," as Stephanie put it. It mirrored, ironically, a pattern that had recurred through his childhood: he would arrive somewhere new—the smart, clever child of the sea who had always lived on a boat—and people were initially fascinated by him, but then all those things that made him different, his otherness, would leave him feeling ostracized and isolated. Now having come to a place he thought should be home, Thomas had, after the initial wave of good feeling subsided, ended up in pretty much the same place. It served only to harden his edges and, in certain respects, increased his arrogance.

As Stephanie recalled: "Thomas was highly intelligent, and if you did not 'get' him he would act as if you did not exist and would have no regard for you."

But there were many on Culebra who did "get" Thomas. His fervently quick mind, the friendly instinct that had sent him combing anchorages for companionship as a boy, the great enthusiasm he generated when intellectually engaged, his often open concern for and interest in other people he related to, were all apparent to others with open minds and open hearts. Among these, for example, was Kristen Camaret, a young mother with two small children then living on the island, who though well aware of

Thomas's reputation for having a "dark side," saw only his good side.

"I was drawn to him and what I remember most is his smile," she recalled. "He was kind and treated me with respect. He was refined and composed, in stark contrast to his outward appearance and many of the other boat dwellers we knew. He was good with my kids and played with them like a kid himself, riding skateboards or sliding down the hill by the pizza place on cardboard with them."

And those who worked with Thomas, people like Peter Yatrakis, owner of the Kokomo Hotel, and Frank Justicia, a local mechanic who often had jobs for Thomas, appreciated his quick mind, his competence, and the close attention he paid to details.

Thomas had little to do with most of the transient cruisers who stopped at Culebra during the winter months, as he generally disdained modern boats and those who sailed with too much "luxury and convenience." But he did become close to one couple, Michael Fischer and Melanie Wells, who each fall sailed from New York to Culebra on a simple 35-foot fiberglass yawl named *Lady Helen* and spent winters there. The evolution of their relationship with Thomas is illustrative.

Michael and Melanie's first impressions were largely negative, as they'd seen Thomas in town, collapsed with eyes glazed over, all zoned out on drugs they assumed. Then one night a kayak they had tied off behind their boat went missing, and Michael in the morning set out in a dinghy to search for it. Some locals he queried suggested Thomas might have stolen it. So he rowed out to Cayo Pirata, where Thomas and Stephanie were then residing aboard *Melody*, and he fell into a conversation with Thomas.

"He was really nice. I immediately liked him," Michael recalled. "It was obvious he could not have stolen my boat."

Two days later the missing kayak was found washed up on shore. Michael and Melanie soon afterward invited Thomas and

Stephanie over to *Lady Helen* for the first of several dinners the two couples shared.

"He was the most gracious dinner guest ever," Melanie remembered. "He would lean over the side after dinner and wash his plate in the ocean and give you back a clean plate. It was so thoughtful!"

As Michael and Melanie returned to Culebra each winter and were usually anchored out at Dakity, Thomas fell into the habit of stopping by to visit in the mornings. He came aboard from his dinghy always with a cup of coffee, usually spiked with some "additional libation," Melanie recalled, and he and Michael often got lost in prolonged discussions about yacht design. Thomas poured his heart into these, sharing drawings of the "dream boat" he'd first started designing on Ryan's computer in Cornwall,[4] as well as the experimental boat models he was still building from discarded bits of foam.

Michael later remarked that he worried about Thomas, that he often smelled of rum in the morning, and he warned Thomas he shouldn't end up "like those crazy old men on boats living alone," but should instead make something of his life.

Melanie also really cared for Thomas.

"Our experience with him was always peaceful," she explained. "He was brilliant. He was engaging. He was respectful. I'm not saying he was like that with everyone, because I heard that he wasn't, but that was my experience with him."

---

4. This was an unusual vessel, a narrow 34-foot three-masted sailboat with a long full keel that was shallow up forward and much deeper aft. Also up forward, just behind the foremast, Thomas drew in a pair of asymmetrical daggerboards. These were to provide lift when sailing to windward, but also could help hold the boat upright when out of the water. There were two cabinhouses, one aft and one forward. In the middle of the boat was a cargo hold for bulk storage of heavy items.

# 9. A FAMILY MAN

IN MAY 2003 THOMAS HAD HOPED to run his current best and favorite boat, the bright yellow nativo *Buenadaga*, in Foxy's Wooden Boat Regatta, which was held each year at Jost Van Dyke in the British Virgin Islands. This was and still is the biggest event for traditional sailboats in the area, and one of the most popular all-wooden boat regattas regularly held in the Caribbean. Thomas managed to borrow a trailer, hauled *Buenadaga* out of the water, and eagerly went to work cleaning and fairing her bottom to prepare her for racing. Unfortunately, his re-arrest and imprisonment that month on the bogus marijuana charge ruined his plan. By the end of 2003, however, Thomas's legal problems and narcoleptic episodes had eased considerably, and he was very ready to compete the following year.

Jost Van Dyke, like Culebra, was a special place. It is an even smaller island, less than three and half miles long, with fewer than 300 permanent residents. Unlike Culebra, Jost Van Dyke has no landing strip for planes, for many years had no regular ferry service, has almost no roads, and is accessible only by boat. Its most prominent inhabitant was Philocianno "Foxy" Callwood, an island-born joke-cracking calypso troubadour who founded Foxy's Tamarind Bar in 1968 at the east end of the narrow white-sand beach that spans the root of Great Harbour, the island's main anchorage. At first Foxy catered to day boats that brought discrete groups of tourists over from nearby Tortola, the largest of the British Virgin Islands, for an afternoon's visit. Later, as the bareboat charter industry established itself and became one of the great drivers of the local BVI economy, more and more boats and people flocked to Great Harbour, often for much longer visits, and Foxy's became known as one of the greatest sailor's beach bars in the world. Foxy had worked on and handled traditional boats as a young man and once sailed to Europe and back on a large wooden schooner. He founded his regatta in 1974, not only to help build his brand and promote his home island, but also to hopefully sustain the tradition of wooden boats built locally in the islands.

Jost Van Dyke was also more than 30 miles as the crow flies directly upwind of Culebra, and to get there Thomas had to sail his 17-foot open-cockpit racing skiff straight into the teeth of the easterly Caribbean tradewind. It was bound to be a wet and bumpy ride. Joining him as crew was Stephanie and also one eager volunteer, Christina Pasquinucci, who was then working on Culebra as an elementary school English teacher. She was two years younger than Thomas and had a keen but as yet untested sense of adventure. She'd heard tantalizing rumors of "the magical hidden island" of Jost Van Dyke and the great regatta there, and though she had no real sailing experience, she buttonholed Thomas and Stephanie the night before they departed and begged them to bring her along.

Not surprisingly, Christina became quite seasick on the hard upwind beat to Jost Van Dyke. She remembered that Thomas "laughed his lungs out, like an old sailor would" as she hung over the side and puked up all the papaya she'd eaten for breakfast that morning. Stephanie meanwhile "became like a mother figure" and helped her to cope with the intense, but mercifully temporary discomfort.

The scene on Jost, as it is colloquially known, was wild. This was the regatta's 30th anniversary, and a huge crowd of competitors and party-goers had gathered at Great Harbour to commemorate the occasion. Christina recalled that Stephanie was the one who organized everything once they arrived, signing up for the races, networking and making friends, cadging discounts and free meals for the *Buenadaga* crew wherever she could, while Thomas wandered about drinking too much. But he redeemed himself on the racecourse and won his class racing *Buenadaga* in the singlehanded series. In the crewed events, meanwhile, Christina proved her courage hiking out far over the water at the end of a trapeze wire on the rugged upwind legs. Many years later Stephanie recalled with a bit of poetic wistfulness the beautiful clouds of "glitter flying everywhere" on the last downwind leg of each race as they emptied out the bags of bright white beach sand they carried as extra ballast. She also remembered how Thomas remarked on one such occasion that he had too many women aboard and joked that perhaps one of them should jump overboard.[1]

When *Buenadaga* wasn't racing, Thomas rafted her alongside a 50-foot schooner, *Ushuaia*, that belonged to his old friend Morgan MacDonald, the naval architect who'd critiqued the design for a singlehanded round-the-world cruiser he'd conceived as a teenager. At night all three members of *Buenadaga*'s crew slept aboard the tiny open boat.

"It was really classic Thomas," Stephanie recalled. "He could sleep on a rock." She and Thomas shared a single air mattress that was slung across the cramped aft deck, while Christina curled up on the sandbags in the open cockpit in the middle of the boat. Despite the primitive conditions, Christina was immediately captivated by the life afloat and enjoyed "the sun, the water, the liberty," as she later described it. She did spend some time ashore socializing during the several days *Buenadaga* stayed at Jost, but what she most enjoyed was making a home of the tiny boat, cleaning it out, airing

---

1. The concept of disposable ballast and disposable crew is not uncommon on traditional island racing boats. Just as sandbags are emptied out on some boats when extra weight is no longer needed, on certain types of boats lead pigs are tossed overboard with buoys attached so that they can be recovered later. In some island races it is also accepted practice for extraneous crew to jump overboard when they are no longer needed.

out the bedding, organizing the food, preparing meals aboard.

Thomas, Christina later recalled, openly "flirted his heart out" with her, often right in front of Stephanie, who didn't seem to mind. Christina always carefully diverted him, laughing him off as though he were joking and acting like he was crazy.

One night during the regatta, she remembered, Stephanie never returned to the boat "and as the sun came out she suddenly appeared, swimming naked, leaving a huge yacht where she had probably slept."

Thomas meanwhile had fallen asleep "fully naked hugging the mast" after coming back to the boat drunk. In the middle of the night Christina found him shivering, so covered him with part of a sail. Thomas suddenly roused himself and called to her in a strange voice: "Woman! Come to me!" She allowed him one chaste kiss, then he hugged the mast and fell asleep again.

In retrospect she could only shake her head: "They had to be the weirdest couple I had ever met!"


CHRISTINA PASQUINUCCI WAS a native-born Puerto Rican, the youngest daughter of an Italian-American English literature professor, Dante Pasquinucci, who came from New York City to teach in Puerto Rico in 1967 and fell in love with and married one of his students. Christina's Puerto Rican mother, Ivelisse, often known simply as Missy, was a small yet dynamic woman, 20 years younger than her husband, warm-hearted, strongly opinionated, domineering, and very outgoing. Missy later recalled that Christina, compared to her two older sisters, was always the problem child, "a free spirit with a mind of her own."

Christina when she was young resisted schooling and often got into trouble in class, but she did appreciate and truly enjoyed attending university and graduated with a bachelor's degree in social sciences from the University of Puerto Rico at Rio Piedras in San Juan in June 2003. She was at the time sharing a house in old San Juan with several friends, and it was here she first heard of a job opening for a teacher on Culebra and of the "blond-dreaded English boy" who had sailed there alone across the Atlantic on his boat. After she moved to Culebra later that year, Christina certainly noticed Thomas, who reminded her initially of both Harpo and Groucho Marx, whose films her father had shared with her when she was young.

"He seemed so funny," she remembered, "with the crazy looks of Harpo and the quickness and smart talk of Groucho!"

After their great adventure together at Jost Van Dyke in May 2004, Christina, Stephanie, and Thomas fell into an odd sort of triangular relationship. Christina and Stephanie had actually become friends prior to the regatta and at one point toured the main island of Puerto Rico together in Christina's Volkswagen van. They particularly enjoyed smoking pot together, a practice Thomas now abhorred, as he was continually afraid it would get him in trouble with the police. At one point during their van tour Christina wondered if Stephanie was hoping their relationship might become physical. Thomas also continued to flirt openly with Christina, and though she was fascinated by him—"such a magical soul, so honest to his nature in every way, strong and at the same time so fragile"—she continued to put him off.

By the end of 2004 Christina had moved off Culebra to Jost Van Dyke, where she took a job running two beachside boutiques for Wendell Callwood, Foxy's son. Early the next year Thomas and Stephanie split up for good, and Stephanie eventually moved off to St. Croix, some 40 miles to the southeast in the U.S. Virgin Islands, claiming Culebra wasn't big enough for the both of them.

Much of that year, 2005, Thomas was at loose ends, hustling to make money however he could, but falling further and further behind financially while he also scrambled to somehow maintain his fleet of boats. As always, this was a pressing concern.

"I have to pump out *Melody* twice a day and *Aquila* at least three times a day," he wrote to the Allcards. "Quite frankly it is getting old."

In August the aluminum lifeboat Thomas used as a workshop was sunk at Cayo Pirata, due to sabotage he believed, and he had to borrow a scuba tank and some 55-gallon flotation barrels to refloat her. Afterwards all the tools and materials he'd kept aboard had to be sorted out and carefully rehabilitated. The following month he reported to the Allcards that he'd had more discouraging bouts of "the flops," which further crippled his ability to get things done.

Meanwhile, Thomas pushed forward on the romantic front wherever and however he could. He sailed *Buenadaga* solo to Jost Van Dyke to join in the 2005 New Year's celebration there with Christina, and again attempted to woo her. "We had so much fun!" she recalled, but once again she coolly blunted his advances. He returned to Jost again with *Buenadaga* in May to compete in Foxy's regatta, with a new female friend, Yari, and also Christina as crew. But Yari was terrified of Thomas, Christina remembered, and quickly hitched a ride on another boat back to Puerto Rico.

Through the middle of that year Thomas cruised through several one-night stands back on Culebra, then got serious about a woman named Brenda, who regularly commuted back and forth between San Juan and Culebra to spend time with Thomas on weekends. Once again, however, she had strong reservations about Thomas's unusual aquatic lifestyle.

Thomas tried his best to overcome these. He taught Brenda to swim, a basic skill she lacked, and worked hard to make the boat he was then living on, *Eric*, a 32-foot ferrocement sloop with no rig on it, into an appealing, comfortable home. In September he took Brenda on her first real sailing excursion, an overnight passage to St. Croix aboard *Bambú*, a 26-foot fiberglass sloop he was caretaking for a friend. Brenda was seasick, passed out on one side of the cockpit, while Thomas catnapped on the other side, popping up from time to time to check on the boat's course and look out for other vessels. At one point, however, he fell hard asleep for a while. On waking he looked up just in time to see an immense cruise ship bearing down on them.

"I don't know how I did it," he later wrote, "but freed the tiller in about 1/5 of a second and slammed it hard over as this juggernaut frothed by not even 50 feet away. It took half an hour and a couple of stiff drinks to sort out my nerves. Brenda just sat there, awestruck."

This did nothing to ease Brenda's concerns, and Thomas ultimately walked away from her, quite literally, on a street in San Juan several weeks later after "she started the whining thing again."

"It was becoming obvious," he later wrote, "she couldn't keep up with me (few people can)."

Finally, in late December, Thomas again returned to Jost Van Dyke. This time he sailed with Christina on *Bambú*, which was loaded with several boxes of merchandise she'd just acquired in Puerto Rico and needed delivered to the boutiques she was managing. Once again Thomas courted Christina, carefully showing her "the respect I had earned," as she later put it. "He understood by now I was not the easy type at all."

And this time, as Thomas described it, "the bomb finally exploded."

The couple spent a few happy days together on Jost, which Thomas later termed "the Island of Love," then he departed aboard *Bambú* on Christmas Day promising to return as soon as he could. Thomas was ecstatic, feeling great, but once again he fell hard asleep as *Bambú* ran off before the tradewinds. He was unconscious for about 12 hours as the boat strayed far from its course, rounding up from a downwind run onto a beam reach. At about 2 a.m. on December 26, he suddenly awoke with a start as *Bambú* slammed onto the rocks on the northeast shore of Vieques, the largest of the Spanish Virgin Islands, some eight miles south of Culebra.

There was nothing Thomas could do. He dropped the sails and sat amidships clinging to the mast, waiting for sunrise, as wave after wave pounded at the wrecked hull of the boat. Once again, as when he was trapped in Porth Cressa Bay aboard *Melody* a few years earlier, one would assume the experience recalled that awful night on Bonaire when he lost his father and sister, but as far as we know he never acknowledged this.

At daybreak a fishing boat appeared, and Thomas swam out to it. A plane from the federal Drug Enforcement Agency had already started circling overhead. The crew on the fishing boat ran Thomas a few miles west to the main town on Vieques, Isabel Segunda, and there Thomas convinced the crew on another fishing boat to take him back to the wreck site and help him salvage equipment from the boat. Soon however a grey police boat powered by three enormous outboard engines also arrived on the scene, and its crew took Thomas into custody. As the police questioned Thomas, obviously suspecting that he'd been smuggling drugs, a helicopter arrived and deposited four men on a nearby beach. They were all decked out in military garb, wearing flak jackets and carrying assault rifles.

Thomas sat in the police boat for three hours—cold, thirsty, and hungry—while the four armed men combed the area on foot as the helicopter overhead swept up and down the shore conducting an aerial search. Finding nothing, the police eventually released Thomas, but declined his suggestion that they drop him off on Culebra, only a few minutes away in a boat as fast as theirs. Instead they left him at Isabel Segunda, where he had to wait to catch the ferry home.

As he later wrote to the Allcards: "Words cannot describe how much I despise those insects (they certainly don't count as humans)."

This was a major setback for Thomas, as he now had to compensate the owner of *Bambú* for the boat he'd just destroyed. But he was not daunted. By New Year's Day 2006 he had returned to Jost Van Dyke on *Buenadaga*—the trip was "rough as hell" he wrote—and was happily reunited with Christina.

"I remember waiting and waiting to see that little yellow boat with huge sails come in," she recalled. "The day he arrived, as soon as he anchored, I paddled out on an old surfboard to greet him."

All the people on the yachts anchored nearby laughed and cheered as they watched Thomas and Christina gleefully embrace each other.

Thomas had intended to stay only four days visiting Christina, but the weather had different ideas. The "Christmas winds," as they are known in the Caribbean, very strong reinforced tradewinds that sometimes blow for weeks on end around the turn of the year, held Thomas prisoner on Jost for 20 days. *Buenadaga* was far too small to risk the huge seas that built up, and during that fateful delay the bond between him and Christina was fully catalyzed.

When Thomas finally sailed away from the island, with a scrap of plywood lashed over *Buenadaga*'s cockpit as protection against the strong 10- to 14-foot seas still running, Christina sailed with him. She hadn't the nerve to tell her boss Wendell she was quitting her job and instead simply left a note behind.

Thomas, in the long letter he wrote to the Allcards soon afterward describing all that had happened, made a bold declaration: "I believe I am now a father. At least, logic indicates that. We get along very well indeed. So we're getting married, most probably March 4. I must admit I'm a bit nervous about it, but I guess I've got to plunge in some day."

THOMAS IN FACT HAD good reason to be nervous about his impending nuptials. Though Christina's mother Missy was not at all enthusiastic about Christina's relationship with Thomas, she knew from prior experience with her two older daughters it would be folly to oppose the union. So when Christina announced she wanted a big wedding on a beach on Culebra, with lots of friends, family, food, and live music, Missy threw herself into helping to organize it. She and Christina went to Ponce, on the main island, to buy a very fine wedding dress. She rented a house by the beach so Christina would have someplace comfortable to change into it and so visiting family would have someplace to stay. She found decorations and attractive cushions to deploy about the beach for guests to recline upon. And she despaired over the logistics of getting a band and sufficient provisions out to the seemingly primitive island of Culebra.

"There is no food on Culebra!" she exclaimed many years later while describing her predicament.

All these preparations, and the prospect of being the focus of such elaborate festivities, were bound to provoke anxiety in Thomas. In response, as the anointed day crawled ever closer, he lapsed once again into protracted bouts of flopping out, sleeping for long periods and apparently incoherent when awake.

Christina, unlike Stephanie, saw these episodes as being directly related to Thomas's drinking. It may be that Stephanie consciously or unconsciously disassociated the drinking and Thomas's flopping out in her mind, to protect herself from feeling culpable for having enabled the drinking to a certain extent, or for some other reason. Or it may well have been that Thomas's condition—his alcoholism, his anxiety, or both—had simply evolved. Or it might have been that Stephanie, as a trained nurse, had a more nuanced perception of Thomas's symptoms and behavior. But Christina's memories of Thomas in the time before their wedding were clear.

"He became more and more nervous and was crazy drunk for weeks," she later wrote, "all red and sweating alcohol and falling asleep in any place. I was terrified and ashamed this would happen in front of my friends and family."

Nor was Christina ever inclined to put a label like PTSD on what Thomas was experiencing. She, like Thomas, did not believe in "playing some kind of bingo" to see what named diagnosis in a psychiatric textbook might best fit him. But she did feel tremendous empathy for him. She understood that Thomas had in some way been damaged by his unusual upbringing and his tragic history, and from the beginning she was drawn to the enormous contrast she saw in him. On the one hand, he was so smart and proud and sure of himself, and she respected and admired that he never pitied himself or ever saw himself as a victim. On the other hand, he was undeniably vulnerable.

"To me he always seemed like a god who came alive when his bare feet touched wood on top of the sea," she once wrote. "There he was free, there he was a master, and had power and strength and was so unnaturally quick. It was magical to see him in this way and then sad to see his sorrows and pain when on land, in contact with humans and society."

Always Christina's base instinct with respect to Thomas was maternal. What she wanted, primarily, was to protect and care for him. In the end she felt she had little choice. She had originally hoped if she scheduled the wedding ceremony in the very early morning, Thomas might be coherent and clearheaded for it. But once she saw Thomas was so anxious this would likely make no difference, she told her mother she could not go through with it. The wedding must be canceled.

Missy was horrified. It was by then much too late to undo the preparations, and several guests, particularly her husband's family from New York, had already booked flights to attend. So Missy apologized to everyone and recast the wedding as a big beach party for family and friends.

Not too long afterward Thomas and Christina did marry informally, without telling anyone, in a very simple ceremony they conducted themselves, just the two of them, aboard the comfortable "houseboat" *Eric*. They exchanged vows and rings and then drank together a bit of the homemade wine, concocted from bananas, cashew fruit, and quenapa fruit, that Thomas had started brewing.

"He was sober and happy and felt secure and peaceful when he was just with me," Christina recalled.

Missy, when she later heard Thomas and Christina were wearing rings and holding themselves out as being married, was understandably confused and also a bit annoyed.

CHRISTINA, FROM THE BEGINNING, was willing not only to live aboard boats with Thomas, but also to go voyaging with him. But she was not particularly interested in mastering the technicalities of sailing, as Stephanie had been. Soon after they got together Thomas bought her a tiny Sunfish sailing skiff, so that she might learn how to sail a boat herself, but Christina spent very little time with it. She did yearn for adventure, however, and was also domestic and nurturing in a way Stephanie had never been. She was more than happy to sustain and support Thomas in the manner his father's chauvinistic example had biased him toward and was very open to the notion of making a home on the sea.

Soon after their improvised nuptials Christina got a good job teaching music on Culebra and urged Thomas to stop working for pay himself, so he could instead focus on repairing and refitting *Melody* so they could eventually sail away on her. Christina also suggested they should perhaps move to Florida, where they could both work well-paid jobs to save enough money for Thomas to build a boat to a design of his own. She mentioned too she had a small property on a mountain in northwestern Puerto Rico, overlooking Lake Guajataca, that she'd inherited from her father (he had died in 2003) and was willing to sell this to help them realize their dream. Thomas was grateful Christina was volunteering to make such sacrifices and contributions, for as he confessed in one letter to the Allcards, he did not feel he could ask for them.

It was a bit ironic then that the advent of Christina in Thomas's life also coincided with the rapid dissolution of his fleet of boats. Immediately after they finally consummated their relationship, he'd lost *Bambú*, which he was responsible for but did not own. Months later he lost his beloved *Melody*, the boat he'd sailed from England on. She was little more than a very leaky hulk by this time and had sunk in shallow water and been refloated at least twice before. But finally one day, as Thomas and Christina were towing her out from behind the reef at Dakity, *Melody* foundered and sank in more than 30 feet of water near the entrance to Ensenada Honda, despite having flotation barrels strapped to her sides.

Christina later remembered this as a "magical" experience, free-diving with a mask and snorkel on "this classical boat lying at the bottom of the sea." But for Thomas she knew it was a nightmare, as he struggled first to save his boat as she started to founder, then dove on the wreck again and again, trying in vain to conjure up some way to get her to the surface again.

And then there was the loss of *Eric*, the boat they were living on. Thomas had determined that Christina should quit her teaching job and they should instead both work on St. John, the most exclusive of the U.S. Virgin Islands, where wages were high.

Because rents on St. John were also quite high, he set out with Christina to tow *Eric* there, a distance of more than 25 miles to windward, with a large outboard-powered skiff he purchased for this purpose. But they didn't get too far, as the outboard engine on the towboat died soon after they exited Ensenada Honda. Thomas anchored *Eric* in open water and left Christina aboard to mind her while he rowed the towboat back into Culebra to get its engine repaired. He warned Christina that if *Eric* started dragging anchor, she should at once set the larger anchor that was stowed on deck.

"It was as heavy as I was," Christina recalled. "I was afraid if I tried to throw it overboard I would go over with it and get dragged to the bottom."

Thomas assured Christina he'd be back within an hour, but three hours later he still had not returned. Christina by then was feeling quite seasick, as *Eric*, with no mast on her to dampen her motion, was rolling heavily in the ocean swell. The interior of the boat, the cozy home Thomas had worked so hard to perfect, was also soon a mess, as the many bottles of homemade wine he'd stored aboard, and also a television set, were smashed to pieces. Christina started waving a red shirt as a distress signal and was eventually taken off the boat by a passing Coast Guard vessel that was out on a buoy-tending mission.

When Thomas finally returned and found Christina missing, he became frantic, fearing she had drowned. He immediately returned to Culebra again to search for her there, but it was some time before the Coast Guard vessel returned from its mission and put Christina ashore. *Eric* meanwhile finally did start dragging anchor, was blown onto the barrier reef spanning the east end of Ensenada Honda, and was destroyed. Christina later noted, a bit ruefully, that Thomas blamed her for this, as she had not stayed aboard and set the larger anchor.

The couple soon afterward set out for St. John again, this time on *Buenadaga*, and quickly found jobs on a large construction crew building high-end condominiums. Christina was hired as a go-fer, fetching tools and materials for the crew, while Thomas toiled as a skilled carpenter doing interior finish work. Between the two of them they made very good money, but after a month Christina tired of working full time while living on a tiny open boat with only a crude makeshift awning for shelter. She left Thomas on St. John and returned to Puerto Rico to live in the simple cottage she'd had built on her property overlooking Lake Guajataca. She had little trouble convincing Thomas to follow her there soon afterwards.

By September 2006 Thomas was living with Christina in the mountains overlooking the lake and wrote to the Allcards that he had "quite astonishingly" lost almost all his boats back on Culebra. His aluminum lifeboat with all his tools aboard, he learned much later, had been seized and cut up for scrap. *Buenadaga* had gone missing and had presumably been stolen. The other boats meanwhile somehow disappeared—Thomas preferred not to go into "all the painful details"—and the sole survivor was a 34-foot fiberglass sailboat, *Grumpy*, which he did eventually succeed in selling.

Thomas seemingly was not too distressed by any of this. As he noted to the Allcards: "It is easier to get over the shock of some of these terrible losses and changes being on a seemingly never-ending honeymoon." With much coaxing from Christina, he had also given up drinking and was, for a while at least, routinely slurping down cups of tea spiked with hot sauce in lieu of booze. On the whole, as he had by now turned 30, he looked back on his days on Culebra disparagingly. "It still astounds me how I could have been so hardheaded as to stay there for so long," he later wrote. Beyond pairing up with Christina, he felt he had accomplished very little in the last 10 years.

But still Thomas had not given up on the ideal of bluewater cruising, of living afloat while roaming the world's oceans, as he had with his father as a boy. In his head, on scraps of paper, or on whatever computer he could lay hands on, he was still designing the "dream boat" he would build someday. And the dream had evolved. He had set aside the drawings for the long-keeled monohull cruiser he first conceived on Ryan's computer back in Cornwall and was now pondering ideas for a proa, an eccentric sort of multihull sailboat originally indigenous to the islands of the western Pacific Ocean.

"Our plan for the future," Thomas assured the Allcards, "is to save enough money so I can build a proa and sail the world—I'm through with boats that don't work, that have to be towed around."

THE ASSUMPTION THOMAS MADE back in January 2006, that Christina must then have been pregnant, proved incorrect. But by the end of that year the couple had conceived a child and calculated it would be born sometime the following September. Meanwhile, primarily at Christina's insistence, they shifted restlessly about Puerto Rico. They moved first from the lake at Guajataca to the small town of Jobos on the northwest coast, a popular surf spot, then soon afterward to the exotic barrio of La Perla, a small shantytown pinched onto a narrow hillside between the walls of old San Juan and the Atlantic Ocean. Thomas was fascinated by La Perla, by its grit and lawlessness, and in describing it to the Allcards seemed particularly pleased that his mother-in-law strongly disapproved of their living there.

"I love it here," he wrote. "We're the third house in from the shore so we have perfectly clean air despite being in the center of the metropolis. The cultural epicenter of Puerto Rico is just a five minute walk away."

During this time Thomas also submitted to some of the conventions of modern life. Having lost his U.S. passport years earlier, he'd had no identification at all for some time and now finally applied for a new passport. He started writing letters to the Allcards on a computer. He also became involved with motor vehicles and eventually obtained a learner's driving permit. He had briefly had access to a car on Culebra, soon after splitting with Stephanie, but now Thomas boasted of having driven a Pontiac Sunbird that had belonged to Christina's father most of the length of Puerto Rico. It was, he noted, "quite novel for me." By the end of 2006 he'd acquired a vehicle of his own, a small motorcycle, a 24-year-old Honda 450. Unfortunately, Thomas soon crashed and destroyed this while riding drunk on the streets of San Juan after a minor dispute with Christina.

"On the list of the most stupid things I've done, which is a rather lengthy one, it must be a heavyweight contender for first place," he wrote, concluding: "The moral is I don't want to have anything more to do with liquor."

During the spring of 2007 Christina proposed that she should sell her house at Guajataca so she and Thomas could instead buy property on Vieques, the larger sister island of Culebra. Like Culebra, Vieques for many decades had belonged mostly to the U.S. Navy, which used it primarily as a firing range. Unlike Culebra, the Navy had stayed much longer on Vieques, not leaving until 2003, after years of local protests, so the island then was even less developed. Thomas feared it might be hard to make money on Vieques, but he also thought investing in property there might be smart, as he'd seen how quickly things had developed on Culebra during his time there. In the end, instead of selling the Guajataca property, Christina and Thomas borrowed money against it. The piece of land she and Thomas purchased on Vieques was on a hillside in an area known as Monte Carmelo, southeast of Isabel Segunda.

"It is just large enough to be able to build the boat (the Proa)," Thomas wrote to the Allcards in early August 2007. "We have a small view of the sea to the north there. I'll start building the little house I designed very shortly."

Christina gave birth on August 19 in the yard outside a tiny house the couple was temporarily renting on Vieques. They called it the "Love Shack." Their child was a boy they named Gaston, after the Belgian comic book character Thomas had enjoyed when he was young. Thomas and Christina were firmly united in favoring a home birth, despite some resistance from Christina's doctor, who at one point threatened to report her to social services.

Thomas and Christina were also united in their attempt to manage the force of nature that was Christina's mother. They had agreed not to notify Missy when it became clear the baby would soon be born, as they felt her presence during the birth would be "detrimental." Christina did call Missy immediately after Gaston's birth, and Missy within hours appeared on Vieques to see her new grandson.

"She didn't come to visit us at all," Thomas wrote with some bitterness soon afterward, "but to force us to take Gaston to the doctor."

According to Missy's version of events, related years later, she discovered on arriving at the scene that Gaston was having trouble latching on to his mother's breast. "He could not suck!" she exclaimed and believed the child would soon starve. She warned Thomas and Christina: "You will fall asleep, and when you wake up the baby will be dead!"

According to Thomas's version, related to the Allcards in a letter at the time, Missy warned them they were required by law to take the baby to a doctor within a day of its birth, or the baby would be taken from them, which turned out not to be true. On arriving at the local hospital, after Missy buttonholed the doctor alone for a moment, it was announced the child had to be airlifted by helicopter to the hospital in Fajardo.

In the end Gaston spent 11 days at Fajardo being treated for what Missy, a firm believer in conventional Western medicine, remembered was a bacterial infection. Both her daughter and son-in-law were furious with her.

"Thomas cursed me in Spanish," Missy recalled. "I think it was the last time he ever spoke to me."

THE YEAR AND A HALF AFTER Gaston's birth was for Thomas filled with more family reckonings. The first came in the form of a visit from his younger half-sister Virginia in the spring of 2008. Though it was Thomas who had cut Virginia's umbilical cord when she was born aboard *L'Artemis de Pytheas* more than 22 years earlier, the two siblings had had little contact since Virginia's mother Florence left Peter Tangvald in Florida in June 1988. Virginia wasn't even two years old at that time, and in the intervening years, as she came of age in Montreal, she had imagined and hoped she might somehow forge a bond with her older brother. She had written several letters to Thomas when she was younger, but she never quite worked up the nerve to send them to him.

Now that Thomas had a wife and son, and Virginia had a newborn nephew, it seemed a good time to take the plunge. But Virginia's reunion with Thomas proved disastrous. She flew into San Juan with a boyfriend, a musician, and the day before her arrival Thomas traveled from Vieques to San Juan and spent the night with a friend of his. Thomas and his friend stayed up until all hours drinking, and the next day, when Thomas collected Virginia and her friend in the old Pontiac Sunbird that had belonged to Christina's father, he was perhaps still drunk. It was a terrible crash. The Pontiac was totaled, and Virginia, who was sitting up front next to Thomas, was seriously injured. Her head and face were badly cut up, with glass shards embedded in various parts of her body, and she was rushed to the University of Puerto Rico hospital in Carolina, just east of San Juan. Her boyfriend, meanwhile, suffered only superficial wounds, and Thomas escaped unscathed.

The member of the family who worked hardest to look after Virginia after the crash was not Thomas, the guilty party, but Christina's mother. Missy, with her large heart and meddlesome ways, was a major presence hovering about the wounded young lady in the hospital. Thomas meanwhile retreated to Vieques, and Virginia, once discharged, declined to follow him there. Instead she stayed with Missy at her home in Camuy, where she spent some time with Christina and Gaston. As badly as Virginia had wished to connect with Thomas as abstract kin, in the end she was, understandably, frightened by her brother in the flesh.

Thomas's next familial reckoning was more productive. In May of that year, not long after Virginia's visit, there came to Vieques a Norwegian film crew led by a larger-than-life character named Alex Rosén. Alex was a celebrity in Norway, a rock musician turned comedian and TV personality who had been sailing since childhood and of course knew of the famous Norwegian bluewater sailor Per Tangvald. In 2002 Alex had participated in a televised voyage deep into the Arctic aboard a tiny 27-foot fiberglass sailboat named *Berserk*. The young skipper was a controversial Norwegian sailor, Jarle Andhøy; the other crewmember an American, David Mercy. Together the three men had sailed via the Svalbard archipelago to a bit higher than 82 degrees north latitude, which they claimed was the farthest north anyone had ever sailed in open water.[2] During

---

2. The "open water" distinction is significant in that the Norwegian vessel *Fram*, in an expedition led by Fridtjof Nansen, had in 1895 reached a higher latitude, of over 84 degrees north, after intentionally getting frozen into the Arctic ice pack and drifting north in it. All three members of the *Berserk* expedition were charged in Norwegian courts with various environmental crimes, including intentionally provoking a polar bear, after the television series documenting their adventure was released.

this daring expedition Alex took along a copy of Per Tangvald's last book to read and was deeply impressed by it.[3] He resolved he would one day track down Thomas Tangvald, sole survivor of the wreck that killed Per Tangvald, and lead him back to the island of Bonaire, where the tragedy had occurred.

"I was thinking these would be great scenes in a TV program," he later explained.

Alex had done his research before flying to Puerto Rico to meet Thomas in person. He had contacted various members of the Tangvald family in Norway and concluded there was one in particular he should bring with him to Puerto Rico and Bonaire. This was Gjermund, Thomas's nephew, who as a joke had taught him obscene pickup lines to try on girls last they'd seen each other, when Thomas was a teenager visiting family in Norway.

The arrival of the Norwegians, descending like a comic Viking horde, was a major event on the sleepy island of Vieques. Alex played the part of a jesting ringmaster while Gjermund acted as his foil, dragging piles of luggage about at his behest. With the working film crew in train, they raided the local supermarket, purchased huge quantities of food and beer, then hauled these provisions to Thomas and Christina's property, where Thomas was still building the house he'd designed for his family to live in. In an absurd echo of Thomas's toddlerhood, when he'd thrown himself into a swimming pool and disabled the PA system at the Norwegian ambassador's party in Manila, he, Christina, Alex, and Gjermund together celebrated Norway's Constitution Day on May 17. They marched about the plywood shell of the house blowing horns, sawed discordantly at a violin, and waved tiny Norwegian flags.

---

3. This was *På liv og død* ("Of Life and Death"), Peter Tangvald's autobiography, which was first published in Norway prior to his death. It was republished in English as *At Any Cost* after his death.

Running beneath the frivolity was a dark undercurrent. Part of this involved Gjermund's state of mind. When he was younger he'd served in the Telemark Bataljon, a prestigious Norwegian military unit, and in 1997 was posted to Bosnia with a NATO peacekeeping force. Following a series of extreme encounters, including being trapped in a minefield and taking hostile fire with orders not to fire back, Gjermund began experiencing periodic bouts of intense anxiety. A year or so after his trip to Puerto Rico and Bonaire, he was formally diagnosed with PTSD, but at the time was struggling to understand what was wrong with him.

Soon after Gjermund arrived on Vieques, as he and the other Norwegians settled into their hotel rooms and before they'd gone to see Thomas, Alex's television producer, Per Hustad, marched into Gjermund's room. Nervous about mind-altering substances that might interfere with Gjermund's performance on camera, he preemptively confiscated a bottle of Valium he found. Though Gjermund had a prescription for the Valium, he did not protest.

As he later explained: "I didn't have the courage to say OK, but I need that for my mental health."

Per retreated to his room on the third floor, just below Gjermund's on the fourth, and a moment later saw Gjermund streaking through the air past his balcony window. This wasn't a suicide leap but a calculated "death dive," a Norwegian extreme sport Gjermund was well practiced in.[4] He splashed down safely into the small shallow swimming pool far below and at once felt better for it.

"I just needed to get stuff out of my system," he later explained. "I needed to relax, and it really helps me to relax to do a stunt like that. It helps me focus again."

---

4. Death diving, or *dødsing* in Norwegian, has been a recognized amateur sport in Norway since 1972. The goal is to hold a spread-eagled pose as long as possible after jumping from a great height. Just before hitting the water the diver curls into a ball, then immediately spreads out again underwater to decelerate as quickly as possible.

Gjermund didn't stay long in the hotel and soon moved in with Thomas and Christina as a family guest for the rest of the week the film crew was on Vieques. Thomas and Gjermund had a chance to reestablish the bond they'd forged when they were younger, and Gjermund harbored some hope he might be able to talk to Thomas about the problems he was having. He broached the subject of mental illness in a general way, testing the waters carefully before saying anything specific about himself, but Thomas quickly shut him down.

"His reaction was that mental illness is made up," Gjermund recalled. "To him it was a hoax, something the West made up to earn money for the pharmaceutical industry."

From Vieques the Alex Rosén circus flew on to Bonaire, where the immediate goal was to see if Thomas could find the spot where his father and sister had been killed. Then hopefully they would dive on whatever remained of *L'Artemis de Pytheas*. Soon after they arrived Thomas studied a map of Bonaire's east coast, then led Alex, Gjermund, and the film crew out to the area where he had emerged from the sea on his surfboard 17 years earlier.

Both Alex and Gjermund were amazed at the alacrity with which Thomas identified the precise bit of coral rock where *L'Artemis* had crashed ashore. Gjermund recalled Thomas was energized and excited to be back at the scene and that something within him led him right to where he wanted to go. "Thomas looked up once at the sun," he later exclaimed. "Just once! And then pop! Pinpointed the rock right away."

"It was great to watch it, because I could just feel him thinking," remembered Alex. "He used the in-built navigator in his head and immediately found that spot. It was such a moment."

Thomas paused to make sure he was in the right place, walking a few paces in different directions across the maze of jagged coral to check his bearings. Great plumes of spray kicked up by the wind-driven waves as they crashed into the shore blossomed in the air around him, the same grinding, merciless surf that had killed his father and sister. Speaking to Gjermund and to the camera, Thomas's voice trembled faintly with emotion. Then he searched the ground carefully and soon found affirmative evidence. Corroded copper rivets. The very rivets his father had used to bind together the two layers of planking in the hull of *L'Artemis*.

And then he started weeping. Gjermund grabbed him reassuringly by the shoulder, but Thomas tried to downplay the moment. "I guess I don't really try to think about it too much," he confessed. The film crew, out of respect, shut down their camera. It was, as far as anyone knows, the first time Thomas had ever cried publicly over the loss of his family.

THE DIVE ITSELF was challenging. The shelf of coral rock where *L'Artemis* was wrecked dropped off steeply into the sea before it, and sharp, white-capped waves driven by the relentless tradewind were constantly crashing on to it. The action of the water on its surface, and the surge of the seas under the water, was tremendous. Only one of the several dive boat operators on the island, a retired U.S. Marine named Larry, was willing to take Alex and company out to dive in this area, so close to the dreaded Iron Shore.

The operation was conducted over the course of two days. Both Alex and Gjermund were certified divers so could legally rent scuba gear, but Thomas, though he had some diving experience, had no certificate and had to settle for the basics—a mask, a snorkel, and a pair of swim fins. The agreed-on maximum dive depth was 24 meters, just under 80 feet. Larry briefed the team on what they could expect. The surge rushing into and away from the shore would be strong as waves pushed by overhead and were reflected off the coral shelf. This action would only grow stronger, like a lung inhaling and exhaling harder and harder, as they moved into shallower water closer to the shore. They had to time their movements to account for this and had to be especially careful not to get caught in any breaking white water that could throw them into the sharp claws of the shelf face.

The goal during the first phase of the dive was simply to search for whatever debris field L'Artemis might have left on the bottom. After their survey ashore, Alex had marked the spot where Thomas believed the boat had crashed with a small buoy. This provided a reference and enabled the dive team to locate the remains of L'Artemis fairly quickly. Ultimately, a fair amount of debris was discovered in about 40 feet of water. There were hundreds of pieces, most of it metal or crockery, as the wooden bits of the boat that had fallen into the water had rotted or been swept away. The defining feature was a line of lead ballast blocks that had been bolted to the keel of L'Artemis and now lay strewn across the bottom like a broken spine.

The next goal was to recover as much debris as possible. Gjermund remembered this was where he came closest to getting into trouble. The trick was to spot a piece of debris to pick up from some distance away, ride an inrushing surge to get in close to it, grab the item, then exit on the reciprocal outflowing surge. Gjermund mistimed one of his runs and ended up clinging to the bottom as he was caught in a cloud of tingling white water that tore at him like an underwater wind. Fortunately, he got away safely.

As he later remembered: "When I saw it on film I was pretty disappointed. The dive was way tougher than it looks in the show. I guess the big reason was that the cameraman had to stay in deeper water."

This was also where the dive team played a bit of a trick on Larry, who was standing by aboard the dive boat. Thomas, with just a mask and snorkel, was quite limited in what he could do, but towards the end of the recovery dive he shared air from Gjermund's tank via an auxiliary line and regulator, known as an octopus, so he could get a much closer view of the wreck site. To Larry, from his vantage point on the surface, it seemed Thomas might well have drowned, as he disappeared and stayed underwater for a very long time. Larry was much relieved when Thomas finally reappeared, but he went ballistic when he realized what had happened. After the team reboarded the boat, he chewed them out at length, yelling coarsely, as only an ex-Marine can.

"Then he smiled, and it was like nothing had happened," recalled Gjermund. "He was so cool and so professional."

Thomas was certainly interested in what they recovered from the wreck. There were porthole frames, cleats, winches, chainplates, many fasteners, and most poignantly, a fragment of his father's old sextant, as well as the twisted remains of a small gong. This originally had belonged to his grandfather Thor and had served as the ship's bell aboard *L'Artemis*. But Thomas was at heart an intensely practical young man, and what he most wanted out of all this was not merely wreckage but something he could actually use.

It seemed likely that anything useful from the wreck must have been salvaged by local Bonairians long ago. Thomas and his tragedy, however, were well remembered. Amado Felix, the local businessman who had done so much to help when Thomas was stranded on the island 17 years earlier, again came to his aid and arranged for him to broadcast a plea on the local radio station to anybody who had salvaged gear from the wreck. One response came immediately from a marine salvage and antiques dealer, an old wreck diver, who thought he might have the anchor from

*L'Artemis.* This was on Thomas's 32nd birthday, May 23, and while driving over to the dealer's shop in their rented truck with a camera running, Alex and Gjermund lustily sang "Happy Birthday" to him.

Out of a large collection of anchors hanging on a wall outside the dealer's store, Thomas instantly recognized the one that had belonged to his father. This was a unique folding seaplane anchor, forged in stainless steel, which was still in excellent condition. The dealer graciously bestowed it upon Thomas as a gift, and Thomas was overjoyed.

"It's like I almost have the boat again or something," he happily declared on camera afterwards. "It's only a very small part of it, but it's like trying to undo what happened. Or come to terms with it." But then, curiously, he undercut the significance of the moment by adding: "I've never really been very disturbed by it. Of course it affects you, but not terribly. But now I feel more… OK, it's done."

The final stop Thomas and company made before leaving Bonaire, at the cemetery where Peter and Carmen were buried, belied any emotional ambivalence. Amado Felix had reminded Thomas where he could find the spot. And here again he wept openly. Gjermund, who this time fully embraced his uncle as he broke down, recalled later that Thomas cried much more over his sister's grave than his father's.

It was, in the end, a powerful positive experience for all concerned. Alex to this day remembers this as the best television program he ever made.[5] Gjermund meanwhile was thankful to have reconnected with Thomas and to have shared in his catharsis.

---

5. The show in question was *Folk i farta* ("People on the Move"), a series of profiles of Norwegians living and working abroad that was hosted by Alex Rosén and produced by NRK1, Norway's oldest and most popular television network. The treatment of subjects was often lightly comic and sometimes controversial. The two half-hour episodes concerning Thomas were broadcast on March 5 and March 12 of 2009 and are still available for viewing online. A search for "Tangvald Folk i farta" will lead you straight to them.

As for Thomas, Christina recalled later that there was "a whole new aura in him" when he returned home to Vieques, "like a part of him was clean and in peace and much happier."

THE LAST OF THE RECKONINGS Thomas navigated in the long wake of Gaston's birth was perhaps more sublime. It was not as dramatic as the diving expedition to Bonaire, but it was certainly more typical, something most of us do—taking a new child to meet extended family. But there was a twist. The family members in question were not Thomas's Tangvald relations in Norway, but his Balta relations, his mother's family in France, Belgium, and Germany.

The connection, long lost, was made not long before Thomas left for Bonaire. His mother Lydia's father, the old French Catholic missionary Gustave, now aged 81, had been bitter after his daughter took off with Peter Tangvald and was shot to death on his boat. He did not like to be reminded of the tragedy and had largely written off the Tangvalds, including Thomas, his grandson. But he relented when he somehow received word that Gaston, a great-grandson, had been born. Now he reached out to Thomas, and in spring of the following year he paid for the family to fly to Europe to meet him.

Thomas had always disparaged the concept of a vacation. He wondered how anyone could settle for a life so miserable and mundane that they felt it necessary to take a break and get away from it. But for Christina, at least, the family trip to Europe became one of the highlights of her time with Thomas. He had always been a very busy person, wholly engrossed in whatever project of the moment he was focused on, and now at last he had a chance to relax a bit.

"I finally really had time to enjoy my husband as a husband and father," Christina later wrote. "He was always working! Always!!! Being unable to work made him so much closer to me and Gaston, and we spent really nice days just enjoying nature and life, food, family and actually resting. It was very healthy for Thomas to have time like this."

The family first flew together to Paris, where they visited two of Thomas's aunts, Lydia's sisters. Thomas, Christina remembered, was particularly interested in some Roma gypsies they met at the base of the Eiffel Tower. They carried on to Dijon, where they stayed with Gustave in a house both Christina and Thomas agreed had an unusual aura about it. Gustave, it turned out, shared with Thomas a taste for weird electronic music and had a small studio where he created and composed music of his own. He also was an author of science-fiction novels. Christina was very struck by the old man.

"I have never met such a magical person in all my living, conscious life," she wrote. "He was so mysterious, yet friendly, enchanting in a way that gave you the creeps."

From Dijon the family traveled into Germany to meet another aunt, then on to Belgium to visit Lydia's only brother, Patrick Balta. Patrick, like Thomas, was an avid sailor and was also a professional yacht designer, so the two had a great deal to talk about. They spent hours poring over designs and computer files together. Patrick had lots of advice for Thomas and shared with him several computer programs he'd spent years developing. Christina, meanwhile, appreciated that Patrick's home had lots of toys and a big play area that was of great interest to Gaston.

Finally the family went on to Andorra to visit Clare and Edward. For Christina this was the most relaxing part of the trip, as she enjoyed the tiny nation where Spanish was often heard and spoken and also felt quite comfortable around the Allcards. Clare was very impressed with Christina and was pleased Thomas had ended up with a woman who cared for him and seemed to ground him so well.

The visit in Andorra also gave Thomas a chance to reconnect with his old tutor and mentor, Don Madden, the retired European Space Agency physicist, a man for whom he still felt great respect and affection. Don came over to the Allcards' house to visit with Thomas and family a couple of times and was struck by how normal and convivial these encounters seemed. He remembered Thomas as being very solitary, reserved, and wary, and he had been astonished when Clare told him Thomas had married.

"I was very pleased he'd got to the stage of meeting somebody and marrying them and having a family," Don later recalled. "I wasn't sure he could have that kind of intimate relationship with other people. I was surprised when I heard about it, and then he appeared here and I met them, and everything was nice. It was easy. I was very glad he was apparently stable and happy."

# 10. ESCAPE FROM BABYLON

WITH A WIFE AND SON to provide for, with a nice piece of property and a house to call his own on Vieques, it did seem that Thomas had achieved some measure of stability. He inevitably put a great deal of effort into building his house, crafting and constructing it as carefully as he would a boat. It was dirt simple, with plywood cladding and galvanized tin roofing, water caught and plumbed from cisterns, and a trickle of power run in from a pirated electrical connection. But it was an elegant structure—an open air, open concept "eco-chalet," as Thomas termed it. It was framed above and below in hardwood, not cheap pine, each floor beam was carefully buttressed, and there were three heavy galvanized wire stays—a very sailorly touch—running at a wide angle from roof to ground to hold everything in place in hurricane-strength winds.

On the grounds surrounding the house, Thomas also had a chance to properly exercise his green thumb. He had been keenly interested in horticulture ever since university, back when he grew cannabis and mushrooms in his room. During his years afloat at Culebra he'd struggled to grow plants that interested him in pots on the decks of the various boats he inhabited, as he was generally thwarted by the biting breeze and burning salt air. Even before he'd built the house in Monte Carmelo, Thomas had anticipated cultivating the property and was raising favored flowers in pots. In a letter to the Allcards, he boasted of an exotic flowering Brugmansia plant he'd nurtured from a cutting, with an amazing fragrance emitted only at night. He ultimately planted this upwind of the house, together with some wild flowering Plumeria, which was fragrant by day. "That way as the days progress, the house is always smelling of flowers," he explained, "but the smell keeps changing so it never gets dull."

Thomas, characteristically, was also interested in agriculture and wanted very much to grow food. His goal was to be as self-sufficient as possible. He thought of the property as a "micro-farm" and on it grew, among other things, tomatoes, corn, peppers, ginger, okra (known in Puerto Rico as guingambo), avocados, and coconuts. One neighbor, Elisabeth Pouplard, an older Frenchwoman, remembered he made his own hot sauce from his red peppers. "To me it was not edible, really like liquid fire," she recalled, "but he loved it."

Thomas also kept chickens for the eggs and developed a sophisticated "aquaponics" system, wherein he kept fish and used the nutrient-rich water they lived in to sustain plants grown hydroponically. The plants in turn cleaned the water for the fish, in what Thomas described as "ecosystem replication under strictly controlled conditions." One of his favored consultants in orchestrating all this was his old friend and surrogate dad Elm Van Pelt, from Boquerón, who had by now moved ashore into a house in the hills behind the bay and was well versed in organic farming techniques.

In addition to feeding his family, Thomas also made a bit of money off his farm, selling excess produce and plants at the weekly street market, a trick he found quite gratifying. "I [am] fairly amazed," he wrote, "at just how much money can be made with just a few plants." Christina meanwhile, soon after the family first came to Vieques, had purchased an old step-van and with Thomas's help converted it to a food truck. Operating as "Pasta Rasta," she sold pasta dishes, fried food, and hot dogs. "For drinks we sell bottled water, which is all the rage nowadays," wrote Thomas to the Allcards, "and the mark-up is sensational—about 500%!—and

I brew tea in gallons, which I then freeze, as well as fresh-squeezed lemonade, and it sells!"

Thomas also still made a bit of money here and there working on boats and began more actively nurturing a dream that he might someday make a living actually designing boats. He designed and built on spec a small pram in plywood and managed thus to attract at least one order to build another. He started up a website, t3-boats.com, to publicize his skills and availability, and through the site he connected with a potential client in Argentina, a wealthy man who was thinking he might like to build a custom 100-foot motor yacht. Though he knew this was very much a long shot, Thomas happily developed a detailed preliminary design. Nothing came of this, but Thomas shared the design with a few interested friends and hoped if he kept pushing he might eventually land a real commission.

BUT THERE WAS A FLY in this ointment. Living on shore in a more established situation, Thomas had more regular access to the Internet and to news of the outside world, and his active, inquisitive mind chewed on this like a terrier with a bone. He had always been at odds with modern society and now had little trouble marshaling evidence to support his view that it was on an unsustainable trajectory. The bald conclusion he had reached at the end of his university years, that there were simply too many people on the planet, was now folded into a more sophisticated analysis of humanity's fate.

It all came down to energy and food, Thomas figured. Industrial society was entirely dependent on fossil fuels, a finite resource, and based on his research he did not see how renewable alternative energy sources could possibly replace them. "A typical reaction is 'I'm sure they'll think of something,' which is about the least useful response possible," he wrote. "This not only downplays the gravity of the situation, but also reveals humanity's hubris and arrogance."

His gravest concern was that the food production required to support the world's enormous load of humans was especially reliant on fossil fuels.

"Depending on which study you read, between 10 and 14 calories of fossil fuel energy goes into producing one calorie of food," he explained. "This is less than parity ERoEI (energy returned on energy invested), which is clearly untenable, but which has permitted, temporarily, for us to vastly exceed the earth's normal carrying capacity."

Compounding this grim assessment was the dramatic unfolding of recent current events. Like many others, Thomas saw the U.S. invasion of Iraq in 2003 and American conduct there, replete with tortured prisoners and rank incompetence, as fundamentally immoral. Just five years later, in the summer of 2008, the entire global economy was teetering on the brink after the insanely inflated American mortgage-securities market suddenly collapsed. In Puerto Rico, as elsewhere, this had very palpable effects. Tourism slowed to a trickle. Thousands of government workers were laid off. Strikes in protest paralyzed the main island for several days. For an intelligent soul such as Thomas, it was easy enough to worry about what might come next.

Thomas's mind during this time was bubbling over with opinions and ideas about the state of the world on both a micro and macro level, and he was very eager to share them. His e-mails to the Allcards, for example, were peppered with conclusive proclamations and various Internet links to articles, videos, and podcasts on such subjects as economics, the environment, agribusiness, genetically modified food, energy production, exotic toads, and flower pollination. He ultimately decided he must harness all this in some constructive way and made a presumptive announcement: he would write a book! "That way instead of wasting so much hot air boring people with my ramblings, those that are actually interested can just read them," he wrote to Clare in an e-mail entitled "An emerging thot."

Just a couple of months later, it seemed he was making good progress. "I was hung up about not knowing how to type correctly," he wrote, "yet I somehow managed to whack out 17,000 words just over the last week and a half!" And he worked up a list of chapter headings:

> Money dynamics
> Biology and economy
> Energy
> Agriculture and water
> Historical snippets
> Holistic health, medicine and witchcraft
> Perspectives on the future

"Should keep me out of trouble for a while," he noted. He soon excerpted a portion of his burgeoning manuscript as a report he entitled "Tipping Point" and sent it around to a few friends. In it he concluded, "We may be close to a global systemic collapse in our economy and by extension our civilization."

When he was younger Thomas had been content to simply observe the unfolding of humanity's dark future, but now he decided he must take action. "I had something of an epiphany," he later wrote. "I realized we must move to Brazil." It seemed a startling conclusion, but Thomas had his reasons. Some were coldly rational. As he pointed out in one e-mail to Clare, Puerto Rico had 411 inhabitants per square kilometer, while Brazil had only 20, and while Brazil was largely self-sufficient when it came to food, Puerto Rico had to import over 80% of its food. The Puerto

Rican economy was suffering badly in the Great Recession, while Brazil's economy was comparatively much stronger. "So there is not too much of a mystery why I'm anxious to move," he asserted.

But some of Thomas's other reasons for wanting to emigrate seemed less rational. In urging that the southern hemisphere was the safest place to be, he sent Clare a video link that featured a left-leaning Canadian policy wonk gravely predicting that the United States would soon start World War III by attacking Iran. When Clare protested that he was scaremongering, Thomas demurred but did not back down.

"You are absolutely right, and I am sorry if I gave you the impression of trying to scare you," he wrote. "However, for a variety of reasons I do think the specter of major war is becoming more probable.... The US's psychopathic-megalomaniacal attitude and behaviour is something that is real and getting more and more out of hand by the day."

Ironically, too, just as his father once worried about Thomas's own "street rat" proclivities when he was younger, Thomas now started fretting over how "the influence of Americana" might affect his toddler son. He complained of the rampant materialism and popular "Bronx bad-boy gangster" youth culture and concluded: "If we were to stay here it would be almost impossible to prevent him picking up the manners."

None of this in fact was very prevalent on Vieques—a small, relatively isolated island with only 9,000 inhabitants on the outermost edge of the American empire—but Thomas did have a positive vision of what life in Brazil might be like. He was not unhappy with the life he and Christina had built on Vieques and wanted simply to transplant and expand upon it in what he felt was a much more secure location. There were vast quantities of vacant public land in Brazil, and farmers there were tacitly and sometimes actively encouraged to usurp and develop it. The rights of squatters living on neglected private land were also being strongly reinforced by the then left-leaning government. Thomas thus saw himself on a larger, more productive self-sustaining farm, obtained hopefully at little or no cost, feeding his family, perhaps starting some sort of business, and designing yachts on the side.

And of course it was perfectly obvious how he should get his family to Brazil.

"For most of my life I have lived on, and owned boats," he explained in a magazine article he later wrote. "Now we had to find another one and sail her to Brazil. With such a mobile home we would have all the time in the world to carefully explore the country's immense coastline and find the perfect place for us."


THERE WAS ONE OTHER more pedestrian reason why Thomas was eager to move his family to Brazil: he wanted to get his wife and child away from his mother-in-law. He did not perceive Christina's mother Missy as being a "wicked" person—"quite the contrary," he insisted. But he did feel Missy was "addicted to stress," always worried and complaining about things, and full of "negative energy." Though he and Christina lived a good distance from Missy's home on the main island, Christina and Gaston often went to visit, sometimes for protracted periods, and Thomas resented this. He also believed that Gaston had a tendency to urinate "in totally inappropriate places when being flooded with female attention."

"[Thomas] had no problem in saying it," Christina remembered. "He wanted to take me away as far as he could from my mother. He used to say that once women married they belonged to their husbands and no longer to their mothers. I just laughed at his crazy possessive remarks and made jokes about it, but he was dead serious!"

Still Christina's sense of adventure and her desire to go voyaging with Thomas had not diminished, and she was willing to sail with him to Brazil. "Why NOT go along for this ride?" she later wrote. "Life at sea, new cultures, new foods... then search for land to buy by the beach to make a dream house with our babies? A dream come true! I am always in for building and creating and for the romantic side of LIVING!"

Thomas started searching for a boat very early in 2010 and at first had little luck. His requirements were particular. He wanted a boat that would not cost much money but was also very rugged and could sail well to windward. It was a long way from Puerto Rico to Brazil, about 1,300 miles to the nearest corner of that vast nation, and over all that distance Thomas and his family would be sailing mostly upwind, against the strong tropical tradewinds.

As Thomas himself noted: "Boat hunting can be frustrating for a boat snob like me." He looked at and dismissed a few worn-out fiberglass boats, and then, on January 12, learned that a well-known nativo racing sloop named *Oasis* was for sale. For Thomas this was an incredibly appealing opportunity. *Oasis* was a full-size nativo, 34 feet long, not a mini, like his old *Buenadaga*. She was built in wood in 1981, framed in mahogany from the El Yunque rainforest, by Thomas's old acquaintance Don Gelo, the recognized master of nativo builders. Many believed *Oasis* was the finest boat Don Gelo had ever created.

"I was incredulous; this was my favorite of them all!" Thomas later wrote. "I vividly remember admiring it when I was a young teenager and had already decided back then that it was the best example of all the Puerto Rican nativo sloops." As he explained in an e-mail at the time: "It is definitely the best proportioned of all the nativos. Perfectly fair, which is astounding given none of these boats are built to lines plans."

The owner of *Oasis* wanted $12,000 for her, which was money

Thomas did not have, and over the next few months he scrambled to raise it. He and Christina had already decided to sell the lake house at Guajataca to help finance their move to Brazil, and now this took on added urgency. Thomas was anxious to sell the house before its value declined below the amount of the loan they'd taken out against it. "It's happening to a lot of people," he noted grimly, "and it is a nightmare situation." He also remembered the painting of his father's that Simonne was holding for him, the old portrait of Norway's early 19th-century French-born king, Jean Bernadotte.

This was supposed to be valuable and was the last significant asset from Peter Tangvald's meager fortune. Thomas had been forced to spend the modest inheritance he received from Peter's estate on bail bonds and legal fees, back when he was harassed by the police on Culebra, and he'd always been upset about this. He knew his father would not have approved, but now he figured his father would certainly approve of his using this last piece of his legacy to help buy a boat to take his family on a voyage. So Thomas wrote to Simonne, asking her to sell the Bernadotte painting and send him the proceeds. Simonne, who was by now failing and in poor health, was enraged by this. For her it seemed the very last in a long line of Tangvald betrayals, and in a fit of spite she burned the painting. Thomas was enraged in turn when he learned this and never communicated with Simonne again. It was a very sad end to what had once been for him a nurturing and supportive relationship.

Finally, in the summer of 2010, the lake house sold. The loan against it was paid off, and Thomas took some of the proceeds, $10,000 in cash that he stashed in a cigar box, and went to the small harbor of Naguabo on the southeast coast of the main island, where *Oasis* was moored. In the end, after what Thomas later described as a long conversation "about how hyperbolically astounding the boat was," the owner accepted the tempting pile of cash. Thomas hoisted anchor as soon as he had the bill of sale in hand and sailed the boat back to Vieques. Once there he stashed *Oasis* in a tight, well-protected bay called Puerto Ferro on the island's south coast, just in time to save her from an oncoming Category 4 hurricane, Earl, that passed just north of Puerto Rico on August 31.

Soon afterward Thomas wrote an e-mail to his oldest friend, Agnita Twigt, his Dutch playmate from when he was just six years old in Martinique, with whom he'd recently reconnected online. She, like Thomas, was very interested in sustainable living and hoped humanity might somehow find its way to a stable post-capitalist future.

"I bought the *Oasis*," he declared triumphantly. "We now have a boat to escape Babylon. There is still much work to be done, but things are coming together very well."

BOTH AT THE TIME and later, in retrospect, there were those who believed that sailing a nativo sloop from Puerto Rico to Brazil, some 1,300 hard miles upwind, was not a wise idea. These boats are closewinded, with very deep keels, and do sail well to windward, but they are also very low-slung, with little freeboard, and were not designed for long-distance ocean sailing. Agnita Twigt, on learning that Thomas planned to move to Brazil, had put him in touch with an old friend of hers, an experienced bluewater sailor from Sweden named Anders Eriksson, who once had sailed to Brazil himself and settled there for 10 years. Anders was impressed with Thomas and gave him some advice on immigrating to Brazil, but he was concerned about *Oasis*.

"I just saw a few pictures, but it's not the kind of boat I would choose for what he was planning to do," Anders later recalled. "He seemed to be very sensitive to my opinions about his boat. I had a feeling it was a touchy subject."

Patrick Balta, Thomas's yacht-designer uncle, was also quite critical and later explained he felt it was grossly irresponsible of Thomas to take a wife and child to sea in such a "DIY" boat with no engine or lifelines around the deck to help keep crew on board.

But what Thomas proposed to do was not without precedent. His old friend Morgan MacDonald, a credentialed naval architect, was, like Thomas, an aficionado of Puerto Rican nativos and once had converted one into a bluewater cruising boat. This was a boat named *Colibri*, the nativo Don Gelo had built just prior to *Oasis*, which Morgan had purchased in 1980 when she was just nine months old. He cut down the boat's oversized racing rig, built a cabinhouse on deck, installed interior accommodations, but never bothered to install an engine or any lifelines. Morgan was living and cruising aboard this boat the very first time he met Thomas in 1985 in Grenada, soon after Thomas, his father, and his sister Carmen arrived there after losing Ann overboard.[1] Morgan subsequently sailed *Colibri* from the Caribbean to New England and back and was still living on the boat with his wife Mandy when he again encountered the Tangvalds on *L'Artemis de Pytheas* in Culebra in 1988, not very long after Florence left Peter. In Tangvaldian style, Morgan's first child, a son named Tristan, had also been born aboard *Colibri*, at anchor in the British Virgin Islands, in August 1987.

So it was that Thomas, in a similar manner, set out to convert *Oasis* to his purposes. He first started working on the boat on Vieques while simultaneously continuing to perfect the Monte Carmelo house so it could be sold. But the boat work went slowly, and by the end of that year Thomas had made little progress. To speed things along he decided to shift his base of operations. He

---

1. Though this was the first time Morgan met Thomas, he had met Peter Tangvald at least once before, during the early 1970s, also in Grenada. Morgan at that time was a young man working for his uncle, Don Street, the famous American yachtsman, author, and chart surveyor.

had a friend with a house on the water at Guayama on Bahia de Jobos, a calm, sheltered bay on the south shore of the main island. Thomas arranged to rent this, rented out the Vieques house, and in early January 2011 with a load of clothing, tools, and lumber sailed *Oasis* with Christina and Gaston over to Guayama.[2]

It proved a perfect place to work on the boat. It was just a short walk from the rented house to where the boat was kept. There was a covered basketball court nearby, an ideal spot to lay out sails. There was even a sunken sailboat in the bay, with its mast canted over the water at a steep angle so that Thomas could use it as a fixed crane to lift his own mast out with a block and tackle. Over the next several months, he succeeded in converting *Oasis* from an over-canvassed open-cockpit racing sloop to a very crude but beautiful cruising boat. He first lowered the cockpit floorboards to increase interior space and extended the floor into the bow and stern of the boat. He next built a small cabinhouse over the cockpit directly behind the mast and cut in some deck hatches to help keep things cool below.

The interior accommodations were excruciatingly simple. Up forward Thomas tacked in a small bunk berth for Gaston to sleep in, and in the middle of the boat, on either side of a narrow open passage leading up to Gaston's space in the bow, he built six open storage bays. A simple galley was installed just under the companionway hatch at the back of the cabinhouse, and this, when the hatch was open, was the only space inside where it was possible for Thomas to stand up straight. The master stateroom, such as it was, was in the very back of the boat, in the slit-trench space under the aft deck, where Thomas and Christina could lay flat side by side with just a few inches of clearance overhead.

---

2. Thomas and Christina produced and published a short YouTube video of this brief passage, entitled "Trip to Guayama," that is still online. Thomas had hoped to create a film of their voyage to Brazil, but nothing came of this scheme.

As Thomas later noted: "The advantage with this sort of boat is that the modifications can be made rough and ready and it doesn't clash with what is already there."

The biggest job was modifying the rig. This involved first pulling out the 56-foot mast, which was originally, as is common on nativos, an aluminum light pole. Removing all the existing stainless steel hardware, fastened with screws now seized tight with corrosion, proved an awful ordeal. "There was only so much I could do per day," Thomas later wrote, "as the huge effort would tear the calluses off my hands." He next cut eight feet off each end of the mast, then laminated custom wooden plugs to fit in at the top and bottom. He also cut eight feet off the 37-foot wood boom and built a 14-foot gaff spar, so as to convert the once triangular Marconi mainsail to a more traditional quadrilateral gaff sail with a lower center of effort. Finally, after re-rigging and re-stepping the shorter mast, Thomas cut down the existing sails to fit them to the new spars, carefully saving all the sail edges and corners so he could reinstall them in their new positions. The end result was a more than 25 percent reduction in the boat's sail area, from 1,150 to 850 square feet.

In the midst of all this work, in August 2011, Christina learned that she was pregnant again. On the one hand, this was good news, as this had always been part of Thomas's master plan—that he and Christina would have another child soon after reaching Brazil, a so-called "anchor baby," and this would ease their path to Brazilian citizenship. On the other hand, they hadn't planned on Christina becoming pregnant quite so soon, and now they were suddenly confronted with a hard deadline. The baby was due in early May, and they had less than eight months to get to Brazil.

"There was still plenty of work to do on the boat," Thomas later wrote, "plus the actual sailing there, so it certainly put the pressure on."

THERE WAS YET ANOTHER PROBLEM, which was Thomas's continuing fondness for alcohol. Christina had been coping with this since the beginning of their relationship, always encouraging Thomas to drink less, with varying degrees of success. He was very much a sexual creature, and this did give her some leverage.

"I told him I could smell the alcohol so strong in his breath and his body sweat, that it was not pleasing and interfered with my desire for him," she recalled. And she learned it was wise to carry a thermos of tea and a bottle of hot sauce with her, "like milk bottles for babies," to feed to him instead of rum.

Christina also noted that Thomas tended to drink less when he was living on shore, away from boats. Though there were some lapses, he had remained relatively sober during the time they lived in the house on Vieques. But after they moved to Guayama and Thomas started working on *Oasis* full time, he started drinking regularly again. It got much worse in May, after the family moved out of their rented house into the cramped quarters on *Oasis*. Thomas again was getting crazy drunk and falling hard asleep, impossible to wake, in all sorts of crazy places. This presented Christina with a dilemma. She had always been very protective of Thomas, had always felt a strong desire to care for and mother him, but now she also had a child to care for.

"I almost did not make the trip to Brazil," she later wrote, "because I was so tired of his drinking I wanted to separate."

Christina left Thomas for a while alone in Guayama and retreated with Gaston to a house that belonged to one of her sisters. It was there she discovered she was pregnant.

"I thought it was God's sign of wanting me back with Thomas and doing the trip!" she remembered. "I went back to him for some days without Gaston and told him the news of the second child. He cried like a little boy he was so touched by it. Still his drinking never became less."

It wasn't until the very end of October that Thomas and family at last sailed *Oasis* out of Guayama. They stopped first at Salinas, just a few miles west, where Thomas spent a few days making money working on some of the yachts that often gathered there. Then it was on to Vieques, where Christina and Thomas went to work putting away their life on shore, selling those possessions that had value, throwing away others that didn't, paring it all down to what was essential and could fit on the boat. Thomas remembered there was "much wrangling and harrumphing" when Christina insisted on trying to bring too much stuff, but that finally they "managed to get the boat tolerably well stowed."

Ideally Christina and Thomas would have sold their house on Vieques before taking off for Brazil, so as to have a bit of capital in hand for starting their new life there. There was also more work to do on the boat. But with Christina's slowly swelling belly bringing them each day closer to the birth of their next child, they didn't have time to wait for a buyer for the house to appear. They left the house listed for sale and hoped for the best, and Thomas figured he could keep working on the boat as they island-hopped their way through the Caribbean towards Brazil.

They finally departed Vieques in late November. Their neighbor Elisabeth Pouplard later remembered sitting on the top floor of her house with her partner, watching *Oasis* sail away east in the distance toward the Virgin Islands. "Their boat looked so tiny it gave us a shock," she wrote. "We were wondering if we'd ever see them again."

Once again Thomas was realizing the dream that had animated so much of his life—the dream he had put on hold, intentionally or not, when he got so badly bogged down on Culebra; the dream his wife Christina had agreed to share with him. He was voyaging again. He had a boat under his feet. He had the wind in his sails, and before him lay an open horizon.

But in the months to come, as *Oasis* made her way across the arc of the Lesser Antilles, it seemed the dream was going sour. It certainly didn't help that the boat was so small. Years earlier, when Thomas sailed *Melody*, an even smaller boat, across the Atlantic, he had been alone and much younger. The physical discomfort meant nothing to him. But now, sailing with a family, the contrast in size between the boat he grew up on, 50 feet in length, and his current boat, some 16 feet shorter, was significant.

For Gaston, now four years old, who had not been reared on a boat as Thomas had, this meant a dramatic shrinking of his home life. He lived wedged up in the bow, a much smaller space than that which Thomas had inhabited on *L'Artemis de Pytheas*, and when the boat was sailing, plunging and crashing through the water, he was very aware he was the tip of the spear. As he later explained in a grim voice: "If we ever hit a ship, I would be the first to die."

Like his father before him, Gaston was never allowed on deck while the boat was underway, and his physical existence was thus constrained into the boat's interior, a space not much larger than a walk-in closet. But unlike his father at the same age, Gaston could remember a previous existence, on land, and he longed to get back to it. Throughout the months on *Oasis*, he announced repeatedly he wanted to return home to live with his grandmother. Whenever the family was ashore somewhere and he found a piece of flotsam to play with, Gaston would pretend it was a boat and push off for Puerto Rico.

Christina recalled: "He kept telling me: 'Sorry, Mom, I love you, but I am leaving for Missy.'"

Christina was torn. She had expected the trip would be tough, but she loved the excitement of visiting new places and a part of her still thrilled to the sensations of life afloat. She did suffer while the boat was underway, enduring hours lying in her berth, seasick and pregnant, without even room to sit up, throwing up and relieving herself in the same bucket they used to bail out the boat. But she found some solace in her galley, the domestic center of the boat, where she could stand beneath the companionway and breathe clean air. She also spent time with Gaston, home-schooling him and doing art projects. On deck meanwhile Thomas was scrambling about—like "a one-man circus," as Christina later described it—sailing the boat on his own, with no harness or lifelines to help keep him aboard.

"So many times I thought of what would happen if he went overboard!" Christina later wrote. "It would be the end of me and my poor baby, brought along on a trip he really did not enjoy. I was ignorant and stubborn, but I needed to do this trip. I would not give up."

Even for Thomas it now seemed the allure of the cruising life was fading. He did still enjoy the bluewater sailing community and his notoriety within it. As he and his family crossed the Caribbean, they were treated almost like royalty by certain sailors and spent many hours visiting aboard other boats. Thomas often met people who knew him or had known and respected his father, and he appreciated this. But he was also, Christina remembered, growing tired of the relentless grind of maintaining and working on a boat with such limited resources.

After departing Vieques, *Oasis* stopped first at Charlotte Amalie in St. Thomas for some time, and here again Thomas's drinking was an issue. This was home base for Thomas's friend Morgan MacDonald, and he set Thomas up with a famous local character, Manfred Dittrich, a traditional sailmaker, originally from Germany, who was based on Hassel Island, an idyllic oasis just across the harbor from the main town. Thomas needed proper reef points installed on his cut-down sails but had little cash, so Manfred agreed to a work exchange. It helped of course that Manfred had crossed paths with and had befriended Peter Tangvald, back when they were both young men cruising the Caribbean in the 1960s.

"I did not realize Thomas was drinking heavily at the time, and Thomas had difficulty fulfilling his side of the bargain," Morgan later wrote. "Ultimately, Manfred was unhappy I had brought Thomas into his circle."

To Morgan it seemed Thomas was depressed and also quite stressed. "The time-frame he had set up for himself was very, very optimistic, and he had a family he was trying to feed, and he was short of money," he remembered. "He also had his father's very high standard for himself that he wasn't living up to."

It was indeed supremely ironic that Thomas now, consciously or unconsciously, was mimicking the crisis in his father's life that had led to his own birth. Just as Peter Tangvald had raced across the Indian Ocean with a heavily pregnant wife on his way to a new opportunity, here was Thomas "racing the clock, or rather the fetus," as he himself described it, on his way to Brazil and the ideal existence he imagined he would find there.

As for Christina, she was captivated by Manfred's compound on Hassel Island. "It was like a story book!" she wrote. "Gaston and I had magical days there. The smell of the sea inside the garden, the kitchen that felt like a sunken pirate boat. The meals with German sausage every night, and the parrot who had her own chair and plate at the dinner table!"

But Thomas's drinking, she noted, "ruined some of the greatness of it."

Morgan recalled that Thomas sometimes behaved abusively toward Christina when he was drunk. For Christina the near breaking point came when Thomas went ashore in the dinghy to

Manfred's yard one evening with her laptop computer to check his e-mail. He never returned, and in the morning she hitched a ride ashore to find him "dead drunk asleep on the ground." He was soaking wet, as it had rained during the night, and her computer was ruined.

"I was so mad I remember being SO close to leaving him!" she later wrote. "I even asked for help to get to the airport, but then because of love, I guess, or my interest in getting to Brazil, I stayed."

Christina remembered also that in St. Thomas some kind soul tried to give Thomas an EPIRB to take along on the voyage. This was a relatively small battery-powered electronic device, an Emergency Position Indicating Radio Beacon, that when activated sent an automatic SOS signal, complete with GPS position coordinates, via satellite to search-and-rescue authorities on shore. Most modern sailors wouldn't think of sailing offshore without one of these, and to Christina it did seem like a very valuable bit of gear to have onboard. But Thomas, channeling his father no doubt, disdained it and refused the offer, claiming the device would take up too much room on the boat.

FROM CHARLOTTE AMALIE Thomas and family sailed on to Jost Van Dyke, the "Island of Love" where Thomas and Christina had cemented their connection six years earlier. They stayed here for a couple of weeks, as Thomas found paid work to do on other boats, had more work to do on *Oasis*, and got a commission from Foxy Callwood to build some special trophy shelves in his bar. But once again his drinking drove Christina away from him.

"[H]is drinking made me feel so helpless and alone!" she later wrote, and for a time she moved off the boat with Gaston into a small cabin that belonged to her old boss Wendell, Foxy's son.

While at Jost, Thomas met another sailor, the writer Fatty Goodlander. This was the man who had worried so about Thomas's father and his sister Carmen when he met them in St. John in early 1991, just months before the shipwreck in Bonaire, while Thomas was living aboard his little boat *Spartan* on his own. Foxy's wife Tessa had asked Fatty to speak with Thomas, as she was worried about his behavior and his drinking. Once Fatty realized who Thomas was, he too became very worried. Here it was happening all over again: Thomas following his father down a seemingly self-destructive path, on a boat that to Fatty looked a bit like a joke, with a child and pregnant wife in tow.

"He had this understandably strange relationship with his father," Fatty remembered. "On the one hand he was in awe of his father, and on the other hand he had big problems with his father. He'd say stuff like: I'm doing this on my boat; my father could do this in 10 minutes and I've worked on it three days. He was always singing his father's praises and putting himself down."

Very soon, after the New Year of 2012 rolled in, Thomas sailed alone on a short hop over to Tortola, hoping to get *Oasis* hauled out for a bottom job. But the boatyard he had in mind was closed, as the owner had recently suffered a stroke. Here Christina and Gaston rejoined him, and from Tortola the family sailed together to St. John, in the U.S. Virgin Islands, where Thomas spent some time temporarily patching a leak in the hull with some epoxy putty. From there it was on to St. Martin, the family's first hard beat to weather in truly open water, 80 miles across the rugged Anegada Passage, a taste of what was to come.

Thomas remembered one wave that struck the bow so hard "the entire boat shook from end to end and all sorts of apparently well stored items below were sent scattering fore and aft."

"I threw up so much I thought I would die," Christina later

wrote. "My poor Gaston was like a dead little leaf lying on the floor."

*Oasis* spent some two months at St. Martin, a half-Dutch, half-French island—over-developed and over-populated—with many facilities, most particularly for boats. Here Thomas easily found work on what he described as "luxury yachts" and earned enough to have *Oasis* hauled out for a bottom job at the Time Out Boat Yard, just outside Marigot, the main town on the French side.

The family was left with some fond memories of St. Martin. Christina, Thomas wrote, was "blown away" by the genuine French pastry on offer in Marigot. A trip to the famous Maho Beach on the Dutch side, directly adjacent to one end of the airport runway, was an exhilarating experience for Gaston, as arriving jumbo jets blasted by just a few feet overhead. Christina, who had "a passion for the circus life," as she put it, also insisted the family put on a show at the boatyard, performing a "true Sea Gypsy Circus as the Sailing Tangvald Family." All three dressed in fanciful costumes— Christina now so pregnant she was bulging out of hers—and put on some magic and music, with stunts by Thomas hanging from the mast, bare-chested in gold lamé trousers and a blue paisley vest.

But by far the biggest treat for both Christina and Gaston came when Missy flew in from Puerto Rico and put the family up in a hotel for several days.

"My mom's visit was such a great joy!" Christina later wrote. "Hotel, pool, restaurants, and BATHS!!! My mom almost cried to see how dirty both Gaston and I were. We did take baths in the boat yard with buckets and a hose, but I guess that wasn't good enough."

BY THE TIME THE FAMILY left St. Martin it was late March and Christina, as Patrick Balta later noted with some disdain, was "pregnant up to her eyeballs." The new baby was due in less than six weeks. Thomas steered first for Barbuda, some 70 miles across open water to the southeast, where the family anchored for a while but had difficulty getting ashore due to "the enormous crashing surf." From there it was a short hop to neighboring Antigua, then came a longer leg, some 100 miles bypassing the French island of Guadeloupe, to Dominica. Here Christina went to the local market and topped up on fresh food. Thomas, who navigated with no electronics, as his father had before him, checked the accuracy of his sextant as he prepared now to sail out of sight of land for days on end. Finally, on April 9, he hoisted anchor, sailed around the north end of Dominica, and set out for South America.

He later wrote: "The sun [was] beating down hard on the azure seas, and we watched as the lush mountains of Dominica slowly faded into the distance."

But now there was some debate as to where exactly in South America they should aim for. Back in St. Martin, Christina and Thomas had befriended another couple who had sailed up to the Caribbean on a cruise from Guyana on their boat. They had a place down there, on the Essequibo River, and had extolled its virtues. The living was cheap, they claimed, and land could be had practically for free. Christina had seized on this as an attractive alternative destination, as Guyana was three whole countries closer than Brazil, about 550 instead of 900 miles distant from Dominica. Thomas had initially dissembled when Christina continually urged they should change their plan. But two days out from Dominica, seeing how miserable his wife was, he at last relented and reluctantly assured her he would steer for Guyana.

"Christina is a sport," he wrote, "but she had only ever done daysails with me, and she was not doing well on these longer trips."

Thomas later described the voyage as a sailor would, in terms of sailing angles and daily runs. He was in his element now and wouldn't think of letting a drop of rum pass his lips. Drinking on shore was bad enough, but drinking on passage was sacrilege, an insult to his father's memory. With the wind blowing steadily from the east, he kept *Oasis* closehauled on port tack sailing southeast, shaping his course to keep the wind as close to his bow as possible. When the wind shifted too far toward the south, he tacked over, but these shifts, he noted, never lasted too long. With the sails properly trimmed and the tiller tied off, *Oasis* mostly sailed herself. Thomas was pleased and proud that she was so fast, covering between 120 and 170 miles every day, save for two when the wind died and the mainsail slammed about angrily as the boat rolled back and forth.

Christina and Gaston were mostly seasick at first, and to ease their suffering Thomas reefed the sails and slowed the boat down whenever the seas got too steep. Thomas later claimed he was "de-facto singlehanding" on this passage, but Christina did take some turns standing watch. She stood her watches mostly at night, so Thomas could sleep, and sat quietly in the companionway keeping an eye on things. She sang to herself to stay awake and was afraid to venture out on deck. There was no cockpit to sit in, as all of the deck aft of the cabinhouse was flush with no footwell. There were no lifelines, only a shallow strip of gunwale rimming the edge of the deck, and she was very afraid of falling overboard. When she was below and heard Thomas working on deck, she tried hard not to think about the awful predicament she'd be in if he fell overboard.

Each day at local noon, when the sun was highest in the sky, Thomas got out his sextant and took sights. He recalled that Christina at these times was ever anxious and impatient, asking again and again how far they had sailed and how much longer it would take to reach Guyana. "I would say that the current was stronger than I had thought," he later wrote, "or that it was hard to estimate, because I can't guess what the wind will do tomorrow, or I would just say we'll get there when we get there, stop asking me that!"

Five days out of Dominica, Thomas had noted that *Oasis* passed through huge mats of Sargasso weed. These were yellow-brown islands of bubbly plant tendrils, teeming with marine life, which stood out brightly against the vivid blue ocean water. Some days later the color of the water shifted from the gorgeous blue to a dull green. Eventually the seas decreased, the boat's motion grew easier, and Christina was emboldened to sit outside in the afternoons. Gaston, when he wasn't sleeping, playing with Legos, or studying picture books, stuck his head out the companionway to have a look around.

On April 23, at last, the water turned a light muddy brown color, a sure sign that *Oasis* was approaching land and a river mouth. A series of squalls blew through, and Thomas was kept very busy—taking in and letting out sail, taking regular sextant sights to be sure of his position, constantly casting his sounding lead to see how deep the water was. When finally the lead found bottom, in 40 feet of water, there still was no land in sight.

"Eventually, land ho!" wrote Thomas. "A thin, grey strip hardly visible at first and then quite quickly resolving into an unbroken stretch of trees disappearing in the distance in both directions. Oh, to get inside the river before nightfall!"

But it was another two hours before they sighted the opposite riverbank, with a lighthouse on it, and by then the sun was setting. Thomas kept pushing on into shallower water until it was pitch dark, then finally dropped anchor. He recalled: "We spent quite a rough night anchored at the entrance in the middle of this immense estuary, with the current against the wind creating small breakers which would, periodically, wash right over the boat."

At daybreak they set out again and two hours later suddenly ran aground. Thomas struggled to get free of the mud, but *Oasis* was very deep, drawing more than seven feet of water, and the tide was running out. Soon it was clear they'd be stuck until it came back in. Some curious fishermen appeared. They lightly grounded their own boats, shallow canoes designed to work in these waters, then waded over to visit with the strangers they'd found.

Thomas was eager to get information from these men. When would the tide turn? What was the tidal range? Where was the deep water further upriver? He gabbled away for a couple of minutes, until finally Christina realized Thomas wasn't speaking Spanish or English, but Portuguese. He had tricked her. They were not in Guyana, at the entrance of the Essequibo River, as she expected, but rather at the mouth of the Rio Oiapoque, on the border between Brazil and French Guiana.

IT TURNED OUT THE tidal range at the river mouth was quite large, on the order of 15 feet. By the time the tide had ebbed away entirely, *Oasis* was left lying full on her side at a very flat angle, thanks to her deep keel. Christina later described this not as a grounding, but as a "shipwreck." Hours later, when the tide finally came back in, the boat did stand up and float again, but not before a good deal of muddy river water flooded down the companionway and made a mess of the boat's interior.

From there it took another five days to get the boat 30 miles upriver to the river's namesake town, Oiapoque, on the south bank in Brazil. At first the current ran hard, at about four knots, and there was no stemming it with sails or the sculling oar when it was foul. Christina, for one, didn't mind the slow pace. After all the time at sea, she now enjoyed the quiet and the calm, watching the trees and fishing boats slip by, anchoring and sleeping peacefully at night.

"The entire way is completely deserted, apart from three tiny Indian settlements of hardly 50 people," Thomas wrote later. "The rest is all just towering Amazonian jungle rising straight out of the water on both sides, harboring millions of colorful parrots and red ibis. There was also the eerie call of the howler monkeys, which sound a bit like the wind in a powerful hurricane."

By the fifth day *Oasis* was far enough inland that the incoming tidal current was too weak to be helpful, and Thomas convinced a passing fisherman to tow them the last several miles to town. First past the smaller community of St. Georges on the French side of the river, under a suspension bridge that carried the only road for many miles in all directions, arriving finally at what Thomas described as "a bustling fishing town of 50,000 people, with shops everywhere selling everything and anything."

Christina gave birth to her second son, Lucio, aboard *Oasis* just three days after their arrival. She awakened early that morning, May 1, and felt her labor was already well underway. The first contractions, she realized, must have started during the night while she was sleeping. She wanted to be outside, so Thomas draped sheets over the mainsail boom to create a private tented space on the aft deck behind the cabinhouse. At first Christina was screaming as the contractions tore through her, but this attracted attention from the fishing boats tied up around them. She switched to chanting in Spanish—"*Indios de la selva dan nos vida*," or "Indians of the jungle give us life!"—and lapsed into what she later described as an intense spiritual trance.

After about 15 minutes of chanting, Lucio's head emerged, but his umbilical cord was wrapped three times around his neck. Thomas shouted to Gaston to bring the razor blade that was in the pot boiling on the stove and managed to cut the cord and unravel it safely. As the newborn infant cried out for the first time, the fishermen on the next boat alongside burst into applause.

Lucio—after his father and his grandmother Lydia—was the third in his line born afloat.

# 11. IN A FAKE COUNTRY

THOMAS HAD ALWAYS HAD TROUBLE dealing with bureaucracies and paperwork. This was in essence an original sin, ingrained in him from his creation, when his father first brought him to shore, introduced him to human society in Singapore, and struggled in vain to promptly document the fact that he had been born and now existed. Thomas had learned well enough during the intervening years how important paperwork could be, but he seemed never to grasp the logic of it. As if there was any logic to it.

He had, for example, never figured out exactly what had happened with his university degree. Back on Vieques, when he started soliciting work as a yacht designer via the Internet, Thomas had written to Clare Allcard asking that she send on a copy of his diploma, so he could tout his credentials. He repeated this request over the next couple of years. But Clare had no diploma, as one had never been sent to Andorra after Thomas finished his last year at school. At that time, she recalled later, the head of the University of Leeds had written to her asking if Thomas intended to return and take his last two exams. He had skipped those tests back in June 1997, just before he left Leeds on *Melody*, because, as he later explained to Clare, he wasn't interested in graduating from school "with honours." It seems he had not realized this had prevented him from graduating at all.

So it was with immigrating to Brazil. Thomas had done enough research to understand that U.S. citizens needed visas to enter Brazil, but he had not actually obtained any visas. Christina was not any better about this sort of thing. "I am not good with the law or instructions," she later noted. "I was in charge of cooking, taking care of Gaston and my big belly, and he was in charge of the paperwork and permits."

Besides arriving in Brazil with no visas, Thomas also had lost his U.S. passport back in St. Martin. Fortunately, he did have a photocopy, and the immigration authorities at Oiapoque were not overly zealous. Though they did not beneficently waive their requirements when they learned of Lucio's birth, as Thomas evidently hoped they might, they did allow a one-month grace period before ordering the family to leave the country to replace the missing passport and apply for visas. During this time, Christina rented a small shop stall in town that served as a shore base for the family. She later recalled she and the boys spent most of their time each day there, while Thomas stayed aboard working on the boat, cleaning out the mud and filth that had come aboard during the grounding at the river mouth. She and Thomas also did succeed in documenting Lucio's birth as a Brazilian, though Thomas could not be listed as the father, as he had no proper identification.

Lucio, meanwhile, was not exactly a healthy infant. Christina remembered his eyes became infected soon after his birth, and she went half-crazy shooing away the flies that swarmed about his face. He also developed some sort of bronchial infection and had a bad rash that caused his skin to peel. Christina later chastised herself over this: "Can you believe I was so stupid that I bathed him with river water? Thomas assumed this disgusting water filled with all kinds of shit was great for us to bathe in, and I never thought whether this could be harmful for a newborn's skin!"

When it came time to leave, the family had little choice but to move on to Cayenne, the capital of French Guiana, about 50 miles up the coast from the mouth of the Rio Oiapoque and the nearest place outside Brazil where they might apply for the papers they needed. Thomas, in a brief e-mail, later described to Clare how they spent a week at the river's entrance "waiting for the times of the tides to be compatible with the trip."

"Pretty nerve-wracking sailing my extremely deep boat in strong currents, over shoals that hardly appear on my charts, as well as tend to shift around, in muddy water so there's no way to eyeball the depths," he elaborated. "I must have thrown out the lead line a thousand times."

He failed to mention that he and the family also had an encounter here with some men who appeared to be bandits. Thomas in fact had given some thought to this before leaving Puerto Rico, as South American rivers do have a reputation for piracy.[1] He consulted with his nephew Gjermund, a military veteran, and they had discussed whether Thomas might repel boarding thieves with Molotov cocktails or perhaps a paintball gun loaded with marbles. Gjermund had urged that proper firearms would be the best deterrent, but it seems Thomas ultimately declined to carry any sort of weapon.

Christina recalled she was washing clothes on deck when a large outboard-powered canoe with a plastic tarp covering its midsection "suddenly came up very close and fast." One young crewmember from the canoe immediately jumped aboard *Oasis*, startling both Christina and Thomas. They nonetheless kept their cool and tried to act friendly.

"The guy started speaking some French, but when Thomas spoke back in Portuguese he got friendlier," she later wrote.

Once the stranger had peeked below and understood that *Oasis* had no engine and that there was a baby aboard, the situation was defused. Other young men hiding under the tarp revealed themselves, the intruder retreated back to the canoe, and the gang

---

1. By far the most famous victim of a South American pirate attack was Sir Peter Blake, a racing sailor from New Zealand who won the 1989-90 Whitbread Round the World Race and later won the America's Cup for New Zealand in 1995. After retiring from racing Blake commanded a large research vessel, *Seamaster*, which explored the Amazon basin during 2001. On December 5 of that year he was murdered by pirates who boarded the vessel at Macapá, near the mouth of the river. Like Thomas's mother Lydia before him, Blake was shot and killed after suddenly appearing on deck with a rifle.

quickly departed. Christina and Thomas felt sure the men had intended to rob them, but they had realized "we needed more than they did," as Christina later put it.

THE FAMILY FINALLY SAILED into Cayenne on June 3, 2012. Thomas's life in one sense had now come full circle. This was where the romance between his parents that led to his conception had been initiated; this was where the boat he'd been born on had been built. As far as we know, he never remarked on this, and he certainly never seemed very pleased with the place. In an e-mail sent to Clare Allcard a week after the family's arrival, Thomas noted simply that he much preferred Brazil. He complained too that the food was very expensive.

French Guiana was an integral part of France, as the French, unlike other colonial powers, normally administer their foreign possessions as departments of the mother country. During the 19th century and on into the mid-20th century, they had maintained a large penal system here. This included Devil's Island—*l'enfer vert* ("the green hell")—an isolated offshore leper colony that evolved into an infamous dumping ground for political prisoners. These days French Guiana is significant in that as a part of France it is also a part of the European Union, the only EU territory in all of South America.

Thomas's father had been reasonably comfortable when he was here during the late 1960s and early '70s, living in a house on an oceanside beach just east of the city of Cayenne, with enough room in his yard to build a 50-foot sailboat. Thomas's family of four, by comparison, now found themselves cramped aboard their 34-foot boat in a small dilapidated marina at Degrad des Cannes, well south of the main city, on the muddy banks of the Mahury River, just upstream from a gritty container port. Christina enjoyed life in the marina nonetheless. It was the first time during her sojourn aboard *Oasis* that she'd been able to step off the boat on to a dock any time she wanted. She also appreciated the friendly sense of community, as many of the other boats on the three crowded marina pontoons were also inhabited. There were a few transient sailors, adventurous types who had wandered far from the popular routes followed by most cruisers, and also several local residents, living on less functional boats, who couldn't afford the rents in the city's notoriously expensive housing market.

But Christina didn't stay in Cayenne for very long. She was anxious to introduce Lucio to her mother and her two sisters, and her mother was more than willing to finance a visit home. Little more than a month after the family's arrival, she took the two boys and flew back to Puerto Rico, a process greatly complicated by the fact that Lucio had no passport and his birth had not been registered with U.S. authorities. Christina and the boys were thus delayed first in Dominica for two days, and then in Barbados for nearly a week, while Missy wrangled furiously with U.S. authorities in San Juan and finally won permission for Lucio to enter Puerto Rico with his U.S. paperwork still pending.

In all Christina spent nearly five months in Puerto Rico, a lengthy separation that left Thomas feeling alone and depressed. He did succeed in finding some work: "Carpentry in the shade, the usual bread-earner stuff," as he described it in one of a few terse e-mails he sent to Clare during this time. He also received a commission to write an article about the voyage to Brazil from *All At Sea*, a Caribbean sailing magazine. He was at first enthusiastic about this, but later struggled through "a crisis of confidence," afraid he was creating "a bunch of drivel" as he worked at drafting the story.[2] In the midst of working on it, his computer broke down, and for a few awful days he was very afraid he'd lost all his data.

---

2. This article eventually ran as a three-part feature series in *All At Sea*. Entitled "Two Thousand Miles to Brazil," the series appeared in the magazine's March, April, and May issues in 2013. I encountered the first in the series while sailing in the Spanish Virgin Islands that spring.

"Five years of boat designs, 24,000 books, the books I was writing, everything..." he lamented to Clare. "Just keeps on getting better and better."

Fortunately, with some of the money earned from his carpentry, Thomas was able to get the computer repaired and did recover most of what he thought he'd lost.

Meanwhile, back in Puerto Rico, one great ray of hope briefly presented itself when Christina thought she'd found a serious buyer for the house on Vieques. A self-described Christian missionary, one John Rios, who purported to be moving from West Africa to Puerto Rico, responded to a direct listing for the property she had posted online. Rios offered by e-mail to pay the asking price, no questions asked, and without mentioning any sort of sales agreement he proposed to immediately wire a down payment along with an extra amount to be handed to an "inspection agent." Thomas at once suspected this might be a scam, and it very likely was, as the mysterious Mr. Rios eventually evaporated and no down payment ever arrived.

Christina finally returned to Cayenne in late December, unfortunately with no house-sale proceeds to help finance the family's new life in South America, but with a healthier Lucio, whose skin and infections had long since cleared up. Again, because the application for Lucio's passport had yet to be processed, it proved a complicated journey. Christina and the boys first flew to Suriname, made their way to the eastern border, took a riverboat across the Maroni River into French Guiana, then got a car ride Thomas had arranged halfway across the country to Cayenne.

Christina was not immediately pleased with what she found there. Thomas's drinking had again escalated, and *Oasis* was by now uninhabitable. Thomas had stripped out much of the boat's interior to make repairs, but the work had stalled, and several rodents had moved aboard. Meanwhile he had moved into a room in an abandoned beachside hotel, taking it as a squatter, a common practice in Cayenne. There were several others also squatting there, most of them illegal immigrants who had come to French Guiana from all over South America, hoping to somehow move on to Europe.

Thomas had made an effort to make the squat comfortable for his family before they arrived. He was building in furniture, with beds raised up high to maximize living space, but the work was incomplete. Christina's first impression was that it looked like a construction site, with a lot of lumber lying around, from Thomas's work in the room and also from the boat.

"I was very upset," she remembered. "But I did not get mad. I told myself: just breathe, just breathe. Then I started cleaning up."

The old hotel was largely a ruin. The squatters all lived on the first floor, as the upper floors were overrun with rats. There was a communal outdoor kitchen, but the politics of using it—whose food was whose, cleaning up, who could use what utensils—were quite complicated. Christina much preferred to have a space of her own, so she set up a little kitchen in a broom closet close to their room.

"It was infested with frogs," she later recalled. "I never saw the frogs, because they came only at night. But I always saw their excrement, and every morning I had to clean it up. It was impossible to keep clean."

To make matters worse, the family was soon plagued with scabies, tiny mites that burrow under the skin causing a persistent itchy rash. Baby Lucio had a particularly bad case, Christina recalled, while Thomas, she noted with some irony, seemed largely immune. To combat the infestation she spent hours every day steam-cleaning all the bed linen over pots of boiling water, then cleaning the room and all the children's toys with disinfectant, to little avail.

CHARLES J. DOANE

Thomas's appraisal of this living situation was a bit more upbeat than Christina's. In a long e-mail to Clare, he described the squat as "an apartment" and while admitting it was "nothing luxurious," he urged that Christina "needs to realize the only way forward is to live below one's means." He cited a few things he liked about Cayenne: there was no genetically modified food, the police were friendly, and there were no "USanians," as he now referred to Americans. But he also confessed: "It's hard not to notice that I'm operating at the very bottom strata of society, and despite large efforts to lift our standard of living, it just never seems to happen. Kind of makes me feel like a failure in the role as provider for the family, and creates a lot of friction in the relationship."

Christina could only take so much, and after little more than a month in the squat—fighting a hopeless battle trying to keep things clean, coping with scabies and Thomas's drinking—she started threatening to leave again.

"Just to be safe I hid their passports, but now she keeps bugging me to give them back," Thomas noted in a follow-up e-mail to Clare. "She is not so good at delayed gratification, a result of how she was brought up. Maybe someone can talk some sense into her. I know I can't take another long separation, so this time it would be final."

Christina had always been an optimistic person, and she did try to inject some positivity into her life and those of her children. She organized family picnics on the beach. And when the 2013 carnival season came around, soon after her return to Cayenne, she seized on the opportunity. With a pair of friends from the marina she dressed herself and the boys in wild costumes and marched in parades.

"How I loved this!" she later wrote. "It was like an angel of art sent to me at such hard times to give me a window of light and interest in living again."

Thomas meanwhile did relent and after a couple of months agreed to move out of the squalid hotel room. While he looked for a new place, the family lived in a tent on a bit of open ground between hauled-out boats in a makeshift boatyard a short distance downstream from the marina. *Oasis* was anchored nearby, in anticipation of another bout of work Thomas hoped would make her seaworthy again. Though camping in the boatyard had been Christina's idea, she soon regretted it. There was no room for Lucio's portable crib inside the family's "broken tent," so it was placed outside, with Lucio sleeping in it during the night. The mosquitos, as Christina later wrote, were "something spectacular," and it broke her heart when she went out in the night to find her baby boy soaking wet from passing tropical rain squalls.

"I remember thinking then," she later declared, "this was all very wrong."

The family's next home was another squat. This was in an abandoned house with fewer inhabitants than the ruined hotel, in what had once been the house's kitchen. It was much more pleasant than the hotel, and the working kitchen, Christina remembered, was in what had been the living room, where each family in the house now had their own space to cook, an improvement over the broom closet, with no defecating frogs to worry about. Unfortunately, however, the scabies followed the family to their new abode, and Christina was still saddled with the daily chore of steam-cleaning linen and disinfecting everything. She also had the baby to care for and was home-schooling Gaston, as Thomas would not allow the boy to be vaccinated so that he could attend the local school.

Thomas was still intent on immigrating to Brazil and around this time, on March 8, 2013, led the family on a day trip back to Oiapoque to amend Lucio's birth certificate. He had by now received his new passport and at last could be documented as the father of his Brazilian-born child. The family first hitchhiked overland some 60 miles to St. Georges, on the French side of the Rio Oiapoque. They made quite a picture—Christina with her baby in a sling, Gaston sternly holding out the sign proclaiming their destination, Thomas dressed neatly in a clean polo shirt and long trousers—all with a small pile of luggage by the side of the road, including Lucio's crib, and the rain forest looming behind them. From St. Georges they took a short water-taxi ride across the river to Brazil.[3] In addition to seeing to the birth certificate, Thomas also now opened a bank account in Lucio's name, so as to create one more link between the family and their future homeland.

But soon afterward, in April, Christina decided she'd had enough. The breaking point came one day when Thomas had taken Gaston to the boatyard with him, as a favor to Christina, to give her one less child to manage. Thomas returned drunk that evening, two hours late for dinner, weaving along the road in the dark on his bicycle with Gaston perched on the handlebars. Christina later learned from Gaston that when he'd complained to his father at the boatyard that he was hungry, Thomas had simply handed him a beer.

A few days later, while Thomas was out at the boatyard again, Christina packed up the boys, found their passports, and checked into a hotel in the city to wait there for a flight she'd booked out the following day. It was for her an extraordinarily difficult decision. Her affection for Thomas had always been rooted in his need to be cared for, and in her desire to take care of him. She knew him well enough to understand the forces that had bent him into the person he'd become, and for every time her heart had railed against him,

---

3. Construction of the Oiapoque River Bridge, under which *Oasis* passed when Thomas and family arrived at Oiapoque in 2012, was completed in August 2011. The bridge was not opened to traffic until 2017.

that same heart had also empathized with him. She had yearned for a life of adventure, and he had given her that—in spades. But now she had children to care for too.

"If it was just me I probably would have stayed and tried to work through it," she later recalled. "But I could not watch my children suffer."

Christina had sworn the other squatters in the house to secrecy. But one of them evidently told Thomas what was happening, and the next day, as Christina and the boys were waiting for their flight, he suddenly appeared at the airport, searching for his family. Christina's heart froze when she saw him. She knew if Thomas pleaded with her directly, in person, her resolve would crumble. "In my mind I just resigned myself to fate," she later explained in describing that moment. She watched Thomas nervously as he stalked up and down the terminal and waited to see which it would be: a reunion with Thomas or an exit from *l'enfer vert*.

Thomas was so frantic and anxious he could not see his family, though they were in plain view, waiting in line to pay their departure tax. At one point Christina saw that Gaston had also noticed his father, and she was wracked with guilt. But finally, after what seemed an eternity, Thomas gave up. She saw him leave the terminal and then disappear on the back of a motor-scooter driven by one of his squatter friends.

Once again, because Lucio still had no U.S. passport, the trip home to Puerto Rico was not easy. The family was again detained in Dominica, and this time Christina insisted they be sent on not to Barbados, but to the Dominican Republic, just one island west of Puerto Rico. Here her mother, through her church connections, arranged for them to stay in a Catholic convent in Santo Domingo. Christina later remembered that the nuns were thrilled to have two children living with them. She noted also that they "tortured" her by making her attend mass every day.

Missy again zealously lobbied the immigration office in San Juan, this time with no success, and the family was stuck in Santo Domingo, in bureaucratic limbo, for nearly a month. Christina eventually did send Gaston, who did have a valid U.S. passport, on ahead to her mother, while she stayed behind with Lucio in the convent. The impasse was finally broken when she went down to the ferry terminal in Santo Domingo and staged a sit-in. She stayed there with her baby boy, refusing to move, holding up a sign that read: "This is How the U.S. Treats its Children." Then finally they were allowed to board a ferry to Puerto Rico.

AS IT HAPPENED, CHRISTINA'S DEPARTURE from Cayenne was one in a series of misfortunes that now rained down on Thomas in rapid succession. He had earlier succeeded in getting *Oasis* out of the water and had done some serious work on her, replacing two suspect frames and five planks, repainting the bottom, and recaulking several seams. Soon after his family disappeared, Thomas took advantage of a high spring tide and relaunched the boat.

"The whole process was a bloody nightmare and took a week, during which I slept a total of about six hours," he complained soon afterward in a bitter e-mail to Clare.

The big tides were bringing huge tree trunks, root balls, and other forest detritus down the river on the swiftly flowing current, some four and a half knots worth. In kedging *Oasis* off the slipway, Thomas lost two anchors when their rodes were fouled and severed. One of these was the cherished Northill seaplane anchor from his father's boat that he had reclaimed in Bonaire. He then had to spend days aboard the boat while waiting for dock space in the marina to open up and was up at all hours fending off the heavy flotsam that continually snagged on the rode to his last remaining anchor.

Finally, at the conclusion of this ordeal, all the ballast from *Oasis*—nearly 9,000 pounds of lead pigs that Thomas had laboriously offloaded and stored temporarily on a nearby ramp—was stolen. "In less than an hour!" he marveled. "I still don't understand how they achieved it."

Poor *Oasis*, with no ballast to hold her upright in the water, was left canted over on her side at a dramatic 40-degree angle. Thomas had more work yet to perform aboard, the temperature was over 100 degrees Fahrenheit below deck, and he had no idea how he might replace the ballast, without which, he admitted, "the boat is useless."

"I'm seriously considering burning the boat," he wrote to Clare. "I'm not going to sell it for a pittance to someone who won't take care of her."

To add insult to injury, two bicycles belonging to Thomas were stolen around the same time. Some valuable tools he had stored aboard another boat at the marina also disappeared soon afterward.

In spite of all these setbacks and distractions, Thomas, spurred on by what he saw as Christina's betrayal, did at last seriously address the problem of his drinking. He had never been in denial about this. He had always admitted it *was* a problem. Christina later recalled one electric moment in their exodus to Brazil, as they were sailing out of St. John on *Oasis*, when Thomas suddenly declared in a grandiose epiphany: "You know? I've realized my abuse of alcohol is all that has prevented me from becoming a millionaire!"

So now finally, in seemingly desperate circumstances, he set out to realize some of his potential. Searching for information online, as was his habit, Thomas found there was a drug, Baclofen, that might help alleviate cravings for alcohol. But he soon concluded he didn't need a crutch like this and could instead brazenly white-knuckle his way out of drinking.

On May 24 he wrote a long e-mail to Clare:

> Apparently I do not need any pills. The last time I bought rum was the 2nd of May. My new routine is one beer Sunday evening before dinner. The first week I did have the odd beer. The second week none, but was anxiously awaiting Sunday. Third week I almost forgot about the Sunday beer. Next step will be to skip a Sunday and see how it affects me. If I get irritated I'll have to cut that one out too, but if it does not affect me, then it's no longer an issue. That saying, "once an alky, always an alky," seems a bit pathetic to me, although it may be true for certain people. The bottle I bought on May 2 is still under my desk with some in there. If I have to run away from it, then I still have a problem. That's why I'm leaving it there.
>
> I feel quite a bit better; more lucid, focused, get more stuff done. Surprisingly, my self-confidence is much higher. Also my willingness to humour people has almost vanished. My patience for fools, never my strong point, is now almost nil. I feel a whole lot more mercenary. I feel no urge to cloud my mind or lose control.

Thomas also reestablished contact with Christina. She had reached out via e-mail soon after leaving Cayenne, and eventually he grudgingly responded. They traded accusations. Thomas urged that if she truly loved him, Christina should have stayed to help him kick his habit. She argued she had tried, but he had "always fallen into the same thing." Now it was time for him to do the work of quitting booze on his own. "It is your way of doing it," she wrote, "you are a very independent being, and when you decide on something you achieve it."

Christina also confessed she still had strong feelings for Thomas. "I have not removed the ring and I do not intend to," she wrote. "I trust that this love is stronger than the episodes in life that sometimes put us to the test."

And Thomas in return freely confessed his remorse: "If I feel anger against you, I am not blaming you as you said, because I feel twice as much anger against myself."

ALTHOUGH HE WAS NOW, as he described it, "heart-broken, angry, balancing on the edge of a nervous breakdown," Thomas resolutely forged ahead with his life. He was still very determined to move to and live in Brazil, with or without Christina, and he still hoped to establish himself as a yacht designer.

In Brazil, though he had spent little time there, Thomas saw a final answer to an annoying question that had dogged him through all his life: where are you from? It was such a simple getting-to-know-you query, posed as a common throw-away line in countless casual conversations, that had always confounded him. Ironically, one of the things that initially had bound him to Christina, for which he was always grateful, was that she had never asked him this. But now, at last, he admitted he did not disdain the question but yearned instead to respond.

"Can't wait to get to a real country, and a reasonably free one," he wrote to Clare, in explaining his passion for moving to Brazil. "I am really hoping I can finally integrate myself into a place where I can say 'I am from here.' I look forward to getting a Brazilian passport and being able to show it to the incredulous 'so where are you from-ers'."

And to get to Brazil, Thomas still believed, he needed his boat. He had a large pile of heavy tools and a portable generator he wanted to bring with him, and *Oasis,* he believed, was the simplest, cheapest vehicle in which to transport them. So he set about the daunting task of replacing her ballast. Lead was both hard to find and expensive, so his first idea was to use steel instead, in the form of scrap cylinder heads from old car engines. He soon shifted his sights to junked air conditioners, which were easy to find all around the city. He first laboriously transported these to his squat on a trailer he built to haul behind the "crappy" bike he'd bought to replace the stolen ones. There he stripped out the heavy compressors, rich with copper plumbing that was both denser and more valuable than steel, and hauled these in turn to the boat, an hour's bike ride away.

Thomas's plan, as reported to Clare in one e-mail, was to collect about 6,600 pounds of replacement ballast, which was about 25 percent less than the original amount. "The boat will be under-ballasted," he admitted, "but I'd rather take my chances with nature than with humans."

As he worked to rehabilitate *Oasis,* Thomas also worked to perfect several speculative boat designs that he planned to eventually showcase online. As a precursor to a site dedicated solely to his designs, Thomas in August launched a blog site he titled *Tangvald: Sailing Adventures and Boat Design,* in which he discussed his unusual background, various technical issues, and his general design philosophy.[4] The designs he drew meanwhile were eclectic and varied. They of course included sailing vessels. One surviving example was a long, narrow sailing yacht with twin daggerboards, two separate cabinhouses fore and aft, a deep spade rudder, and

---

4. Thomas by now had allowed his first website, t3-boats.com, to lapse into nonexistence. His blog site, as of this writing, was still online at tangvald.wordpress.com. The last entry, on traditional Brazilian sailboats, was posted on January 8, 2014.

a rotating wing-mast. Another was a very innovative design for a lug-rigged Mini Transat 6.50, a class of radical 21-foot ocean-racing yachts in which several designers have launched successful careers. There were also some motor vessels, including a design for a fancy high-powered speedboat. In addition to all this work, Thomas started participating in an online wooden boatbuilding forum, where he published not only free design drawings but also detailed building plans for a small dinghy, so as to help get his name out and plant the budding seeds of a reputation.

While developing these concepts and designs, Thomas taught himself a programming language, VBScript, and wrote some original software to aid in complex stability calculations. He also reached out for advice and feedback from two men he considered mentors of a sort. One of these was Jacques Mertens, the father of Florence, Thomas's last stepmother, who had worked with several boatbuilders over the years and was now designing small boats and selling building plans and supplies online. Jacques had great respect for Thomas and well remembered several days they had spent together in Florida, when Florence and Peter were still a couple and Thomas was age 11. The boy had impressed him at that time, and Jacques later described him as a genius. He recalled that young Thomas then had built a 10-foot sailing dinghy without plans and had also quickly figured out how to work the first computer he ever encountered. Jacques was happy to help him now.

Thomas's other perceived mentor, his uncle Patrick Balta, was less helpful. Although Patrick had been encouraging when the two first met in Belgium in 2009, he had since grown critical of Thomas's unconventional lifestyle and the seemingly dangerous choices he made. Now when Thomas reached out to him as a fellow designer, Patrick did not respond. Worried something might have happened to his uncle, Thomas wrote to his grandfather Gustave, who informed him that Patrick refused to aid in furthering Thomas's design career and believed he should instead pursue some other calling.

"He could have at least told me himself!" Thomas fumed to Clare. "Thousands of little things like that foster my attitude of deep cynicism and contempt for humanity."

Later that year, in September, Thomas succeeded in landing a paid job as a designer. This came from a local boatbuilder, a fellow called Maido, originally from Madagascar, who had immigrated to French Guiana 30 years earlier. He had heard rumors of a transient sailor with serious design skills and had come down to the marina looking to hire this person. He first gave Thomas a commission to design and draw up building plans for three small aluminum outboard-powered skiffs. Soon Thomas was boasting to Clare via e-mail: "Just got paid for my design work. €1,500 for about ten days work. Air-conditioned office, flexible hours. Makes a change from all the other grotty jobs I've had. Monday I'll start designing two more motorboats for him."

The first three commissions were followed by orders from Maido for some larger powerboat designs, and by late October, Thomas had a lead on another potential customer who wanted a large sailboat "to charter around the world." He noted to Christina that he was now making about €4,000 a month and was sending money to the bank account he'd opened in Oiapoque. Still he felt he was being underpaid by Maido. He complained to a friend at the marina, a young marine biologist named Arthur Alt who was living on a boat there, that his compensation was insulting. He had only accepted the jobs, he claimed, because he really needed the money. Even so, Thomas clearly was proud he was at last getting paid to do work that was meaningful to him. In an e-mail to Clare, he noted that these small designs, although "nothing special," were "important stepping stones" in advancing his career.

"My long-term goal," he boldly declared, "is to become

recognized as one of the world's top small (under 100 tons) boat designers. Sounds ambitious and possibly cocky, but I really think I deserve it."


DURING THIS TIME THOMAS was regularly in touch with Christina, usually by e-mail and sometimes by phone, engaged in a protracted, tangled debate over what sort of future they might have together. They both, very clearly, yearned to be reunited, but both were wary of falling into the same old traps.

Christina, for her part, was worried about Thomas's drinking. She generally seemed willing to accept his affirmations of abstinence, but she was always concerned it was a habit he might lapse into again. "I want to be sure that having stopped drinking is something serious on your part," she wrote, "and not something you will start to do little by little until you return to the same old shit."

Still it was Christina who took the lead in maintaining communications, chastising Thomas when he responded slowly to e-mails, and urging him to call more often so his two boys could hear his voice and feel connected to him. She showered Thomas with declarations of affection and also took the lead in proposing ways they could get back together. At various times over the ten months they maintained this arm's-length long-distance relationship, Christina allowed she might be willing to return to Thomas on her own to see if they could together find a place in Brazil that would be safe and comfortable for their children. But she also made it clear what she really wanted was for him to simply return to Puerto Rico.

Christina had quickly reestablished herself on her home island, moving in with her mother in Hatillo on the north shore, enrolling Gaston in a school that he enjoyed, and working as a tutor to make money as she cared for Lucio. From a practical point of view, it made perfect sense that Thomas should come to them rather than the other way around. He needed no visa or plane ticket to return, but could simply sail downwind from Cayenne to Puerto Rico.

"Yes, I am upset," she wrote. "I am the one who always has to give to your side. You just want us to leave everything here and throw ourselves back to you when you are already doing what you have always wanted to do, and you only need a computer to do it, and can do it from any place on the planet."

Christina painted a very positive picture of life on the north shore of Puerto Rico and urged Thomas at last, unlike his father, to make his family his first priority.

"I gave you the opportunity to show me your version of a better life for all of us," she wrote, "and through illness and health I was by your side, exposing my life and those of my innocent babies to danger. If your lifestyle is not dangerous, why is your mother dead? Your stepmother? Your sister? Accidents happen, of course, but your father's focus on only him and his passions cost the lives of others who loved him."

Thomas, in the face of these entreaties, was adamant. He refused to even consider coming back to Puerto Rico to live. "I already tried that for 12 years," he wrote. "On the other hand, you never tried Brazil." And, he noted, he had also already lived on the north shore, during their time together on the lake at Guajataca.

"My sailing to Puerto Rico in 2000 was not a decision made with any logic," he explained. "It was pure and simple nostalgia. I will not repeat the mistake of doing things out of nostalgia."

To reiterate all the reasons why he had decided they should leave Puerto Rico, Thomas peppered Christina with Internet links on the weak economy there and urged apocalyptically: "When our children are older Puerto Rico will be very poor, most likely under Chinese command."

And there was also the intractable problem of Christina's mother.

"Of the seven years we were together, I spent almost two alone just because you were with your mother," he complained. "You have no idea how that affected me. I hoped this would go down to a more reasonable level if we were much further from her, but the result has been precisely the opposite, which leads me to believe you prefer your mom to me."

Despite all the problems he'd encountered, Thomas was still very sure of his goal: "What is going to happen, if there are no unforeseen events, is I'm going to Brazil. If there are no bad surprises there, I stay as planned, and I'm going to become a millionaire. If you really love me and care so much about our family, I am sure you will join me. If not, then enjoy Puerto Rico. I'm sure it is going to be interesting."

Thomas did allow one small concession and in mid-November, at Christina's insistence, seemed willing to consider flying back to Puerto Rico for a two-week visit over Christmas. But then, on December 2, he sent a note apologizing. He could not do it: it was too expensive, he did not want to fly, and he could not leave the boat unattended. Christina, who had already told the boys their father was coming to see them, was badly disappointed. Later, the day after Christmas, she told Thomas she was willing to sail with him to Brazil if he paid for her plane ticket to French Guiana, but that afterwards she felt she must return home. "That is not where I want to spend the rest of my life," she wrote. "I love this land!"

In another exchange a few days later, on New Year's Eve, it seemed at last that Thomas had closed his heart.

"Thanks for teaching me two things," he wrote. "Without money no woman is going to stay with me, and no man is going to respect me. Love is a nice fantasy, but it doesn't really exist. So I'm going to get rich, and I'm not going to fall in love anymore. I feel sorry for the kids, but I can't be a long-distance father. It is futile."

THROUGH ALL OF THIS, through the wrenching exchanges with Christina and the minor triumph of his design work, Thomas kept struggling to prepare *Oasis* to go to sea again. It was certainly a grind. He could not leave tools and materials at the marina for fear of theft, and each bout of working on the boat entailed a two-hour commute to the marina and back by bicycle, hauling his heavily loaded makeshift trailer behind him. With his friend Arthur Alt he spent days dragging the river, hoping to recover his father's seaplane anchor, but had no success. Meanwhile, having exhausted the supply of scrap air-conditioner compressors he could easily lay hands on, Thomas turned next to using wet sand to re-ballast his crippled craft. He found she was now also leaking badly, the result most likely of her planks having shrunk up in the unforgiving tropical sun while she was canted over on her side without any ballast to hold her upright.

By now, as the year 2014 got underway, Thomas had been in Cayenne for over a year and a half and was increasingly anxious to leave. He had grown to loathe French Guiana and was determined to be gone before the rainy season, which had started in December, was too far advanced.

"Oddly enough, I ended up by accident in another fake country," he wrote to Clare on January 7, "a colony by the French, not the USanians, along with the symptomatic colony diseases. Here in this most unhappy place I have learnt to be racist and also why the French have such a poor worldwide reputation, which was always a mystery to me before."

He seemed too to have given up on reuniting with his family, as he also wrote: "Christina is not coming back, despite me beating the drink demon, which is what I imagined all along."

Though he was normally honest in admitting his faults, Thomas was disingenuous here, as he had not quite beaten the demon. He earlier had confessed to Christina he'd fallen off the wagon for a few days, through boredom, waiting for his computer to be repaired. And Arthur Alt later remembered he'd seen Thomas drunk more than once, usually when he was talking about Christina, or after he'd just been in touch with her.

"I think he was very, very sad about the situation," Arthur recalled. "Every time he told me about her his words were very angry, but every time he finished by saying she would join him with the two children in Brazil. For him it was the plan. If he managed to arrive in Brazil, she would come back."

The last burst of e-mail correspondence between Christina and Thomas began on January 27, when she wrote him a long note that began with a bold pronouncement: "If it is true, and I ask for your honesty here, that you are no longer lost in the madness of your eternal vice of drinking, we will return to you." And she added: "I want to return to my funny, romantic, adventurous husband!"

Christina was proposing to come with the boys to French Guiana in March and there apply for visas for Brazil, which would take two weeks or more. Thomas's response was noncommittal. The boat was almost ready to go, he wrote, and though he did not say as much, he clearly implied he was not inclined to wait around for something that might or might not happen. There followed a series of exchanges on the logistics and paperwork and expense of getting Christina and the boys to Brazil at some later date, and on the ever wished for possibility of selling the house on Vieques.

By February 10 it seemed Thomas was on the verge of departure: "I already have everything packed, and I am making the last arrangements. It has me a little in suspense. It is a long trip, and I am alone and poorly equipped. Between the robbery and the awful weather here nothing works on the boat anymore. But if I don't go, the boat will end up lost, that's for sure."

The last e-mail Christina ever received from Thomas came on February 18. It was very brief, in response to some photos she'd sent him of her and the boys participating in a circus performance back in Puerto Rico. "I am downloading the photos," he wrote. "I'll look at them quietly later on my computer, as I always do now, because of the rush of being online on other people's computers."

It was never clear exactly where in Brazil Thomas thought he was going. Later it was commonly reported he was bound for Fernando do Noronha, an archipelago of Brazilian islands more than 200 miles off the coast. Christina had always believed his ultimate destination was Salvador in Bahia, as they had often discussed reuniting there. Thomas had told Arthur Alt he planned to sail to Natal and open a bicycle shop. In his last e-mail to Jacques Mertens, he said he hoped to visit several Brazilian islands, including Fernando do Noronha and also Trinidade and Martin Vaz, which are almost 700 miles offshore and much further south.

According to friends at the marina Christina communicated with later, Thomas "went crazy sick drinking again and got in fights and trouble with everyone there" during his last days in Cayenne. He finally left on March 4. At some point that day, Thomas Thor Tangvald untied his dock lines, sailed away from Degrad des Cannes, out the muddy brown Mahury River, and was never seen again.

# 12. A PRINCE IN HIS REALM

ANY SINGLEHANDED PASSAGE lasting longer than a few hours inevitably involves a certain amount of risk. Significantly, any voyage where a solo sailor must take time off to sleep, for any amount of time, is technically prohibited under Rule 5 of the International Regulations for Preventing Collisions at Sea. This states: *Every vessel shall at all times maintain a proper lookout by sight and hearing as well as by all available means appropriate to the prevailing circumstances and conditions so as to make a full appraisal of the situation and of the risk of collision.*

Things to watch out for on a sailboat include not only vessels and other objects one might collide with, but also changes in wind speed and direction that call for sails to be reefed or trimmed.

Despite Rule 5 and the inherent risks of sailing alone across the ocean, singlehanded bluewater sailing is a fairly common activity. For many decades there have been various singlehanded ocean races, some lasting just a few days, others going on for weeks or even months,[1] and there has always been a small minority of bluewater cruising sailors who sometimes, or even always, sail alone. For contemporary sailors the dangers of singlehanding can be significantly reduced with modern technology. I've made a few solo passages myself over the years, between New England and the West Indies via Bermuda, and have felt reasonably safe and secure doing so. Modern marine radar units can be set to sound an alarm when they detect anything within a predetermined

---

1. The longest singlehanded sailing race is the Vendée Globe, which starts and finishes in Les Sables d'Olonne, France, and runs every four years non-stop clear around the world. The boats raced are very sophisticated 60-footers, and the current record elapsed time is 74 days, 3 hours, 36 minutes, set in 2017.

"guard zone" around a vessel, and targets will reliably include not only large ships but also rain squalls and thunderstorms that may bring abrupt, potentially dangerous gusting winds. More recently, Automatic Identification System (AIS) technology allows vessels at sea to automatically recognize each other from a distance and continually evaluate collision risks via VHF radio frequencies, and this too can sound an alarm when necessary. With both radar and AIS units maintaining a constant electronic watch, a sleeping solo sailor stands an excellent chance of being roused in time to cope with the most commonly encountered threats.

Thomas, thanks to the influence of his anti-technological father, enjoyed none of these advantages when he departed Cayenne. Indeed, he was positively disadvantaged in that he was sailing an under-ballasted and possibly quite leaky boat. If he did strike out to the southeast down the Brazilian coast toward Fernando do Noronha and Natal, the closest of his declared destinations, he was also working against the natural flow of the Atlantic Ocean's winds and currents. The easterly tradewinds he had previously battled coming from the West Indies can prevail for some distance past the Rio Oiapoque, as far down as the Amazon and beyond, depending on conditions. More importantly, he had to fight against the strong North Brazil Current, which runs at three to four knots to the northwest up the northeastern shoulder of South America.

Once clear of the North Atlantic's tradewind zone, Thomas next would have confronted a different sort of obstacle. The Inter-Tropical Convergence Zone (ITCZ), more commonly known as the Doldrums, is a broad stripe of fickle, variable wind that separates the tradewinds of the South and North Atlantic and stretches roughly from West Africa to the eastern horn of South America, with its exact position varying widely. Conditions in the ITCZ can be frustrating, particularly for a sailor in a vessel with no engine. Long periods of little or no wind may be interspersed with shorter, sudden intervals of strong, squally wind, and to make progress under sail alone one must take full advantage of whatever wind appears, whenever it appears. A solo sailor seeking to make use of any squalls, while also avoiding being overwhelmed by them, needs to be alert and awake as much as possible.

Meanwhile, the Amazon River itself was a potential source of trouble. The Amazon and the Rio Tocantins, the next river east, form a single enormous estuary some 180 miles across, through which an incredible quantity of turbid fresh water and rainforest detritus is expelled into the ocean. For many miles out to sea there is some risk, particularly for a small, more easily damaged boat, of running into flotsam, and the outflowing current, cutting across the North Brazil Current, can create confused seas. Along the whole of the northern Brazilian coast there are also countless fishing boats at work, many of them poorly lit at night, maintaining haphazard watch systems, and behaving unpredictably while pursuing their catch. To avoid such threats, with no AIS or radar to rely on, a solo sailor like Thomas would need to be both vigilant and a bit lucky.

The simplest way to dodge inshore hazards and also stay out of the worst of the North Brazil Current while sailing Thomas's presumed route is to run well out to sea, and there is good evidence this was his intention. In one e-mail to Christina, he stated he planned to sail toward Natal while staying 200 to 400 miles offshore. It is also an old adage of ocean sailing: the farther you are from land, the safer you are.

The distance from Cayenne to Natal or Fernando do Noronha is roughly 1,300 nautical miles. If Thomas did try to sail this one long leg non-stop well offshore, as seems likely, one might conservatively expect him to take about two weeks doing so, or perhaps a bit longer if the Doldrums gave him much trouble.

Archived weather data from the two weeks after Thomas left

Cayenne shows he initially would have enjoyed fair conditions. The tradewinds were blowing solidly from the northeast, or even a bit north of northeast, at between 15-20 knots, with some patches of slightly stronger wind. Though he would always need to keep an eye out for squalls, as these do sometimes occur in otherwise stable tradewind conditions, Thomas would have been able to make good progress down the coast while also steadily putting distance between himself and the shore. If all had gone well, he might have been at least 200 miles offshore and just clear of the Amazon delta after his first five or six days at sea.

From the Amazon delta onwards, if he made it that far, the wind eventually shifted against Thomas, coming from a more easterly direction. It also became lighter, blowing generally at 10-15 knots, or perhaps just 5-10 knots, depending on where he was exactly. This certainly would have slowed him down. And the farther east he got, the likelier Thomas was to encounter the less stable conditions around the ITCZ. Not only was the ITCZ shifting alternately north and south in this region during this time, like the wagging tail of a dog, but archived satellite data also indicates there were several clusters of robust squalls developing along it.

Finally, after more than a month with no word from Thomas, people started getting worried. By April 10, 2014, according to an e-mail from Christina to Clare Allcard, Thomas had been reported as missing to the French Maritime Gendarmerie in Cayenne. They in turn notified the Brazilian navy, which is responsible for search-and-rescue (SAR) operations in Brazilian waters. The U.S. Coast Guard in San Juan was also notified, and on May 5 they notified Christina that they were receiving reports from both the French and the Brazilians.

But the fact is no physical search for Thomas was ever conducted. Because no one had any specific idea where he might be, because there was no reasonably defined area in which SAR "assets"—planes, helicopters, ships, or patrol boats—might be deployed, it made no sense to do this. Instead descriptions and photographs were circulated, and port officials all down the Brazilian coast and as far south as Uruguay and Argentina were asked to keep their eyes peeled and to check their records to see if Thomas and *Oasis* had booked in anywhere. Bulletins were also sent out to all commercial vessels transiting the South American coast, asking them to keep a look-out for a boat resembling *Oasis* or for any signs of possibly related wreckage or debris.

Nothing ever came of any of this, and eventually, by the end of May, Thomas was officially declared "lost at sea."

FOR CERTAIN PEOPLE IT WAS, and still is, difficult to accept the notion that Thomas Tangvald, a veritable son of the sea, might somehow have perished while on passage. These people, as well as others who concede Thomas must be dead, have developed varied theories about who he really was and what likely happened to him. It is as though his life and his disappearance have formed a convoluted Rorschach blot that those who knew him are bound to interpret in different ways.

Clare Allcard, for example, was initially not too worried that no one had seen or heard from Thomas for a while. She immediately recalled an episode from her own life when Edward, bound solo across the Indian Ocean aboard *Sea Wanderer*, disappeared for four and a half months, leaving her alone with their baby daughter to wonder what had become of him. Like Thomas, Edward carried no radio and had no way to communicate with shore, but he did turn up eventually, in the Seychelles rather than in Kenya, his intended destination. He was more than three months overdue when Clare, who was waiting in Nairobi, suddenly received a cheerful telegram:

"Delete Mombasa substitute Seychelles have found love nest come soonest." It turned out the weather had been very contrary, and the voyage had simply taken much longer than anticipated.

But after some five months passed with no word of Thomas, Clare eventually lost hope. "He still might have decided to start afresh in some other corner of Brazil, or he could even now be rowing his dinghy towards the shore," she wrote to Dan Axon, one of Thomas's old university friends. "But I doubt it. As you can imagine I have thought and thought and thought about it, and I have now come to the conclusion that Thomas did indeed drown—whilst still praying I am wrong."

Clare was well aware of the narcoleptic symptoms Thomas had sometimes exhibited, and she felt this may have contributed to an unfortunate fate—that he was sound asleep below, perhaps unable to wake up, as *Oasis* was overwhelmed in some emergency.

Jacques Mertens was another who was at first reluctant to conclude that Thomas must be dead. "I still have some hope that Thomas is on anchor somewhere drinking cocktails and will reappear to surprise everybody," he wrote to me that May. Nearly a year later there was at least one slim branch of kindling to feed the flame of that hope when his granddaughter Virginia, Thomas's half-sister, reported she had received what appeared to be a missed call on her phone from Thomas's number. Ultimately, however, both she and Jacques have accepted that Thomas most probably is gone.

Thomas's nephew Gjermund has also accepted this and has developed a firm view that he must have been killed by pirates. "Absolutely. I am so sure of it," he insisted to me during one conversation we had. He believes pirates shot Thomas dead from a distance, then boarded *Oasis*, stripped her of valuables, and sank her with Thomas aboard: "That way there's no evidence, like nothing ever happened. So that's how they did it."

He added, as though this somehow must be persuasive: "His mother was also killed by pirates."

Thomas's alternative father figure, Elmer Van Pelt, believes just as firmly that Thomas must still be alive and is thriving. "No way is he gone," he told me as we stood in a pasture on a sunburnt hillside, looking down on Boquerón Bay as his three-legged dog gamboled about us. "I'm sure by now he is king of a lost tribe up a river somewhere."

Melanie Wells, who was often Thomas's neighbor in the anchorage at Dakity, also believed, or has at least hoped, that Thomas might still be alive. "I always wondered and hoped that Thomas would appear on some tiny island," she told me. "That he had lost his memory and was still roaming the earth."

And Elm and Melanie aren't the only ones. Some four years after Thomas disappeared, I found one friend from his teenage years in Puerto Rico who declined to say much about Thomas or the Tangvald family, but noted: "I wonder if he will resurface or not. It doesn't quite feel like his energy has dissipated."

There are a few others like this, who cannot believe a sailor as competent as Thomas could be claimed by the sea, but were shy about sharing their memories of him, as though this would be a concession he has not survived.

Of course the one person most immediately concerned with whether Thomas was alive or dead was Christina. She knew him well enough—his capacity for anger, and the betrayal he felt he suffered when she left him in Cayenne—that she could not rule out the possibility he had landed somewhere in Brazil and gone into hiding. On May 7, 63 days after Thomas had sailed out of Cayenne, she decided she would bait him, to see if he was "just being an asshole," as she put it. She sent Thomas an e-mail, the last she ever addressed to him, and announced if she had not heard from him by May 24—80 days since his disappearance, and the day after his birthday—she would organize a funeral for him to be held on Sunday, June 8.

"Many of us are full of hope that you are well, and if you are well and not communicating, you are a brute!!!" she wrote. "I strongly doubt this, but don't make me waste money and energy (especially energy) if you are alive and just being a bastard."

Christina received no response to this message and later that month, instead of organizing a funeral, wrote to Gustave Balta. She was thinking she might leave the boys with her mother in Puerto Rico and travel to Brazil to search for Thomas on her own, and she wanted to know what Gustave thought of this.

Gustave's answer was harshly critical of Thomas, who, as he put it, "preferred to abandon his family to risk his life for a foolish dream." He urged Christina to focus now on caring for Gaston and Lucio and concluded: "Brazil has destroyed Thomas. If you go to Brazil, Brazil will destroy you."

In the end Christina never did go to Brazil to search for Thomas, nor did she hold a funeral. She remembered the bank account Thomas had opened in Lucio's name in Oiapoque and reasoned that if Thomas were indeed still alive, he would likely have accessed it. But she was never able to find out if this had happened. She wasn't sure which bank held the account, she had no account number, and she had no record of Thomas's passport number. All she was left with, sadly, was uncertainty.

When I first started communicating with Christina in 2016, she seemed finally to have accepted that Thomas must be dead. "In my opinion, maybe not in a conscious way, Thomas did commit suicide," she wrote in one early exchange. Yet her opinion, during the time I have known her, has wavered. As recently as February 2021, seven years after Thomas disappeared, she wrote to me she thought *Oasis* might well have sunk in the first rainstorm she met. But she added: "What I am not sure about yet is him. He could have made it somewhere. He had the life of a cat. I still can imagine HE would have made it out alive somehow."

Christina is a strong woman and has resolutely moved ahead with her life. She found a new partner, has given birth to a third son, and has been steadfast and collected in helping me research Thomas's story. She lives with the uncertainty and mystery of Thomas's fate and seems to have made peace with it somehow, but still the ragged emotion inherent in her memories of Thomas can surface at odd moments.

I will never forget an afternoon spent in Christina's company with Elm Van Pelt and his partner Claudia Medusa, who also knew Thomas, in their home in the hills outside Boquerón. We were sitting in an enclosed verandah and strapped to the ceiling overhead there was an old wooden rowing dinghy. Claudia told us how it got there. Thomas had come by one day years earlier, looking for Elm, who was away, and found the dinghy sitting neglected in the yard. It was a good boat, he insisted, and should not be left out to rot. So with Claudia's help Thomas pulled it inside, found some line, and mounted some blocks on the ceiling beams. He then hoisted the boat aloft and secured it up there.

Christina sat quietly as Claudia described all this. She stared up at the boat and the lines that held it in place. "You mean Thomas tied those knots?" she finally asked.

Yes, answered Claudia, he did. And we all sat silently for a moment, gazing up at the boat dangling from the ceiling, a memorial to Thomas, crafted by his own hands.

And slowly Christina's eyes filled with tears.


THERE CAN BE NO ANSWER to the question of what really became of Thomas Tangvald; there can in the end be nothing but opinions. There is not enough evidence, one way or another, to draw any definitive conclusions. Because no wreckage or remains were ever found, we cannot rule out the possibility that he might still be alive somewhere. Perhaps he really has found a refuge and is secure at last within some carapace he has fashioned to protect and hide himself from the modern world. But the likeliest scenario, I believe, is that Thomas did in fact die at sea.

It is easy enough to imagine what might have happened. Gjermund's colorful pirate-attack theory, in my opinion, is not very credible. Though small-time thieves can be found in South American rivers and close to shore, they are not known to operate well offshore, where Thomas was likely sailing. Also, as was the case when *Oasis* was boarded by would-be pirates at the mouth of the Oiapoque River, the bedraggled little boat was not an appealing target. But there are certainly other ways Thomas might have perished. He could easily have fallen overboard. *Oasis* might well have been run down by a ship, as she may not have been showing lights at night and would have made a poor radar target. Or, if she was leaking very badly, she may simply have sunk, leaving Thomas to abandon ship in his plywood dinghy, a low-slung rectangular scow that may have been swamped and sunk in turn. If only Thomas had accepted the EPIRB that was offered him in St. Thomas, he might have activated it in any such emergency, and we would now at least know he had been consciously in distress. He might even have been rescued. Once an EPIRB is activated in any but the remotest waters, a castaway is likely to be picked up by a passing ship within a day or less.

Though some imagine Thomas's great skill as a sailor should have saved him in any crisis, the sad fact is he had lost and nearly lost boats before. He came within a whisker of getting run down and sunk by a cruise ship while sailing the fiberglass sloop *Bambú* in 2005, then soon afterward destroyed the boat when he ran her into the coast of Vieques. Earlier, in 1998, he was lucky not to have destroyed his cutter *Melody* when he ran her aground on a beach in Cornwall. Significantly, all three of these mishaps were the result of Thomas having fallen fast asleep while underway. As Clare Allcard believes, there is a good chance this was also a factor in his disappearing aboard *Oasis*.

It might all have happened very quickly. Because *Oasis* was under-ballasted and thus less stable than she should have been, and because her ballast was not secured in place, she was vulnerable to being capsized. If a common squall or thunderstorm came along without Thomas noticing and unleashed a sudden burst of strong wind into sails set to a much lighter breeze, the boat in an instant might have been knocked down and flung violently onto her side. The mast on *Oasis* was both hollow and sealed, thus was buoyant, so there likely was no real danger of the boat flipping all the way over into a fully capsized upside-down position. But still the makeshift ballast inside might well have come tumbling out of the very bottom of the boat and then would have piled up in a confused jumble on the cabin's lee side, crippling the craft's ability to swing upright again. If Thomas happened to have fallen asleep with one or more of the boat's three hatches open—as was likely, given he was sailing at or close to the equator—the boat might then have filled with water and sunk in only a few minutes. Even if he had woken up and become alert in the midst of such a catastrophe, there may well have been little he could do to save the situation.

AS EASY AS IT IS to imagine how Thomas's life may have ended, it is just as easy to conjure the alternate life he might have led. He was undeniably talented, highly intelligent, and was possessed by an ambition he might well have fulfilled. All other things being equal, there really was no good reason why he should not have found some success as a yacht designer. His university education in advanced mathematics and fluid dynamics left him with a far stronger technical and theoretical background than many modern designers, several of whom have had little formal training and simply picked up the trade as they went along, much as Thomas's father had when he set about designing *L'Artemis de Pytheas*. The annals of yacht design are filled with prolific "amateur" designers, as well as successful professionals who have never studied naval architecture, much less anything as esoteric as fluid dynamics. Thomas, with his keen aptitude and intelligence, a lifetime of practical experience, and his very relevant education, was well positioned to excel in this field.

Yet there was something in his nature and personality that prevented this from happening. Thomas's arrogance and the strong traditional biases he inherited from his father did present obstacles. Due to both these traits he alienated his uncle Patrick Balta, who might have been a helpful mentor. But ultimately I think such problems were surmountable. For every person put off by Thomas, there usually was another who understood and appreciated him, and toward the end of his life, in the speculative designs he was drawing to attract attention, he demonstrated a willingness and desire to explore more modern aspects of boat design. And he was always willing to work hard. Thomas was never a lazy person; he was forever busy with something. Yet somehow, after returning to the Caribbean, he was often spinning his wheels, getting nowhere and sabotaging himself.

Thomas's alcoholism obviously played a major role in this, and also, tragically, in his inability to maintain a stable relationship with the mother of his children. This in turn raises the larger question of whether Thomas did perhaps suffer from post-traumatic stress disorder and whether his substance abuse and his apparent sleeping disorder may have been related to this.

Thomas's childhood, from age three all the way up to age 15, was a forest of traumatic events and circumstances. He was an eyewitness as his mother was shot to death and murdered by pirates. He was again an eyewitness, at close quarters, as his first stepmother was badly beaten and nearly raped by thieves in Tunisia. This woman subsequently beat and abused him; ultimately she was lost overboard, and Thomas assisted in searching for her in vain. For extended periods during his early boyhood he was kept locked in a cabin aboard his father's boat and was sometimes left alone, crying for hours. He was frequently bullied and ostracized in the many different schools he attended. He had no mattress and only a straw mat to sleep upon at night and was perhaps at times undernourished. And finally there was the awful denouement—he was the sole survivor of the ghastly shipwreck that killed his father and sister.

As originally conceived, PTSD is a diagnosis describing the trauma experienced by military veterans and other survivors of one-off events such as combat, natural disasters, car accidents, sexual assaults, and other scary, potentially life-threatening episodes. It was first recognized by the American Psychiatric Association in 1980 in its *Diagnostic and Statistical Manual of Mental Disorders* (DSM) after increasing numbers of Vietnam veterans exhibited the disorder during the 1970s. The "clear story line," as one trauma specialist has described it, is "[a] person is suddenly and unexpectedly devastated by an atrocious event and is never the same again."[2] Symptoms include frequent nightmares and flashbacks related to the traumatic event, increased anxiety and hyper-vigilance, persistent insomnia, and increased likelihood of substance and alcohol abuse. Subjects may also engage in risky behaviors that are ultimately self-destructive, such as drunk

2. Bessel Van Der Kolk, MD, *The Body Keeps the Score: Brain, Mind, and Body in the Healing of Trauma* (Viking Penguin, 2014)

driving, chronic gambling, or unprotected sex with strangers. Or they may seek release in extreme sports that induce strong surges of adrenalin, which some believe can be therapeutic.

Certain aspects of Thomas's experience do fit into this diagnosis. Yes, he eventually had problems with drinking and drugs, engaged in risky behavior, and was also a bit of an adrenalin addict during his time in Andorra, with his crazy skiing and crane climbing, similar to Gjermund's practice of Norwegian death-diving. But it is not a good match in other key respects. Thomas was exposed not to one discrete event or situation, but instead endured a series of traumatic events and circumstances that persisted throughout his childhood. As far as we know, he never relived these in nightmares or flashbacks. Most notably, he never had trouble sleeping, a primary PTSD symptom; instead he sometimes blacked out, had trouble waking up, was renowned for falling asleep in unusual situations, and on a few occasions remained mostly unconscious for long periods of time.

There is however an alternative diagnosis that fits better. Complex PTSD (C-PTSD) and a variant specific to childhood trauma, developmental trauma disorder (DTD), which are not officially recognized in the DSM, are increasingly used to describe situations where subjects suffer prolonged and repeated exposure to trauma in environments they cannot easily escape from.[3] In the case of children and DTD, the trauma often involves dysfunctional relationships with caregivers and physical, emotional, and educational neglect, as well as other types of child mistreatment. Symptoms of C-PTSD and DTD can include not only the regular spectrum of PTSD symptoms, including substance and alcohol abuse, but also a host of others, including in some instances

---

3. Though not listed in the DSM, complex PTSD is described in the World Health Organization's *International Statistical Classification of Diseases and Related Health Problems*. It is also recognized by certain government agencies in the United States, the United Kingdom, and Australia.

dissociative episodes induced by stress that are similar to what Thomas experienced—black-outs, fainting spells, and unusual bouts of unconsciousness.

Evaluating Thomas's relationships with his childhood caregivers in terms of these disorders is instructive. He had no conscious memory of his first primary caregiver, his mother Lydia, nor of her being gunned down by pirates in the Sulu Sea when he was but a toddler. This could easily have been a function of his very young age, but it is interesting to note this can also be a symptom of C-PTSD and DTD, wherein a subject may dissociate and completely block out memories of a trauma they have suffered. Similarly, with his stepmother Ann, though Thomas had memories of her, he seemed to have forgotten, or at least never consciously acknowledged, that she had abused him.

Of course Thomas's most important and influential caregiver was his father. This was the critical defining relationship in Thomas's life, and in his presumed demise. Reduced to its book-blurb essence, the story of Thomas Tangvald is that of a young man who destroyed himself striving to follow in his father's footsteps. The great irony of his life was that he could never see nor comprehend how negative his father's influence really was. Thomas always saw his father as a victim of tragedy, and so empathized with him. What he never grasped was that his father was in fact an agent of tragedy.

Other more objective observers saw this very clearly. The sailing author Fatty Goodlander, for example, to hear him tell it, was practically traumatized himself by his encounters with Peter and Thomas. In both instances, when he spent time with Peter on St. John in 1991, not long before Peter sailed for Bonaire, then later with Thomas on Jost Van Dyke in 2011, when Thomas was en route to Brazil, Fatty saw the courses each of them were on could lead only to ruin and agonized over his inability to thwart their self-destruction. Though Fatty had originally revered and looked up to Peter as both a sailor and a writer, his final opinion of the man is damning.

"The truth of it is that Peter Tangvald has been responsible for five people's deaths in the water," he told me during a long phone interview. "There was Carmen, arguably Thomas, himself, and the two wives. That's five people. Nobody should get to kill five people. Nobody should have five people with salt water in their lungs."

Thomas's idolization of his father, and his failure to see his father as a root cause of his own troubled life, are themselves symptomatic of C-PTSD and DTD. Persons in long-term traumatic situations can become preoccupied with caregivers or other people in control of those situations and can develop very distorted perceptions of them. This can include having an overly positive view of a caregiver who is putatively abusive, particularly if the abuse is not intentionally malicious. A subject can be transfixed by an abuser's apparently positive attributes and may become overly focused on seeking affection and approval from them.

Another relevant symptom is negative self-image. Though Thomas often projected confidence, self-assurance, and even arrogance when dealing with others, he could also be quite insecure and unsure of himself in various common social situations. Most significantly, he often saw himself as failing to live up to his father's standards and ideals. As Fatty Goodlander saw very clearly on Jost Van Dyke, Thomas was inclined to berate himself when comparing his life and work to that of his father's.

What is particularly ironic in this regard is that Thomas during his teenage years, prior to the wreck on Bonaire, seemed clearly to be moving away from Peter Tangvald and was striving to escape his all-pervasive influence. Relations between them became much more strained. Thomas, with some help from others, began to question his father's presumptive edicts, and he took the very bold step of preemptively moving onto a boat of his own. This is generally speaking a perfectly normal process in adolescents and young adults, described as "individuation" by psychologists. Had it continued in Thomas's case, he might eventually have gained enough space and perspective to perceive his father more accurately and objectively.

Instead it appears the accident on Bonaire short-circuited this evolution. Instead of Thomas having to do the work of gradually extricating himself from the web of his father's life, the bond between them was violently and abruptly severed in yet another traumatic crisis. Seeing his father suffer this last conclusively fatal tragedy, Thomas likely again defaulted to simply empathizing with the man. Even worse, Thomas may have blamed himself for what had happened. As far as I know, he never spoke directly of this to anyone, but some people I interviewed did get some sense of it.

One of these was Michael Fischer, Thomas's transient cruiser friend on Culebra. Michael never read *At Any Cost* and evidently never knew Thomas wasn't aboard *L'Artemis* when she was wrecked on Bonaire. He knew of the wreck only from a little bit Thomas had mentioned and had a strong feeling Thomas felt very guilty about it. "My assumption, from the way he acted," he told me, "was that Thomas was on watch when it happened. So I didn't ask a lot of questions."

Another was Morgan MacDonald, who discussed the end of *L'Artemis* with Thomas at some length: "He talked about being absolutely helpless, unable to do a damn thing, watching the whole shipwreck and hearing his sister's cries from down below. It was an extremely traumatic event for him. I think he held himself at least partly responsible for not having been aboard."

It would have been unusual if the sole survivor of the wreck that killed Peter and Carmen Tangvald did not feel guilty in some way, if only for having survived. And Thomas did have that one very tangible regret he could torture himself with: if only he had never bought that scraggly little boat *Spartan*, then he would have been at his father's side—standing watch aboard *L'Artemis*, ready to help, wherever they were sailing to—and nothing bad would have happened.

And having thought that, it might then have become very hard for Thomas to blame his father for anything.

I AM NOT THE ONLY ONE who has wondered if Thomas Tangvald suffered from PTSD. Stephanie Labonville, when she saw Thomas flopping out, mostly unconscious for days or weeks at a time on Culebra, felt very sure something like this must be going on. Gjermund Tangvald, who himself suffered from PTSD after his military service in Bosnia, feels strongly this is something he must have had in common with his uncle. And there are others who knew Thomas who have wondered about this. Morgan MacDonald, for example, though reluctant to speak in terms of psychiatric jargon, definitely saw Thomas as being "haunted" and "driven by demons." Even Clare Allcard, despite her own calamitous encounters with psychiatrists as a young woman, over time came to realize that Thomas had serious problems that were likely rooted in his past.

Studying the events of Thomas's life through the lens of PTSD, all sorts of connections can be made. His adrenalized stunts as a teenager; the sudden flashes of anger he sometimes exhibited; his dismissive arrogance and bouts of insecurity; his evident meltdown and inability to cope with that awful moment of crisis aboard *Melody* in Porth Cressa Bay—all these and more might be interpreted as trauma responses. The biggest puzzle is Thomas's relationship to the sea. This was both closely bound up with his relationship with his father and with the traumatic unfolding of his life. It is telling, I think, that Christina's impression was that Thomas's problem with alcohol seemed to abate when he focused on a life on shore and increased when he turned to a life afloat. This may well have been the defining paradox of his existence. The sea, thanks to his upbringing, was inexorably attractive to Thomas. It was always his lodestar, his one true home, a realm in which he was a veritable prince.

Thomas summarized his feelings in this regard very neatly in a leter he sent to Kathy Young, his girlfriend from university, right after he succeeded in bringing *Melody* into the Humber River: "I don't think I've ever felt as alive as when I am sailing. It made me realize just how pampered most people are—and how little freedom most people have. Most humans live hardly at all—they might as well be dead for all the shields they have put in between themselves and L I F E."

Thomas certainly succeeded in stripping away any such shields in his own relationship to life. But it is hard to say he ever achieved anything like freedom. Tragically, it seems instead the sea and sailing may have become for him a source of mind-numbing anxiety.

In the end, however, our memory and appraisal of Thomas must be larger than a mere diagnosis. Thomas himself would have strenuously resisted such an epitaph. Christina, who always shared Thomas's prejudice against playing the diagnostic "bingo" game, still resists it. And a diagnosis, after all, is only constructive if it is correct and leads to successful treatment. Whether this could ever have happened in Thomas's case is debatable.

Clare now regrets she never took Thomas to see someone while he was in her care in Andorra, but there was at the time no real reason for her to think this was called for. Beyond the one slightly disturbing incident at the airport in Amsterdam en route to Andorra, Thomas as a teenager never displayed overt symptoms of any sort of mental disorder. His various idiosyncrasies otherwise could be seen simply as the product of his unusual upbringing afloat—something which to Clare did not seem at all unusual—rather than of his necessarily having been traumatized. At that point, in the early 1990s, relatively little was known about trauma in children in any event.[4]

After Thomas left Andorra, any decision about whether to seek help was ultimately up to him. Except during the extreme flopping out episodes he experienced while being harassed by the police on Culebra, it seems never to have occurred to him that anything was really wrong with him. Even then his profound distrust of modern medicine made it hard for him to believe that conventional doctors could possibly do him any good. Though he obviously did recognize he had a drinking problem, he most likely would not have connected this to any underlying mental disorder. And certainly not to any disorder that had anything to do with his father. Most probably he felt it was a problem he had foolishly created for himself by failing to live up to the abstemious example his father had set for him.

The fact was Thomas was never willing to see himself as a victim or as a damaged person. He refused to be defined by the tragedies he had endured. He was proud he was of the sea and not of the land. He was happy to live outside the boundaries of modern society. And he was very proud he was his father's son, heir to a considerable reputation within the sailing community, to a great fount of traditional sailing wisdom and expertise, and to a minimalist worldview and way of life.

"In spite of all the difficult and traumatic experiences, I don't think Thomas would have changed a thing about the way he was brought up," Stephanie once told me. "When I read he was

---

4. See Dr. Bruce Perry's seminal book, *The Boy Who Was Raised As a Dog*, first published in 2006. Perry's groundbreaking work in childhood trauma only began in 1987.

missing, lost at sea, I was not surprised at all. If I had to predict how this was going to end, that would have been it. And I think that's the way he would have wanted to go."

WHEN I FIRST JOINED the tribe of bluewater sailors in the 1990s, I was very interested in the story of Peter Tangvald. This is the way of any tribe: stories are passed down and resonate with subsequent generations. I soon divined that Peter had directly inspired the generation of sailors who had in turn inspired me. Like a friend found in an anchorage far from the one before, I was not surprised, for example, when I noticed that one early book written by Lin and Larry Pardey, a cruising couple who became very influential in the 1970s and '80s, was dedicated to Peter Tangvald.[5] They hailed him as a supreme example of a "self-sufficient sailor," the epitome of what most bluewater cruisers aspire to. So he seemed something like a hero to me, a man to be respected. Decades later in the Spanish Virgin Islands, when I came across the magazine article that gave me a first glimpse of who and what Thomas had become after his father's death, he too seemed heroic to me, a fellow sailor with some talent and a unique perspective and background who was worthy of my respect.

But now, having come to the end of this long road, I struggle to define these characters in my mind. When it comes to human personalities, familiarity always breeds complexity, and Peter and Thomas were nothing if not complex. Even the most admirable people are bound to have flaws, and sometimes it seems their virtues only magnify these. As one woman who spent some time

---

5. Lin and Larry Pardey, *The Self-Sufficient Sailor* (W.W. Norton & Co., 1982). Lin and Larry Pardey were strongly influenced by Peter's first book, *Sea Gypsy*, and the Pardeys, while cruising on their engineless boat *Seraffyn*, spent time with the Tangvald family in the Philippines in 1978 prior to Lydia's murder. I read several of the Pardeys' books while preparing to go to sea myself and later served as their editor at *SAIL* Magazine.

with Peter and came to respect him put it: "They talked about him being a purist, and they talked about him being everything from remarkable and brilliant to completely insane, but I don't think many people really understood him." The same might well be said of Thomas.

In the case of Peter Tangvald, any positive view of him must obviously be balanced against his miserable record as a spouse and parent. I am a father myself, but I have never tried to rear a child on a boat, much less as a single parent, so I cannot speak personally to the challenges Peter faced while raising Thomas on *L'Artemis*. But I have met several children as they were being raised on boats, and I have a few adult friends who were themselves raised on boats, and I can say this about boat kids: all those I have ever met or heard tell of, with just two exceptions, turned out very well and ultimately benefited from their time afloat.

Laypeople coming to this story may be surprised to hear this, but most bluewater cruising parents do not lock their children in cages while underway. They do go to great lengths to see that their children are properly educated. Most sail on the safest routes during the safest times of the year, and many even shape their itineraries so their kids can more easily make friends their age and stay in touch with them. Properly cared for, most boat kids have a fantastic time. Unplugged from screens and thrust into a world where books seem just as exciting as movies, where they are exposed to many different peoples and cultures, where they are constantly outdoors in close contact with nature, where they are continually in the company of adults who treat them as peers and give them significant responsibilities at an early age, where they have lots of opportunities to play in and around the water, children do tend to thrive. Many cruising kids do not go on to embrace the lifestyle as adults, but for most it is a positive experience.

The first of the two exceptions I mentioned are a pair of

brothers I have heard stories about. They were raised on a cruising boat in the Indian Ocean, based primarily in East Africa, and both went to sea on boats of their own as adults. One was eventually jailed in South Africa on a rape charge; the other is suspected of murder. I have no idea what might have led them to this. The other exception is Thomas, who did none of those sorts of terrible things, but was very likely traumatized by the life he led as a child.

In this respect Peter Tangvald clearly failed to adhere to a core ethic of the bluewater tribe—really of any tribe. He betrayed the next generation, his own children, and he harmed others, quite badly, in pursuit of his own selfish dream. In considering how I feel about him now, I think first of Elm Van Pelt's concise judgment, that you had to respect the man, even if you didn't like him. But I wonder now if Peter Tangvald really is worthy of respect, in spite of his accomplishments, his great skill as a bluewater sailor, and his austere, undiluted exaltation of personal freedom. It has become a common dilemma in this age of tell-all biography. Once we know a celebrated, accomplished figure well enough to see the ugliness within them, must we forgive that and look up to them nonetheless? Thomas presents a harder case. How should we remember him? His great competence as a sailor, his acute intelligence, his great spirit and determination to stand outside of human society as a unique singularity—is all this worthy of our respect, in spite of his manifest flaws? All of us in the end are only human, the product of nature and nurture. We all have something we must be forgiven.

In considering the enigma that is Thomas, it is only natural to compare him to his father. This is the standard by which he often evaluated himself, quite negatively, but I think more objective observers might form more positive opinions. Peter Tangvald was reared in a realm of wealth and privilege and enjoyed all sorts of advantages while growing up. He was eternally a child in many ways, reluctant to accept personal responsibility for his actions, and quick to cast himself as a victim of unfortunate circumstances. Thomas, on the other hand, had a very austere upbringing and had far more unfortunate circumstances to complain about than his father ever did. Yet he usually refused to do this. He was often self-critical and rarely held himself out as a victim of any sort. Likewise we have good evidence that Thomas did feel some measure of guilt and responsibility after surviving the wreck on Bonaire, the defining tragedy of his life. His father seems never to have openly acknowledged feeling any responsibility or culpable remorse for the deaths of Lydia and Ann. Had he somehow survived the wreck on Bonaire, this might also have been the case regarding Carmen's death.

Still Thomas was fully capable of being just as blindly self-centered as his father. Most notably, in his great zeal to immigrate to Brazil, Thomas very much mirrored his father's willingness to put his immediate family at risk in order to achieve his own goal. In the end it was only Christina's willingness to make a very hard decision that saved him from perhaps destroying his wife and the two lives he helped to create.

Any respect we feel for Thomas must be tempered by this. But ultimately I think what most demands respect, and some measure of forgiveness, when it comes to Thomas are the raw, seemingly impossible facts of his history—the existence he both endured and reveled in while growing up; the unique, exalted, and tortured legacy his father so blithely handed to him; all the trauma that loomed so large in his personal rear-view mirror. Though he always hated the idea that he might be defined by his past, it seems the greatest tragedy of Thomas Tangvald's life was that he could neither escape nor transcend it.

# ACKNOWLEDGEMENTS

THE TWO PEOPLE who helped me most in creating this book were Clare Allcard, Thomas's foster mother, and Christina Pasquinucci, Thomas's wife. Clare was considering writing a book about Thomas herself when I first contacted her, and though I made it clear I would defer to her project if she chose to pursue it, she very graciously deferred to me instead. Fortunately for me, Clare is something of a packrat and gave me full access to the mounds of correspondence and documents pertaining to Thomas that she had saved and stored in her basement in Andorra. We've had great fun exchanging bluewater sailing tales and anecdotes over the years I worked on this project. Clare has also been a great source of inspiration and guidance. She has been unrelentingly honest and supportive, has ultimately trusted my judgment in the drafting of the text of this book, and I now count her as one of my great friends within the cruising community.

Christina was also gracious and very brave in providing support to me. She has trusted me implicitly, despite knowing nothing about me when I first contacted her. She answered endless e-mails filled with questions about her and Thomas and received me as a guest in Puerto Rico, where she answered more questions in person and led me to sources who were in turn also very helpful. Ultimately she shared without reservation or restrictions the entire archive of her e-mail correspondence with Thomas.

I would be remiss if I did not mention that while I was writing this book Clare and I formed a syndicate of sorts, together with Thomas's half-sister Virginia, and have helped to finance the private grade-school educations of Thomas's two sons, Gaston and Lucio. In Puerto Rico this does not amount to much money, and we all feel that Thomas's offspring are well worth the investment. Like their father before them, they are unusually bright boys. I have dedicated this book to them, in the hope it will help them understand who exactly their father was.

I feel very strongly that this story is much more Christina's than mine, so I am also committed to sharing with her half of any and all proceeds I realize from this project. I suggest therefore you not pass this book on to friends if you think they will enjoy it. Instead you should urge them to buy their own copies. There may be, I pray, some measure of redemption in the tragic tale of Thomas's life if it can help to support the family he left behind.

While writing the book I shared draft copy with and received feedback from several people. Some of these are subjects of this narrative, as I explained in the preface. Most were more objective parties. Comments from two old friends, Kurt Meinen and John Geoghegan, helped me early on to reorganize the book's structure. James Jordan was unfailingly interested and supportive, with many helpful comments, and his wife Pauline Hopper, a child psychologist, provided a useful critique of the last chapter. Thomas Jackson, a psychologist specializing in trauma, read the entire manuscript, in the midst of a serious battle with brain cancer, and was also very helpful. Jenny Apostol provided several useful comments. Phil and Meg Cavanaugh, Jeff Bolster, and Seth Lapidow also provided supportive feedback.

Most importantly, my wife Clare O'Brien gave me all the space and encouragement I needed to pursue this project and read through all the copy several times, offering advice and comments.

I must also tip my hat to the many interview subjects who shared information with me. These include several members of the cruising community, as well as many others who knew Thomas and Peter. Thomas's Norwegian family deserve special mention, most particularly Gjermund Tangvald, who has been very open and honest in all our exchanges. Stephanie Labonville was a very valuable source. The same is true of Jean Buchanan, whom I fear may have regretted some of what she shared with me. She is a special person, uniquely challenged now in her day-to-day life, and I can only pray she appreciates this final product. Morgan MacDonald, besides sharing what he remembers of Thomas and Peter, also provided me with a detailed tutorial on the design and construction of Puerto Rican nativo sailing sloops. Ken McKinley of Locus Weather, who in the past has provided me with weather-routing advice on a few of my own ocean passages, proved also to be a great "weather historian" and was able to put together a detailed reconstruction of the weather conditions Thomas likely encountered after he departed from French Guiana. Margie Serkin provided invaluable translation services.

Finally, I am particularly grateful to Jon Gosch at Latah Books, who has embraced this project with all the enthusiasm I feel it deserves. Jon, Ben Romano, and Logan Amstadter helped me sharpen up the text. Kevin Breen lent a keen eye to the book's design and appearance.

In the end, obviously, I am the one responsible for this mess. All errors and misjudgments are attributable solely to me, and all those who helped me are utterly blameless.

# IMAGE ATTRIBUTIONS

THIS BOOK HAS BEEN ENRICHED by a variety of images. What follows is a list of the images utilized throughout the text, as well as the people who furnished the photographs.

Chapter 1: Thomas (left) with his father Peter and sister Carmen aboard *L'Artemis de Pytheas* at Curaçao during the 1990 hurricane season. Photo by Jean Heylbroeck.

Chapter 2: Thomas at the wreck site on Bonaire, studying the splintered remains of the boat that was his home for the first 15 years of his life. Photo courtesy of Clare Allcard.

Chapter 3: Thomas with his mother Lydia moments after he was born at sea aboard *L'Artemis de Pytheas*. From the personal collection of Peter Tangvald.

Chapter 4: Thomas (right) with Edward Allcard at the Allcards' home in Andorra. Photo courtesy of Clare Allcard.

Chapter 5: Peter at the helm of *L'Artemis* with Thomas (center) standing with a friend in the companionway. From the personal collection of Peter Tangvald.

Chapter 6: Peter and Florence with all three children—Thomas, Carmen, and Virginia—aboard *L'Artemis* at Culebra. Photo by Olav Hasselknippe.

Chapter 7: Jean Buchanan's son Ryan (left) with Thomas in the Isles of Scilly, with *Melody* at anchor. Photo courtesy of Jean Buchanan.

Chapter 8: Thomas aboard the boat *Aquila*, one of several different boats he lived aboard during his time at Culebra. Photo courtesy of Stephanie Labonville.

Chapter 9: Thomas with Christina and Gaston. Photo courtesy of Christina Pasquinucci.

Chapter 10: Thomas sailing *Oasis* out of St. John en route to Brazil. Note Gaston's arm sticking out the porthole. From the personal collection of Thomas Tangvald.

Chapter 11: *Oasis* out of the water near the marina outside Cayenne, with work in progress. Gaston stands in the foreground. Photo courtesy of Christina Pasquinucci.

Chapter 12: (Photo 1 of Thomas, left) Thomas aboard *Oasis* taking a sextant sight during the voyage to Brazil. Photo courtesy of Christina Pasquinucci. (Photo 2 of Peter, right) Peter taking a sextant sight aboard *Dorothea* during his circumnavigation. From the personal collection of Peter Tangvald.

CHARLES J. DOANE

Charles J. Doane is an active bluewater sailor who has worked as a yachting journalist since 1986. He has logged nearly 100,000 miles sailing offshore, including seven transatlantic passages and a number of singlehanded passages between the West Indies and New England. He has cruised extensively on the U.S. East Coast, in the West Indies, in Spain and Portugal, and in West Africa. His racing credits include runs in the Newport-Bermuda Race, the Fastnet Race, and the Sydney-Hobart Race.

Besides having worked on staff at top U.S. sailing magazines, he is the author of two previous books—*The Modern Cruising Sailboat*, a reference work, and *The Sea Is Not Full*, a memoir. His freelance work has appeared in *The New York Times* and in top international sailing magazines. In previous existences he was an attorney and a daily newspaper reporter.

He now lives with his family in Portsmouth, New Hampshire.

Printed in Great Britain
by Amazon

24916171R00179